# Micrographics

# LIBRARY SCIENCE TEXT SERIES

**Introduction to Public Services for Library Technicians.** 2nd ed. By Marty Bloomberg.

**Introduction to Technical Services for Library Technicians.** 3rd ed. By Marty Bloomberg and G. Edward Evans.

**A Guide to the Library of Congress Classification.** 2nd ed. By John Phillip Immroth.

**Science and Engineering Literature: A Guide to Reference Sources.** 2nd ed. By H. Robert Malinowsky, Richard A. Gray, and Dorothy A. Gray.

**The Vertical File and Its Satellites: A Handbook of Acquisition, Processing and Organization.** By Shirley Miller.

**Introduction to United States Public Documents.** By Joe Morehead.

**The School Library Media Center.** 2nd ed. By Emanuel T. Prostano and Joyce S. Prostano.

**The Humanities: A Selective Guide to Information Sources.** By A. Robert Rogers.

**The School Library and Educational Change.** By Martin Rossoff.

**Introduction to Library Science: Basic Elements of Library Service.** By Jesse H. Shera.

**Introduction to Cataloging and Classification.** 5th ed. By Bohdan S. Wynar, with the assistance of John Phillip Immroth.

**An Introduction to Classification and Number Building in Dewey.** By Marty Bloomberg and Hans Weber.

**Map Librarianship: An Introduction.** By Mary Larsgaard.

# Micrographics

## William Saffady

School of Library and Information Science,
State University of New York at Albany

1978

**Libraries Unlimited, Inc.**
Littleton, Colo.

LIBRARIES UNLIMITED, INC.
P.O. Box 263
Littleton, Colorado 80160

---

**Library of Congress Cataloging in Publication Data**

Saffady, William, 1944-
    Micrographics.

    (Library science text series)
    Bibliography: p. 219
    Includes index.
    1. Microphotography.   I. Title.
Z265.S22          686.4'3          78-1309
ISBN 0-87287-175-4

# PREFACE

This is the first of two independent, but related, textbooks that will, together, provide comprehensive coverage of the most important aspects of document reproduction in libraries, technical information centers, and related agencies. As its title indicates, this book deals with microform reproductions. The second book, to be entitled *Reprographics*, will deal with full-size document reproduction, facsimile transmission, videotape document storage systems, word processing, and the impact of reprography on copyright protection.

This book is designed for practicing librarians and library school students who want a systematic presentation of the basic facets of micrographics as applied to library work. Chapter one provides an historical overview of the uses of microforms in libraries and points the reader to more detailed treatment of specific points in subsequent chapters. Whenever possible, generalizations are supported with examples taken from published literature, thereby permitting more detailed study of interesting applications. Specific micrographic equipment is mentioned and illustrated throughout the text. The selection of particular models was made to illustrate important features and functions and does not necessarily imply endorsement. While the devices depicted are all manufactured in the United States, many of them are available in Canada, Great Britain, and other countries where an English-language textbook might be read.

W.S.

# TABLE OF CONTENTS

**Chapter 4–COMPUTER-OUTPUT-MICROFILM (COM) (cont'd)**

**Chapter 5–MICROPUBLISHING** . . . . . . . . . . . . . . . . . . . . . . . 117

# CHAPTER 1

# MICROFORMS AND LIBRARIES: An Introduction

## OVERVIEW

As defined and described in the next chapter, *microform* is a generic term for any information storage and communication medium containing images too small to be read with the unaided eye. Since the late 1920s, librarians and information specialists have used microforms in five broad application areas:

1) to develop library collections;
2) to manage library collections;
3) to provide reproductions of library materials on user demand;
4) as a component in information storage and retrieval systems of varying complexity;
5) to manage the library's own operating records.

This chapter reviews the development of these application areas, introducing facets of library micrographics that will be discussed in detail in subsequent chapters. The history of micrographics' transition from a photographic novelty to a powerful information storage and retrieval medium of wide applicability has been described elsewhere and will be repeated here only as it relates to the use of microforms in libraries.[1]

## COLLECTION DEVELOPMENT

### Early Acquisition Projects

In the United States, the earliest library applications of micrographics were oriented toward the acquisition of archives, manuscripts, and rare books from foreign libraries. In the 1920s and 1930s, even the largest American research libraries lacked the primary source materials required to support the work of university faculty members, doctoral students, and other scholars.[2] In some cases, libraries or individual researchers were able to obtain a few hand-transcribed or photostatic copies for local study, but the slowness and high unit cost of such copying techniques effectively prohibited the acquisition of entire collections of important books or documents. Consequently, historians, literary scholars, and other researchers specializing in foreign studies were forced to spend considerable time and money in travel.

Between 1927 and 1935, a gift of $490,000 from John D. Rockefeller, Jr., enabled the Library of Congress to replace its existing foreign document copying activities with a well-planned, large-scale microfilming program.[3] Called simply "Project A," the eight-year program resulted in the acquisition of over three million document images from the British Museum and elsewhere. Project A demonstrated the feasibility of micrographics as a major acquisitions tool and, for the next two decades, served as a model for similar programs at the Library of Congress and elsewhere. A 1938 grant from the Rockefeller Foundation, for example, permitted the Harvard University Library to microfilm backfiles of 37 foreign newspapers.[4] In 1939, also with a Rockefeller Foundation grant, Brown University began microfilming selected titles in Mexican and South American libraries to support the development of graduate and undergraduate curricula in Latin American studies.[5] Into the 1950s, representatives of the Bancroft Library microfilmed more than two million documents in Mexican and European archives. In 1951, St. Louis University announced plans to microfilm 30,000 codices in the Vatican Library, thereby making much unique material conveniently available to American researchers.[6]

Such microfilm-based acquisitions programs were not limited to foreign materials. During the late 1930s, the University of Texas, with a gift from the Littlefield Fund for Southern History, conducted itinerant microfilming operations in Southern and Eastern archives.[7] Similarly, researchers working on large-scale historical editing projects—the Theodore Roosevelt papers, for example—found microfilming an effective means for rapidly collecting materials for later analysis.[8] While libraries generally administered such projects, much of the impetus for acquisition-oriented microfilming came from professional and scholarly associations. R. C. Binkley, as chairman of the Joint Committee on Materials for Research of the Social Sciences Research Council of the American Council of Learned Societies, became America's foremost spokesman for microphotography as an economical alternative to other document reproduction methods, on the one hand, and to foreign travel, on the other.[9] The American Council of Learned Societies itself sponsored the microfilming of 280,000 pages of NRA and ARA documents, which it subsequently offered to libraries at four hundred dollars per set, a savings of over five thousand dollars when compared to stenographic copies at two cents per page. In 1941, another professional organization—the Modern Language Association—initiated its Rotograph Project, designed to help literary scholars obtain microfilm copies of manuscripts from foreign libraries.[10]

## The Development of Micropublishing

While many libraries continue to maintain microfilming facilities for use in applications described later in this chapter, most of the microform research materials acquired by today's libraries are produced by third parties called *micropublishers.*[11] The NMA *Glossary of Micrographics* (Silver Spring: National Microfilm Association, 1972) defines micropublishing as the issuing of "new (not previously published) or reformatted information in multiple copy microform for sale or distribution to the public." As discussed more fully in chapter five, library literature uses the term in a less restrictive sense, which encompasses both *original* publication in microform and *retrospective* micropublishing—the recopying in multiple copy microform of material previously published in paper. In either case, the intention of producing multiple copies for sale distinguishes micropublishing from microfilming projects primarily designed to acquire research materials for use in a single library.

Although the first public discussion of the concept of micropublishing dates from 1853, when the British scientist J. W. F. Herschel wrote a letter to the editor of *Athenaeum* suggesting micro-editions of reference works, actual micropublishing began in the mid-1930s when Eastman Kodak microfilmed the retrospective file of the *New York Times* for sale to libraries.[12] The earliest micropublishers followed the lead of library-administered microfilming projects in emphasizing rare research materials from foreign repositories. University Microfilms, for example, began filming items listed in the Pollard and Redgrave *Short-Title Catalogue* in 1938. Readex Microprint Corporation was formed in the following year, although the earliest of its many extensive projects—nineteenth century British Parliamentary Papers and titles listed by Sabin—required several years to complete.[13]

The market for such large research collections remained relatively small but stable through the 1950s.[14] The rapid expansion of higher education during the 1960s, however, produced a second collection development crisis in American libraries. While the microfilming projects described in the preceding section resulted in a significant improvement in the availability of advanced research materials in major older libraries, many smaller or newly established academic institutions faced the difficult task of building basic library collections to support undergraduate instruction as well as graduate student and faculty research. Attracted by increased library acquisitions budgets that were enhanced by readily available federal funds, a number of micropublishers responded with specially prepared core collections consisting mainly of important out-of-print monographs essential for undergraduate term papers and recommended reading. Microcard Editions, for example, offered selected titles from *Books for College Libraries* on microfiche in subject-oriented groups. Similarly, the *PCMI Ultrafiche Library*, developed by NCR, featured several thousand titles drawn from established bibliographies. At the same time, the rapid development of community colleges, with their associated learning resource centers, generated a market for dynamic, subject-oriented information packages in microform.[15] A study by Yerkes-Wolf Associates reported a 104 percent increase in the dollar value of micropublishing products and services for the period 1966 to 1969, with libraries accounting for a substantial share of that growth.[16]

Today, the library market is served by over 75 commercial and institutional micropublishers. While the changed economic climate of the 1970s has resulted in drastic reductions in both library budgets and federal assistance to libraries, a 1975 *Publishers Weekly* projection of library acquisition trends through 1981 suggests that the percentage of total acquisitions budgets devoted to micropublications will increase and reaffirms the continued significance of microforms as a collection development resource.[17]

## COLLECTION MANAGEMENT

### Space Savings

While the first library applications of microforms emphasized the acquisition of research materials, their earliest commercial counterparts involved the reduction of bank checks and other voluminous inactive records to save storage space.[18] Despite the bulk and demonstrable inactivity of many library materials, the literature on library micrographics never considered space savings more than an incidental advantage until the publication of Fremont Rider's controversial book, *The Scholar and the Future of the Research Library* (New York: Hamden Press, 1944). Rider contended that, of the four costs associated with library collections—acquisitions, cataloging, storage, and binding—the cost of storage is the most significant.[19] Yet, he charged, prevailing library accounting practices improperly concealed the cost of storage by treating it as a one-time capital expense. Arguing that research collections double in size every five years, Rider emphasized the urgency of developing alternative storage methodologies and proposed the wholesale conversion of printed book collections to three by five inch *microcards*, stored in catalog card trays and containing a catalog card image on the reverse side.[20]

It is certainly not difficult to demonstrate the space-saving potential of microforms. The First Series of the *National Reporter System*, for example, requires over three hundred feet of shelf space in printed form but only about three feet in the West Publishing Company ultrafiche edition. Although commercial records management practice concedes the economic advantages of microforms over most types of warehouse storage for documents retained longer than seven years,[21] librarians have been generally critical of Rider's proposed solution to the problem of proliferating research materials. A 1957 study by Pritsker and Sadler for the Association for Research Libraries contended that the high cost of converting retrospective library collections to microcards or microfilm is difficult to recover through space savings alone.[22] Unfortunately, the study failed to consider the possibility, through micropublishing, of spreading initial conversion costs among a number of libraries. More substantial criticisms were made by Raffell and Shishko who, in a 1969 case study of cost reduction in the MIT Libraries, refuted Rider's contention that space savings represent a meaningful way to reduce library operating expenses.[23] At MIT, they pointed out, storage costs amount to only 6.4 percent of the library's annual budget. A fifteen percent space savings would achieve a mere one percent reduction in total library expenditures.

The relationship of microforms to cost reduction through space savings is further complicated by variations in the value of floor space depending on time, geographic location, and local circumstances. In the few libraries that have published calculations of the value of their floor space, the cost to store an average bound volume ranges from 13.5 cents per year at the University of Chicago in 1961 to 34.7 cents per year at MIT in 1968.[24] Even at the higher figure, the cost of purchasing a five dollar microform replacement of a 400-page monograph would not be recovered through space savings alone in less than fourteen years. Depending on the application, a combination of weeding, warehousing, or compact shelving may prove a more cost-effective means to reduce total space consumption.[25]

As a result of the many variables involved in the computation of floor space value, public and academic libraries rarely cite space savings as the sole reason for conversion to microforms. Space savings are typically more significant to special libraries in hospitals, business, and industry, many of which occupy expensive rented quarters in crowded urban areas or compete for available expansion space with other divisions of their own organizations. In such libraries, conversion to microforms can reduce the amount of required space, thereby lowering annual rental payments or permitting collection expansion that would otherwise be impossible due to space constraints. At the Martland Hospital Library, for example, the unavailability of space for much-needed expansion proved the decisive factor in the replacement of hard copy periodical backfiles with microforms.[26] In such applications, microforms can be effective in extending the useful life of a library's physical facilities.[27]

## Microforms vs. Binding

A number of libraries leave paper copies of scholarly journals and other periodicals unbound at the end of the volume year and acquire permanent shelf copies on film or fiche from a micropublisher.[28] Following a predetermined period of most active reference—typically one or two years after receipt of the last volume issue—the paper copies are discarded, leaving the microform backfile to satisfy continuing, but diminished, use requirements. This approach to the management of the periodicals collection offers two potential advantages: backfile integrity and economy. Microform backfiles provide some defense against unavailability resulting from theft or mutilation of paper issues. Some technical libraries even prepare their own microform versions on receipt of paper issues to ensure availability. Because microforms must be used with special equipment that is not widely available outside of the library, microform editions are less likely to be stolen.

In terms of economy, it is important to note that, while micropublishers' pricing policies vary considerably, libraries ordering periodical backfiles in microform must generally pay for subscriptions to *both* the paper and the microform editions. Although some space is saved, the bulk of the additional acquisition costs must be recovered through the elimination of expenses associated with binding. These expenses, like the cost of book storage, vary with publication size, vendor, and geographic location. In 1973, the range was reported as $3.85 to $7.88 per volume for a twelve-inch periodical.[29] Labor and overhead charges associated with the preparation and control of materials to be bound may increase these costs by as much as three dollars per volume.[30] Thus, while it may cost eighteen dollars to bind the two semi-annual volumes of *Scientific American*, Xerox University Microfilms offers annual subscriptions to the microform edition for only twelve dollars. Part of this substantial saving must, however, be applied to the cost of purchasing, maintaining, and servicing readers and other use equipment discussed more fully in chapter six.

## The Duplicating Library

Recent attention given to the automation of the circulation activity has confirmed its labor-intensive, and consequently expensive, nature. In most libraries, the hours of circulation service are long. Extensive record-keeping is essential for controlling circulated items and recalling overdues. Returned materials must be sorted and reshelved. Taken together, these costs may easily exceed the purchase price of an item circulated more than a few times. Furthermore, items in circulation are not immediately available to other users.

In an important paper delivered at the 1962 convention of the National Microfilm Association, Laurence Heilprin outlined the concept of a *Duplicating* (D) Library in which an inviolate collection of books and other materials, in full-size or microform, is duplicated and distributed to patrons. The patron may use the duplicated items in or away from the library, keep them or dispose of them when finished. Guaranteed availability of materials, he noted, would result in greatly improved service. Heilprin further suggested that any portion of the copying charges not defrayed by the elimination of labor-intensive circulation activities might be charged back to the user.[31]

This approach to collection management is adopted in part by libraries of all types and sizes. Periodicals, for example, rarely circulate. In many libraries, patrons have the option of note-taking or of using self-service coin-operated copiers. In such applications, the patron pays a modest five- or ten-cent page charge that may not fully cover the cost of copier usage and supplies. The remaining costs are assumed by the library and recovered through the elimination of circulation-related expenses.[32] With respect to microforms, the most significant move in the direction of the D Library involves the maintenance and servicing of technical report files. As will be discussed more fully in chapter five, many libraries order NTIS and ERIC reports on microfiche. Rather than risk file integrity by allowing patrons to use master microfiche, inexpensive distribution duplicates are made on patron demand for local or remote use. The patron may discard these duplicate fiche or retain them in personal microform collections. Equipment and supplies for microform duplication are described in chapter three.[33]

## MICROFILMING AS A REPROGRAPHIC SERVICE

### Reproduction of Research Materials

Although the collection development and management applications described in the preceding sections rely heavily on microforms produced by micropublishers and other outside sources, there are occasions when libraries will want or need to create their own microforms. The potential of micrographics in the reproduction of research materials for personal use or interlibrary loan has been recognized since the 1930s. Despite the current dominance of electrostatic copies in interlibrary loan applications, microforms remain a viable alternative to the full-size reproduction of entire books, archival record series, manuscript collections, and similar voluminous research materials.[34] For such large orders, the use of microforms can simplify copy handling and significantly reduce both the required time of reproduction and the cost of mailing reproduced materials.

In 1940, only about fifteen percent of American academic libraries had microphotographic facilities.[35] By 1975, about fifty percent reported the capability of filling interlibrary loan requests in microform.[36] Growth, while significant, has undoubtedly been deterred by the greater availability and suitability of electrostatic copiers for the wide range of interlibrary loan requests. Because of the considerable investment in the equipment and staff required, library literature has traditionally advised the establishment of microfilming facilities only in larger research libraries.[37] Since 1970, however, the micrographics industry has given increased attention to the special needs of low-volume users in small offices. The acronym SOM is used to denote this *Small Office Microfilm* as a concept, a market, and a product group with distinctive characteristics.[38] The potential SOM market is extensive and includes a sizeable library component.[39] The prospective SOM user typically lacks micrographics expertise or experience and must operate within severe budgetary constraints. The availability of SOM cameras—described in chapter three—provides a library with limited capital funds and only occasional use requirements with the ability to produce high quality microforms for patron use, interlibrary loan, and similar reprographic service applications.

## Preservation Microfilming

Microforms have long been recognized as an effective alternative to slower, more expensive techniques in applications requiring the preservation of the information content of ephemeral library materials, especially newspapers.[40] Archival potential is an important advantage of silver halide microforms. When processed and stored in the manner outlined in chapter three, silver halide microforms will retain their original characteristics for very long periods of time.

An obvious limitation of preservation microfilming is the inability to preserve the physical form of the original document in those applications in which the physical form is significant.[41] In such applications, however, a microform use copy may satisfy many research requirements, thereby preventing much unnecessary deteriorative handling of materials in poor condition.

## INFORMATION RETRIEVAL

### Microforms and Technical Information

The advantages of microforms for the archival storage of inactive records, described in a preceding section, dominated commercial applications through the 1950s. Beginning in the 1960s, however, microform systems designers and manufacturers began emphasizing the potential of microforms in applications requiring the rapid retrieval of information from active files. Proponents of active microform systems stressed the advantages of file integrity and ease of duplication; the possibility of automated retrieval; and the potential for combining human- and machine-readable information on the same medium.[42] During the 1960s and early 1970s, a number of technical libraries and information centers developed specialized information storage and retrieval systems utilizing microforms as a preferred substitute for conventional printed materials. The availability of government-sponsored technical reports on microfiche, for example, spurred the development of complementary systems for other library materials. At the Bell Aerosystems Library, where microfiche are used in a selective dissemination of information program, technical reports not available on fiche from government sources are microfilmed locally and put into jackets.[43] Several universities experimented with microform-based information retrieval systems. The MASTIR System at the Institute of Gas Technology of the Illinois Institute of Technology interfaced microfilmed abstracts in 16mm cartridges with an optical coincidence uniterm index.[44] At Texas A and M University, a file of technical reports on microfiche was controlled by a computer-produced KWIC index also on microfiche.[45]

*Project Intrex*, the name given to the information transfer experiments conducted at the Massachusetts Institute of Technology between 1965 and 1973, was unquestionably the most ambitious and interesting of these university-based information retrieval programs.[46] Project Intrex was designed to examine the potential of new technologies in providing scientists with rapid remote access to both cataloging information and the full text of a data base consisting of professional journal articles. Participants in the Project were seeking alternatives to traditional library procedures in dealing with the increased flow of information resulting from the dramatic expansion of research and development activities following World War II. The Project Intrex data base, which ultimately reached 20,000 articles, was stored on microfiche and supported by an on-line computer-stored catalog and index with abstracts. The fiche themselves were stored in a desktop automated retrieval device adjacent to the terminal used to access the on-line catalog.

The designers of Project Intrex chose microforms for their full-text access system because of the expense of storing large amounts of alphanumeric and graphic data in computer-processable, machine-readable form. Although the cost of computer storage has decreased dramatically since 1965, and the focus of professional interest is increasingly on the development of total on-line systems, microforms remain an economical alternative to digital technology for the full-text storage of large data bases, especially in applications requiring massive conversions of data to machine-readable form. Microforms used in this way interface with on-line or computer-printed index information. At Schering Laboratories, for example, articles, reports, and other source documents containing references to Schering pharmaceutical products or their generic equivalents are converted to microfiche and accessed through computer-produced indexes.[47] Other manual and automated microform retrieval systems and techniques are described in chapter eight.

## Vertical File Conversion

Several libraries have recently reported the successful conversion of vertical files to microform with resulting benefits in ease of maintenance, retrieval, and dissemination. At the Consumer's Association Library in London, for example, a large, active, and frequently updated subject file of clippings and foreign consumer legislation has been converted to microfilm jackets, one jacket per subject.[48] In addition to saving considerable floor space in an area where high rents prohibited much needed collection expansion, the jacket system has simplified both filing and information dissemination. Using a table top camera, documents are microfilmed several times for filing in multiple locations, thereby eliminating cross references. When appropriate, entire jackets may be duplicated for filing under several subjects. In response to information requests, duplicates of jackets from the master file are distributed to patrons for their personal retention. The advantages of microfilm jackets in such applications are discussed more fully in chapter two.

In similar applications, an extensive file of clippings, pamphlets, broadsides, and similar materials maintained by the Schomberg Center are being converted to 175,000 microfiche.[49] At Portsmouth Polytechnic School of Architecture, a 35mm aperture card camera/processor is used to create a data base of archival drawings and student papers.[50] A number of newspaper libraries have converted their clipping files to microform.[51] As described in chapter eight, the Detroit Free Press Library maintains an automated microform-based news clipping retrieval system using Eastman Kodak MIRAcode equipment.

## LIBRARY RECORDS MANAGEMENT

### Microfilming of Operating Records

Records management is the application of systematic analysis and control to the records required to operate a library, business, government agency, or other organization.[52] As noted in a preceding section, microforms are widely used in business to reduce the bulk, or to simplify retrieval, of such operating records as purchase orders, transaction documents, accounts receivable, and personnel files. Although libraries generate as much paperwork as comparably sized businesses, library records management and its relationship to micrographics remain an unfortunately neglected subject. An exception to this statement is the use of microforms in circulation control, an application of micrographics pioneered by libraries.

The advantages of photography in recording circulation transactions were first publicized in the early 1950s.[53] Today, several manufacturers offer inexpensive microfilm systems for circulation control. The Recordak Starfile RV-1 Microfilmer (Fig. 1-1) is especially designed for such service-counter type applications in small to medium-sized public libraries. The RV-1 features an 11.5 by 4.25 inch photographic surface with three compartments designed to hold a book identification card, a borrower identification card, and a transaction slip indicating due date and other information meaningful to the borrower. These three items are recorded in a single exposure to complete a circulation transaction. Following filming, the book identification card and transaction slip are inserted in the pocket of the circulating book. Microfilmed documents, arranged by transaction number, provide the full record for each circulation transaction. When books are returned to the library, transaction slips are removed from book pockets and filed in numerical order. One or two weeks following the due date, this file of transaction slips is examined, missing numbers are determined, and the appropriate microfilm reels are consulted to determine borrowers' names and addresses. This information is then used to recall overdue items. Some libraries employ computer-processable transaction slips, which can be machine-sorted to print a list of overdue transactions.[54]

**Figure 1-1**

**Recordak Starfile RV-1 Microfilmer**
(Courtesy: Eastman Kodak Company)

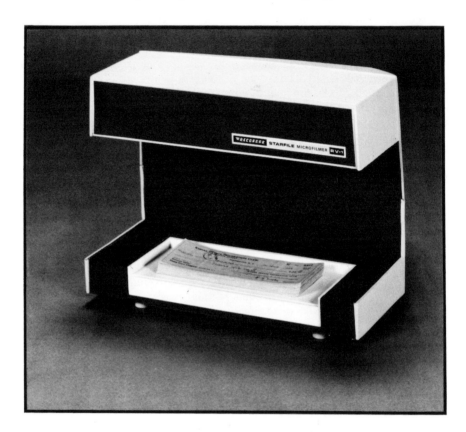

## Microform Catalogs

The library's single most important operating record—the public card catalog—has been faulted for unwarranted space consumption since the 1940s, when Fremont Rider pointed out that, with the doubling of library collections every fifteen years, the card catalog at Yale would require 750,000 drawers and occupy eight acres of floor space by 1980.[55] Despite this dramatic warning, librarians showed little enthusiasm for microform catalogs as space-saving devices through the 1950s. The development of multi-branch libraries and library systems during the 1960s, however, underscored a further liability of the card-form union catalog—its inaccessibility from branch libraries and other remote locations. As an alternative to the high cost of printed book catalogs, several public and corporate library systems microfilmed their union card catalogs, distributing duplicates to member libraries.[56] In addition to the reference value of remote access to information about system-wide holdings, these microform catalogs offered significant potential for cost reduction and improved service. Branch or member libraries submitting loan requests to system headquarters could prepare accurate bibliographic information locally, thereby eliminating much costly duplication of effort and reducing response time. Items unavailable through the system could be identified immediately, permitting alternative sources to be explored at once and eliminating time-consuming communication with system headquarters. By the same token, the Ramapo-Catskill Library System, which converted its 60,000-entry subject catalog to microfiche, reported a significant decline in the percentage of requests improperly diverted outside the system.[57]

Microfilming of card catalogs overcomes the problem of remote access but does nothing to reduce the increasingly high cost of catalog maintenance. At the University of British Columbia, for example, the filing of 813,600 cards in the academic year 1973-1974 required 5,500 hours of clerical effort.[58] The conversion of catalog data to machine-readable form permits computer processing and eliminates manual file maintenance, but batch-processed computer-printed catalogs may be out of date shortly after printing. Furthermore, the bulky output of computer printers occupies considerable space, may prove awkward to handle, and lacks the aesthetic qualities considered desirable by many libraries. Some of these difficulties can be overcome by on-line computerized catalogs, but the cost of developing and implementing such systems remains very high.

Despite the complexities outlined above, a 1975 survey found a significant number of medium-sized and large academic and public libraries considering alternatives to their existing card catalogs.[59] While complete on-line access was invariably mentioned as the most desirable alternative, less than 25 percent of the survey's 77 respondents expected to implement patron-accessible on-line catalogs before 1980. Over forty percent of the respondents—including most of the public libraries participating in the survey—reported that implementation of such a system would not occur before 1985. Increasingly, libraries in the latter group have turned to computer-output-microfilm (COM) for rapid, cost-effective access to machine-readable catalog data. Computer-output-microfilm is a technology that permits the conversion of machine-readable data to human-readable information on microfilm or microfiche without first creating a paper document. COM technology and its applicability to library records are discussed in detail in chapter four.

## REFERENCES

[1] On the history of microphotography, see Frederic Luther, *Microfilm: A History, 1839-1900* (Annapolis, Md: National Microfilm Associated, 1959); Luther, "Rene Dagron and the Seize of Paris," *American Documentation* 1 (1957): 196-206. Reviews of microform applications in libraries include: Ralph H. Carruthers, "The Place of Microfilm in Public Library Reference Work," *Journal of Documentary Reproduction* 1 (1938): 263-68; Rolland E. Stevens, "The Microform Revolution," *Library Trends* 19 (1971): 379-95; Vernon D. Tate, "From Binkley to Bush," *American Archivist* 10 (1947): 249-57; Keyes D. Metcalf, "Implications of Microfilm and Microprint for Libraries," *Library Journal* 70 (September 1, 1945): 718-23; Alfred Gunther, "Microphotography in the Library," *UNESCO Bulletin for Libraries* 14 (1962): 1-22; Philip Rochlin, "Micro Media in the Library: A Once Over Lightly," *Journal of Micrographics* 6 (1973): 99-104; Allen B. Veaner, "Microfilm and the Library: A Retrospective," *Drexel Library Quarterly* 11 (1975): 3-16.

[2] Edward A. Henry, "Film Versus Books," *Library Journal* 58 (1933): 237-40 described this as distinctly an American problem, since European scholars can travel to the great libraries at far less expense. See also Ralph H. Carruthers, "Problems of Mass Reproduction of Material in Foreign Collections," *Journal of Documentary Reproduction* 3 (1940): 169-75.

[3] On the earliest microfilming projects, see T. R. Schellenberg, "Library Applications of Microcopying," *Library Journal* 60 (1935): 289-92; Edward A. Henry, "Books on Film: Their Care and Use," *Library Journal* 57 (1932): 215-27; Grace G. Griffin, "Foreign American History Manuscript Copies in the Library of Congress," *Journal of Documentary Reproduction* 3 (1940): 3-9; Irvin Stewart, "Microphotography for Scholarly Purposes," *Journal of Documentary Reproduction* 4 (1941): 44-52; Lester K. Born, "History of Microfilm Activity," *Library Trends* 8 (1960): 348-58; Born, "A National Plan for Extensive Microfilm Operations," *American Documentation* 1 (1950): 65-75; Born, "Planning for Scholarly Photocopying," *PMLA* 79, pt. 2 (1964): 77-90; Charles G. La Hood, Jr., Microfilm for the Library of Congress," *College and Research Libraries* 34 (1973): 291-94.

[4] John Y. Cole, "Developing a Foreign Newspaper Microfilming Program," *Library Resources and Technical Services* 18 (1974): 5-17.

[5] James H. Case, Jr., "Latin American Microfilming Project at Brown University," *Journal of Documentary Reproduction* 3 (1940): 200-203.

[6] J. V. Jones and L. J. Dailey, "Vatican Library at St. Louis," *Library Journal* 82 (1957): 914-16.

[7] Barnes F. Lothrop, "Microfilming Materials for Southern History," *Journal of Documentary Reproduction* 2 (1939): 91-108. For a similar project, see Grace Lee Nute, "Microphotography at the Minnesota Historical Society," *Journal of Documentary Reproduction* 2 (1939): 109-117.

[8] John M. Blum, "Editor's Camera: The Letters of Theodore Roosevelt," *American Documentation* 1 (1950): 181-84.

[9] Robert C. Binkley, *Manual on Methods of Reproducing Research Materials* (Ann Arbor, Mich.: Edwards Bros., 1936); Binkley, "New Tools for Men of Letters," *Yale Review* 24 (1935): 519-37.

[10] Lester K. Born, "Planning for Scholarly Photocopying," *PMLA* 79 (1964): 77-90.

[11] A few libraries continue to maintain their own acquisitions-oriented microfilming facilities. See, for example, John M. Kinney, "The Texas Consortium to Microfilm Mexican Archival Resources," *College and Research Libraries* 32 (1971): 376-80; Theresa Blake, "Microfilm Publications Sponsored or Published by the Dartmouth College Library," *Dartmouth College Library Bulletin* (November 1975): 34-41; Sister Joan M. Braun, "The Monastic Manuscript Microfilm Library: The Mating of Medieval Knowledge with Modern Technology," *Microform Review* 1 (1972): 281-83.

[12] J. W. F. Herschel, Letter to the *Athenaeum* (July 1853). See G. W. W. Stevens, *Microphotography: Photography and Photofabrication at Extreme Resolution* (New York: John Wiley and Sons, 1968), pp. 363-64.

[13] Eugene B. Power, "University Microfilms," *Journal of Documentary Reproduction* 2 (1939): 21-28; Power, "University Microfilms—A Microfilming Service for Scholars," *Journal of Documentation* 2 (1946-47): 23-31.

[14] Lawrence S. Thompson, "Microforms as Library Resources," *Library Trends* 8 (1960): 359-71 notes the dependence of larger libraries on microforms for collection development.

[15] D. Joleen Block, "Microform Usage in Two Year Colleges," *Journal of Micrographics* 7 (1974): 231-34; Dale Gaddy and Aikin Connor, "Microform Systems in Community Colleges: New Users—New Data," *Journal of Micrographics* 4 (1971): 79-81; Louise Giles, *A Research Project to Determine the Student Acceptability and Learning Effectiveness of Microform Collections in Community Colleges, Phase I: Final Report* (Washington: American Association of Junior Colleges, June 1970).

[16] Charles P. Yerkes, "Micropublishing Market," *Proceedings of the National Microfilm Association* (Silver Spring, Md.: NMA, 1972), II-25-29; Yerkes, "Micropublishing: An Overview," *Journal of Micrographics* 5 (1971): 59-61.

[17] John P. Dessauer, "Library Acquisitions: A Look Into the Future," *Publishers Weekly* 207 (June 16, 1975): 55-68; Dessauer *Library Acquisitions: A Look Into the Future* (New York: Book Industry Study Group, 1976).

[18] H. R. Verry and G. H. Wright, *Microcopying Methods* (London: Focal Press, 1967), pp. 13-28 provides an introduction.

[19] For a brief summary of his main argument, see Fremont Rider, "The Future of the Research Library," *College and Research Libraries* 5 (1944): 301-308; Rider, "Microcards vs. the Cost of Book Storage," *American Documentation* 2 (1951): 39-44; Rider, "Warehouse or Microcard?," *Library Journal* 75 (1950): 832-36, 927-31; R. W. Batchelder, "The Scope and Value of the Microcard," *Special Libraries* 43 (1952): 157-61; J. W. Kuipers, "Microcards and Documentation," *American Documentation* 2 (1951): 89-94.

[20] Rider himself later decided against the storage of microcards in the public catalog. See Grace W. Bacon, "Handling Microcards in Libraries," *College and Research Libraries* 11 (1950): 372-73.

[21] W. E. Allord, "Some Economics—Microfilm and Space," *Records Management Quarterly* 5 (1971): 16-20; Frank W. Bobb, "Microfilm in a Records Management Program," *National Micro-News* 26 (1956): 1-13.

[22] Alan B. Pritsker and J. William Sadler, "An Evaluation of Microfilm as a Method of Book Storage," *College and Research Libraries* 18 (1957): 290-96.

[23] Jeffrey A. Raffel and Robert Shishko, *Systematic Analysis of University Libraries: An Application of Cost-Benefit Analysis to the MIT Libraries* (Cambridge: MIT Press, 1969), p. 22.

[24] Frederick C. Lynden, "Replacement of Hard Copy of Microforms," *Microform Review* 4 (1975): 9-14.

[25] Ralph E. Ellsworth, *The Economics of Book Storage in College and University Libraries* (Metuchen, N.J.: Scarecrow Press, 1969); F. J. Hill, "The Compact Storage of Books: A Study of Methods and Equipment," *Journal of Documentation* 11 (1955): 202-216; Lucinda Conger, "The Annex Library of Princeton University: The Development of a Compact Storage Library," *College and Research Libraries* 31 (1970): 160-68; Drahoslav Gawrecki, *Compact Library Shelving*, trans. Stanislav Rehak (Chicago: Library Technology Program and American Library Association, 1960).

[26] Esther R. Meirboom, "Conversion of the Periodical Collection in a Teaching Hospital to Microfilm Format," *Bulletin of the Medical Library Association* 64 (1976): 36-40.

[27] For examples, see Virginia L. Cuncan and Frances E. Parsons, "Use of Microfilm in an Industrial Research Library," *Special Libraries* 61 (1970): 288-90; Joan M. Daghita, "A Core Collection of Journals on Microfilm in a Community Teaching Hospital Library," *Bulletin of the Medical Library Association* 64 (1976): 240-41; P. R. P. Claridge, "Microfiching of Periodicals from the User's Point of View," *Aslib Proceedings* 21 (1969): 306-311; B. H. Weil, et al., "Esso Research Experiences with Chemical Abstracts on Microfilm," *Journal of Chemical Documentation* 5 (1965): 193-200; Lee N. Starker, "User Experiences with Primary Journals on 16mm Microfilm," *Journal of Chemical Documentation* 10 (1970): 5-6.

[28] The economics of this approach were first delineated by Eugene Power, "Microfilm as a Substitute for Binding," *American Documentation* 2 (1951): 33-39. See also David Peele, "Bind or Film: Factors in the Decision," *Library Resources and Technical Services* 8 (1964): 168-181; Michael Gabriel, "Surging Serial Costs: The Microfiche Solution," *Library Journal* 99 (October 1974): 2450-53.

[29] Frederick C. Lynden, "Replacement of Hard Copy by Microforms," *Microform Review* 4 (1975): 9-14.

[30] Jutta R. Ried, "Cost Comparison of Periodicals in Hard Copy and on Microform," *Microform Review* 5 (1976): 185-92.

[31] Laurence Heilprin, "Economics of 'On Demand' Library Copying," *Proceedings of the National Microfilm Association* (Annapolis, Md.: NMA, 1962): 311-39.

[32] See William Saffady, "Selecting Coin-Operated Copiers for Library Applications," *Library Resources and Technical Services* 20 (1976): 115-22.

[33] See also Edward Gray, "Subscriptions on Microfiche: An Irreversible Trend," *Journal of Micrographics* 8 (1975): 241-44.

[34] Albert H. Leisinger, Jr., "Selected Aspects of Microreproduction in the United States," *Archivum* 16 (1966): 127-50. Researchers in archives and manuscript libraries require convenient, rapid reproduction facilities. See William Saffady, "Reference Service to Researchers in Archives," *RQ* 14 (1974): 139-44.

[35] Harold P. Brown, "A Survey of Microfilm Sources," *Journal of Documentary Reproduction* 2 (1939): 118-24.

[36] Joseph Nitecki, comp., *Directory of Library Reprographic Services/A World Guide*, 6th ed. (Weston, Conn.: Microform Review, 1976).

[37] H. Fussler, "Some Implications of Microphotography for Librarians," *Journal of Documentary Reproduction* 2 (1939): 184-88; Fussler, *Photographic Reproduction for Libraries* (Chicago: University of Chicago Press, 1942); F. Donker Duyvis, "Document Reproduction Services: Their Efficient Organization and Management," *UNESCO Bulletin for Libraries* 14 (1960): 242-59; George A. Schwegmann, Jr., "The Photo-Duplication Services at the Library of Congress," *Journal of Documentary Reproduction* 2 (1939): 176-79. Some larger libraries employ customized equipment. See, for example, Don W. Massey, "The Management and Reorganization of the Photographic Services at Alderman Library, University of Virginia," *Journal of Micrographics* 4 (1970): 35-39.

[38] John Van Auken and Richard Van Auken, "Small Office Microfilm (SOM) Products: A Status Report," *Journal of Micrographics* 5 (1971): 5-11; Stanley Nathanson and Richard Van Auken, "The Emergence of Small Office Microfilm (SOM) Systems," *Information Records Management* 4 (December 1970): 36-40; Richard Van Auken, "The Need for Microfilm Systems Software," *Proceedings of the National Microfilm Association* (Silver Spring: NMA, 1971): 3-7; Alan W. Wilbur, "Microfiche Systems for the Small User," *Journal of Micrographics* 5 (1972): 131-36.

[39] William Saffady, "Small Office Microfilm (SOM) Products: A Survey for Libraries," *Microform Review* 5 (1976): 265-71; Herman Fussler, "Microphotography for Smaller Libraries," *ALA Bulletin* 31 (1937): 41-42; George W. Tressel, "A Personal Microform System," *Journal of Micrographics* 5 (1972): 287-89.

[40] Karl Brown, "Newspapers on Films," *Library Journal* 59 (1934): 471; L. Bendikson, "The Place of Photography in the Reproduction and Preservation of Source Materials," *Library Journal* 59 (1934): 548-49; Sidney H. Houghton, "Preservation of Records by Microphotography in the United States," *Journal of Documentation* 1 (1938): 156-61; Daniel F. Noll, "Some Recent Developments in Public Record Microfilming," *Journal of Documentary Reproduction* 4 (1941): 109-117; William H. Herman, "Microphotographing Bound Milwaukee Newspapers," *Journal of Documentary Reproduction* 2 (1939): 11-20; Ladd Z. Sajor, "Preservation Microfilming: Why, What, When, How," *Special Libraries* 63 (1972): 195-201; Herbert Bouscher, "Microforms: Can They Save Our Treasures," *Journal of Micrographics* 7 (1974): 119-22; Pamela W. Darling, "Microforms in Libraries: Preservation and Storage," *Microform Review* 5 (1976): 93-100; Darling, "Developing a Preservation Microfilming Program," *Library Journal* 99 (1974): 2803-2809.

[41] W. A. Jackson, "Some Limitations of Microfilm," *Papers of the Bibliographic Society of America* 35 (1941): 281-288; L. A. Cummings, "Pitfalls of Photocopy Research," *Bulletin of the New York Public Library* 65 (1960): 97-101; Louis Gottschalk, "Possible Readjustments by the Scholar," *Library Quarterly* 23 (1953): 205-215; H. J. Hanham, "Clio's Weapons," *Daedalus* 100 (1971): 509-519; Walter Rundell, *In Pursuit of American History* (Norman: University of Oklahoma Press, 1970), pp. 202-233.

[42] Klaus W. Otten, "Microform in the Research Library of the Future," *Journal of Micrographics* 6 (1973): 121-27; Otten, "A Hypothesis: Microform Will Become the Major Medium for New Information in Reference Libraries," *Journal of Micrographics* 4 (1971): 265-74; Alan G. Negus and Edward J. Malkiewich, "The Use of Microfilm as a Creative Systems Tool," *Information and Records Management* 6 (September, 1972): 42-46; Ernest P. Taubes, "Microfilm as Systems Tool," *National Micro-News* No. 68 (February 1964): 151-69; Peter R. Scott, "Microform Systems in Education and Research," *Proceedings of the National Microfilm Association* (Silver Spring, Md.: NMA, 1968): 321-25; A. S. Tauber, "The Dynamic Use of Microfiche," *Proceedings of the National Microfilm Association* (Annapolis, Md.: NMA, 1966): 41-51; R. E. Mayberry, "Microfilm— A Means, Not An End," *Proceedings of the National Microfilm Association* (Annapolis, Md.: NMA, 1962): 137-41.

[43] Albert D. Neveu, "Bell Aerosystems Library Information Dissemination System," *Proceedings of the National Microfilm Association* (Silver Spring, Md.: NMA, 1969): 33-44. For other examples, see C. H. O'Donahue, "Microfilm-Based Information Systems and Their Use in an R and D Center," *Journal of Chemical Documentation* 14 (1974): 163-65; M. Arthur Manzelli, "Information Retrieval from Microfilmed Research Reports at Philip Morris," *NMA Journal* 2 (1968): 3-4; G. H. Kieswetter, "Technical Communications in a Decentralized Corporation," *NMA Journal* 2 (1968): 40-43; C. Allen Merritt, "Micro Today and Tomorrow in Information Retrieval," *NMA Journal* 2 (1968): 108-110; Merritt, "Microfiche in an Informational Retrieval System," *Proceedings of the National Microfilm Association* (Annapolis, Md.: NMA, 1967): 3-8; E. Tylicki, "Preparation of a Microfilm File of Company Technical Reports," *Journal of Chemical Documentation* 10 (1970): 20-22; J. E. Crow, "Microforms and Technical Information," *Journal of Chemical Documentation* 8 (1968): 204-207.

[44] Harold L. Mensch, "Cost Analysis of an Information System for the Gas Utility Industry," *Proceedings of the American Society for Information Science* 10 (1973): 147-48. A similar system is described in R. I. Tomlin and R. G. Brunner, "A Total Information Concept: Rapid Retrieval of Microfilmed Documents Using an Optical Coincidence System," *NMA Journal* 2 (1968): 102-104.

[45] Roger E. Elliot and Eugene B. Smith, "A Specialized University Information Center," *Journal of Micrographics* 3 (1969): 95-101. See also Rowena W. Swanson, et al., *Micrographics in Modern Information Systems.* Proceedings of a Conference Sponsored by Texas A and M University (College Station: Texas A and M, 1969).

[46] Peter Scott, "Project Intrex and Microphotography," In *Intrex: Report of a Planning Conference on Information Transfer Experiments* (Cambridge: MIT Press, 1965): pp. 203-215; Carl F. J. Overhage and J. Francis Reintjes, "Project Intrex: A General Review," *Information Storage and Retrieval* 10 (1974): 157-188; Donald R. Knudson and Richard S. Marcus, "The Design of a Microimage Storage and Transmission Capability into an Integrated Transfer System," *Journal of Micrographics* 6 (1972): 15-20; Carl F. J. Overhage, "Science, Libraries: Prospects and Problems," *Science* 155 (1967): 802-806.

[47] Maryann J. Mislovitz, "Control and Dissemination of Drug Related Literature," *Proceedings of the American Society for Information Science* 10 (1973): 157-58.

[48] Peter A. Thomas, "Microfiche in a Special Library," *New Library World* 76 (1975): 43-44; Marion Chinn, "A Microfiche System for Legal Materials at Consumers' Association Library," *Microdoc* 14 (1975): 109-111.

[49] Ottila M. Pearson, "Planning for Preserving the Schomberg Center Vertical File via Microfiche," *Microform Review* 5 (1976): 25-33.

[50] John Perry, "How Microfilm Assists Architectural Information Retrieval," *Microform Review* 3 (1974): 263-65.

[51] Kenneth Janda and D. Gordon, "Microfilm Information Systems for Newspaper Libraries," *Special Libraries* 61 (1970): 33-47.

[52] See William Benedon, *Records Management* (Englewood Cliffs, N.J.: Prentice-Hall, 1969).

[53] Ralph R. Shaw, *The Use of Photography for Clerical Routines* (Washington: American Council of Learned Societies, 1953).

[54] George Fry Consultants, "Starfile/EDP: Two Systems of Circulation Control," *Library Technology Reports* (March 1970).

[55] Fremont Rider, *The Scholar and the Future of the Research Library* (New York: Hamden Press, 1944).

[56] Clara A. Falk, Bell W. Campbell, and Masse Bloomfield, "A Microfilm Card Catalog at Work," *Special Libraries* 67 (1976): 316-38; Anthony W. Miele, "The Illinois State Library Microfilm Automated Catalog (IMAC)," *Microform Review* 2 (1973): 27-31; C. Edward Carroll, "Microfilmed Catalogs: A More Efficient Way to Share Library Resources," *Microform Review* 1 (1972): 274-78; O. P. Gillack and R. H. McDonaugh, "Spreading State Library Riches for Peanuts," *Wilson Library Bulletin* 45 (1970): 354-57.

[57] Katherine Gaines, "Undertaking a Subject Catalog on Microfiche," *Library Resources and Technical Services* 15 (1971): 297-308.

[58] J. McRee Elrod, "Is the Card Catalogue's Unquestioned Sway in North America Ending?," *Journal of Academic Librarianship* 2 (1976): 4-8.

[59] Kenneth John Bierman, "Automated Alternatives to Card Catalogs: The Current State of Planning and Implementation," *Journal of Library Automation* 8 (1975): 277-98; see also "The Future of Card Catalogs," Association for Research Libraries, Minutes of the Eighty-fifth Meeting, June 18, 1975, pp. 40-42.

# CHAPTER 2

# TYPES OF MICROFORMS AND THEIR USES

## INTRODUCTION

### Definitions

*Microform* is a generic term for any information communication or storage medium containing images too small to be read without magnification. This definition excludes eye-legible, reduced-size copies made on a Xerox model 7000 or equivalent copier/duplicator with reduction capability. The term does encompass both transparent (film) and opaque (paper) image supports. The images themselves, properly called *microimages*, may contain textual or graphic information produced by microfilm cameras from source documents such as bound volumes, technical reports, and office correspondence, or from digital data by a computer-output-microfilm (COM) recorder.[1]

In terms of physical appearance, microforms are divided into two broad groups: *roll* and *flat*. The most common roll microforms consist of varying lengths of microfilm, usually 16mm or 35mm wide, wound on a flanged holder called a *reel* or loaded into a cartridge or cassette. The flat microforms include *microfiche*, *microfilm jackets, aperture cards*, and *micro-opaques*. Subsequent sections of this chapter describe the most important microforms and their uses in library applications.[2]

### Reduction

Regardless of physical appearance, all microforms present information in reduced size. *Reduction* is a measure of the number of times a given linear dimension of a document or other object is reduced through microphotography. This measure is expressed as 14X, 24X, 42X, and so on, where the reduced linear dimension is 1/14, 1/24, or 1/42 the length of its full-size counterpart. Alternatively, reduction can be expressed as the *ratio* of the measure of a given linear dimension of a document to the measure of the corresponding linear dimension of its microimage—14:1, 24:1, 42:1.

Reductions below 15X are termed *low*. *Medium* reductions range from 15X through 30X. Reductions above 30X up to and including 60X are termed *high*. Reductions from 60X through 90X are considered *very high*. Reductions above 90X are termed *ultra high*.

The choice of reductions is based on a number of considerations, including the nature of the documents being microfilmed, the microform utilized, and conditions and equipment at the point of use. As a general rule, the reduction ratio chosen must be suitable for microfilming a given document or group of documents without loss of information, and for producing legible duplicate microforms through several generations. The ease of handling that results from having many pages of information on a single microform makes higher reductions attractive, but the varied type faces and poor condition of many library materials make medium or even low reductions mandatory. As a linear measure, reduction does not convey the magnitude of the total reduction in document area achieved through microphotography. The microimage of a letter-size document reduced 24X, for example, actually occupies only about 1/580 the area of the original. When conventional silver microphotographic materials are utilized to make large area reductions, fewer silver halide grains are available in any given area of film to define the shape of individual characters in the original document. If all text were printed on white paper of uniform opacity in sans serif ten-point type without italics or hairlines, higher reductions would pose few problems. But libraries have no control over the physical characteristics of documents in their collections. A National Bureau of Standards study of photometric characteristics of bound serials and monographs in the National Library of Medicine found significant information recorded in type sizes as small as 0.5mm high. Although the total percentage of such characters in library materials is quite low, preservation of their information content is essential to the mission of the library. When works printed in Oriental languages are microfilmed, even minor quality deterioration can change the meaning of symbols. Consequently, the NBS study recommended a maximum reduction of 12X.[3]

Other authorities generally concur in recommending low reductions for library materials microfilmed by conventional techniques. Hawken, following an extensive examination of the typographic characteristics of printed text, suggested a maximum reduction of 12.7X to ensure legibility through several generations.[4] The American Library Association's *Microfilm Norms* (Chicago: Resources and Technical Services Division, 1966) set the standard reduction for library materials at 14X. *Specifications for the Microfilming of Books and Pamphlets in the Library of Congress* (Washington: Library of Congress, 1973) and *Specifications for the Microfilming of Newspapers in the Library of Congress* (Washington: Library of Congress, 1972) both recommend normal working reductions in the range 16X to 20X. For typewritten reports, where individual character size is typically larger than in printed documents, the Committee on Scientific and Technical Information (COSATI) microfiche standard, developed in 1964, provided for an 18X maximum reduction. The widespread use of electric typewriters with carbon ribbons has improved document quality to the point where the current National Micrographics Association microfiche standard of 24X reduction is acceptable for most typewritten reports. Despite improvements in camera lenses and microfilm emulsions, 24X is likely to remain the upper limit of recommended reduction in source document microphotography for the foreseeable future. An exception must be made in applications involving source documents created expressly for microfilming. With the *NMA Microfont* (Fig. 2-1), a sans serif typeface designed specifically for microreproduction, legible diazo duplicates of source documents reduced 30X have been made through as many as eleven generations.[5] In computer-output-microfilming, described in detail in chapter four, close control of type font, size, and image density permits reductions in excess of 40X with legible results.

**Figure 2-1**

**NMA Microfont**
(Courtesy: National Micrographics Association)

ABCDEFGHIJKLMNO

PQRSTUVWXYZ.-,:;

1234567890=÷+−±

@&*?#×''%'( )[ ]°!

¢$/_∠∞Δ≈~∅⊥<>μα

√σδΣγπβθωΩ∴||

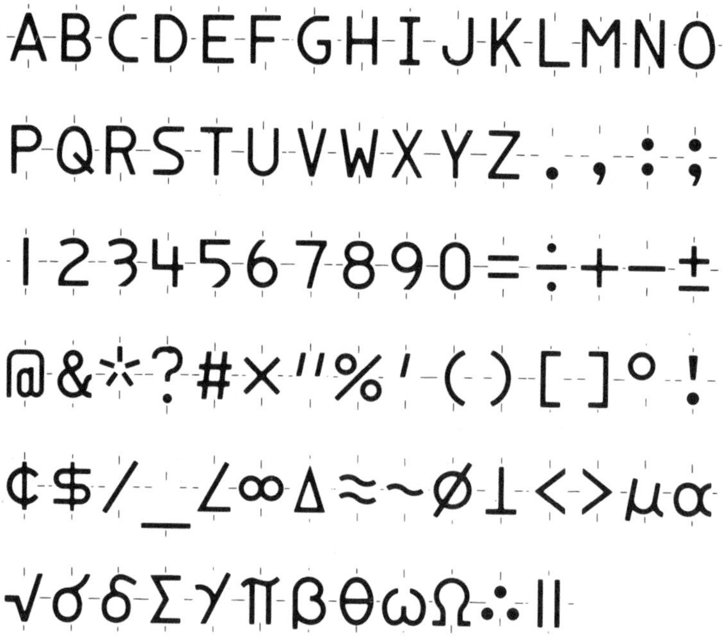

### Standards

As the micrographics industry has matured, early tendencies toward proprietary design have given way to standardization.[6] Standards have, in turn, led to increased user confidence and acceptance. Today, micrographics standards are developed at several levels.

In the United States, the seventeen standards committees of the National Micrographics Association prepare proposed standards that are distributed for comment and vote to the entire NMA membership. If the vote is favorable, the standard is published as an NMA Industry Standard. Industry Standards reflect membership consensus about the state-of-the-art at a specific point in time and are subject to change. The NMA Industry Standard for Microfiche of Documents, for example, has been rewritten several times.

The PH5 Committee of the American National Standards Institute (ANSI) is responsible for the approval of national micrographics standards. Like the NMA standards committees, ANSI PH5 consists of both users and vendors. The NMA now serves as the sponsor/secretariat of the committee, a role formerly played by the American Library Association. All NMA Industry Standards are submitted to the PH5 Committee for consideration as American National Standards.

International micrographics standards are developed out of the prevailing practices of seventy nations by the TC 46/SC 1 Committee of the International Standards Organization (ISO). The NMA represents the United States' interests on this committee. Current NMA, ANSI, and ISO standards are discussed in the applicable sections of this text.[7]

In some cases, individual organizations and institutions have developed their own micrographics standards. The Catalog Committee of the Automotive Advertisers Council, for example, prescribes a proprietary microfiche standard consisting of 49 double frames reduced 24X, to be observed in the micropublication of parts catalogs for the automotive after-market. Likewise, the Aviation Distributors and Manufacturers Association has its own standard for microfiche catalogs, providing 288 frames reduced 40X.[8] In the library field, only the California State Universities and Colleges have developed and published their own standards statement.[9]

Except when mandated in a procurement documents, adherence to micrographics standards is voluntary. Standards benefit both users and vendors, however, in a number of ways: by lowering equipment costs and speeding development times; by insuring compatibility and interchangeability of supplies and components; and by simplifying systems design, procurement, training, and control. Furthermore, when the vocabulary of a discipline is standardized—as it is in the NMA *Glossary of Micrographics*—the interchange of information among interested persons is facilitated.

## ROLL MICROFORMS

### Reel Microfilm

*Roll microform* is a generic term for reel microfilm, microfilm cartridges, and microfilm cassettes.[10] Like motion picture film, most microfilm is supplied and exposed in rolls. Following processing, roll microfilm can be converted to other microforms, but much of it is simply wound onto reels for viewing or storage. Most reel microfilm is 16mm or 35mm wide (Fig. 2-2). In 1971, the Micro-8 Company of La Crosse, Wisconsin, introduced an 8mm roll microform designed specifically for the small office market, a market with a sizeable library counterpart.[11] Despite a relatively low price and attractive equipment, the 8mm microform gained few adherents in the general micrographics user community and none in the library field. The limitations of an 8mm film width necessitated reductions too high for many library materials. While Micro-8 products are no longer available, Information Handling Services still offers its Visual Search Microfilm (VSMF) catalog series, a data base of military and engineering specifications, in 8mm cassettes.[12]

Thirty-five millimeter reel microfilm has such a long history of use in library applications that some authorities consider it, for better or worse, the de facto library standard. The 35mm film width affords the large image area necessary for

**Figure 2-2**

(Courtesy: University Microfilms International)

the reproduction of newspapers, maps, charts, and other large documents at low to medium reductions. The greater film width also permits the recording of deteriorating books and manuscripts at reductions as low as 9X to 12X. While it is the only microform capable of accommodating the full range of library materials, many systems designers contend that 35mm reel microfilm is incompatible with effective retrieval and should, consequently, be avoided whenever possible. Although many libraries have invested heavily in 35mm reel microfilm collections, micrographics equipment manufacturers, with a few exceptions, have not considered the library market sufficiently lucrative to design products specifically for it. Consequently, much 35mm display equipment is archaic in concept and difficult to use. New models are rarely introduced and seldom represent significant improvements in the state-of-the-art. In a 1973 equipment evaluation by researchers at the National Archives, the Recordak MPE and Recordak Model C—two 35mm microfilm readers no longer in production—were rated consistently better than most newer models.[13]

Because 16mm reel microfilm is used in many commercial applications, a wider selection of newer readers and reader/printers is available. For letter-size documents, the 16mm film width requires a minimum reduction of 18X. Most applications utilize a 24X reduction, which is compatible with the NMA standard for microfiche of source documents. Many industrial and technical libraries, contending that these somewhat higher reductions are compatible with acceptable image quality for typewritten or printed source documents in good condition, refuse to buy 35mm microfilm and, instead, maintain their journal backfiles and similar materials on 16mm microfilm reels, cartridges, or cassettes.[14] Commercial micropublishers have encouraged the adoption of 16mm microfilm, since economies are possible through the simultaneous production of 16mm microfilm and microfiche at 24X reduction. Academic libraries with substantial investments in 35mm microfilm readers and reader/printers have generally resisted any change to 16mm. Several years ago, when Xerox University Microfilms announced that its micropublished serials would henceforth be available only on 16mm microfilm or microfiche, the protest from academic libraries was so great that the announcement was rescinded. At the California State Universities and Colleges, a microforms acquisition policy approved by the Board of Trustees specifically prohibits the purchase of 16mm microfilm.

Regardless of film width, reel microfilm has significant strengths that account for its continuing popularity in libraries. These strengths include the following:

## Economy

In terms of both equipment and labor, reel microfilm is the least expensive microform to create. For 16mm reel microfilm, several excellent cameras, described in the next chapter, are priced within the budgets of most medium-sized libraries. Cameras that accept 35mm microfilm are usually more expensive. In both cases, production techniques are straightforward.

## Storage Density

The microimage capacity of a 16mm by one hundred foot reel depends on reduction and image orientation but generally exceeds 2,000 letter-size documents reduced 24X. Reel microfilm is, consequently, well suited to very large document sets, such as newspaper and serial backfiles or archival collections.

## Format Flexibility

The *USA Standard Specifications for 16mm and 35mm Silver-Gelatin Microfilms for Reel Applications* (New York: American National Standards Institute, 1967) recognizes four types of image placement (Fig. 2-3), which together accommodate a wide range of document sizes. In position *1A*, the text of the document runs perpendicular to the edges of the film and a single document appears in each film frame. In position *2A*, the image orientation is identical, but two documents appear in each film frame. Positions 1A and 2A are often called *cine mode* orientations because of their similarity to the orientation of frames on motion picture film. In position *1B*, the text of the document runs parallel to the edges of the film and a single document appears in each film frame. If two documents appear in each film frame, the image placement is *2B*. Positions 1B and 2B are often called *comic mode* orientations because of their similarity to the orientation of panels in a comic book. The choice of image orientation depends on the dimensions of the original document and the reduction used. When filming average-size newspapers at 18X reduction on 35mm microfilm, for example, position 2B is preferred. Position 2A is possible with tabloids and can result in greater information compaction. Position 1A is required for oversize newspapers and other very large documents. This flexibility in image placement—typically not possible with other microforms—also facilitates the microreproduction of the variously sized source documents commonly encountered in archival and manuscript collections.[15]

## Vital Records Protection

The reel is an excellent microform for vital records protection. In the event of fire or other disaster, a library card catalog on reel microfilm can be reproduced at full size on card stock using a Xerox Copyflo machine.

## Flexibility

Sixteen millimeter and, to a limited extent, 35mm reel microfilm can be converted to cartridges, cassettes, microfiche, microfilm jackets, or aperture cards as requirements change. The shape of other microforms cannot be altered as easily.

Despite these strengths, reel microfilm suffers from some serious disadvantages that limit its utility. The necessity of removing a reel of microfilm from its container, mounting it with more or less difficulty on a reader, threading the proper amount of leader through the film gate, rewinding the film, and returning the reel

Figure 2-3

American National Standard Image Placements

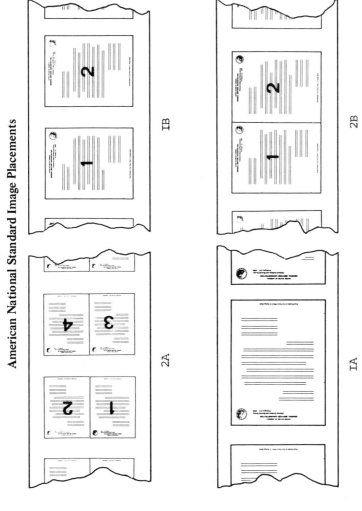

to the proper container when finished constitutes not only a genuine inconvenience but a potentially insurmountable psychological obstacle to many users. Librarians who have supervised microform reading rooms are aware of the problems: reels are returned to the wrong containers; patrons, unable to thread the microfilm, are too embarrassed to ask for help; an entire reel of microfilm, inadvertently wound onto the reader's take-up spool, is replaced in the container, backwards, for the next unfortunate user to find.

In some applications, roll microforms compound this inconvenience by limiting the user to serial access. Once the reel has been correctly mounted on the reader, the user seeking a particular microimage must pass through all preceding microimages. Readers with motorized film advances can reduce the traverse time to the desired microimage, but such readers are more complex and expensive than their manual counterparts. Reel microfilm readers cost more than flat microform readers in any case. A high-quality microfiche reader can be purchased for about two hundred dollars. A reel microfilm reader of comparable quality costs twice as much.

Apart from splicing, there is no way to add or remove microimages from reel microfilm. This makes the reel an unacceptable microform for dynamic document collections, such as library vertical files. Reel microfilm can be duplicated, but expensive equipment is required and selective duplication of microimages is difficult. A library patron who wants a microform duplicate of one twenty-page technical report contained on a 16mm reel with other such reports must accept a duplicate of the entire reel.

Because it is difficult to handle and it limits the user to serial access, reel microfilm is rarely the microform of choice in applications involving the brief examination of documents scattered on many separate reels. It is, however, acceptable for the detailed study of many documents on a single reel—as is often the case with microfilmed manuscript collections or newspaper backfiles—or for microforms that will rarely be consulted and for which the expense of other formats cannot be justified.

## Cartridges and Cassettes

The unique advantages of other microforms are, in many ways, responses to one or more of the disadvantages of reel microfilm. Cartridges and cassettes are designed for users who want the advantages of reel microfilm—especially high image capacity and internal format flexibility—without the inconvenience of manual film handling. While they share a common purpose, cartridges and cassettes differ in design. A cartridge (Fig. 2-4) is a plastic, *single-core* microfilm container. When mounted on an appropriate reader, microfilm from the cartridge is automatically threaded onto a take-up spool built into the reader itself. The microfilm passes out of the cartridge during use and must be rewound into the cartridge prior to removal from the reader. A cassette is a plastic, *double-core* microfilm container that encloses both a supply and take-up spool in a single housing (Fig. 2-5, p. 40). Cassettes require no film threading and can be removed from the reader at any time without rewinding.

**Figure 2-4**

**16mm Microfilm Cartridge** (Courtesy: Microfilm Enterprises Marketing Company)

**Figure 2-5**

**16mm Microfilm Cassette** (Courtesy: Bell and Howell)

Cartridges were introduced in 1959 by Eastman Kodak for the catalogs of the Sears Roebuck Company, one of the first applications involving the active use of microforms for information retrieval.[16] They have since been successfully used in libraries for the maintenance of periodical backfiles and card catalogs.[17] At the Learning Resources Center of Prince George Community College, the conversion of a 3,000-reel microfilm collection to cartridges resulted in a significant decrease in both user resistance and required professional assistance to users.[18] Cassettes have been used successfully for computer-output-microfilm catalogs in British and Australian libraries.[19] In the United States, the Wayne State University Libraries chose cassettes in preference to cartridges for its microform serials holdings list because rewinding film back into a cartridge before removing the cartridge from the reader created undesirable complications in a public use application.[20]

While the conversion of reel microfilm to cartridges or cassettes is technically simple—requiring only a relatively inexpensive loading device, special leader and trailer, and some splicing tabs—the time and labor involved, combined with the cost of the cartridges or cassettes themselves, can prove prohibitive in libraries with large reel microfilm collections. A 1970 analysis of the cost of converting 30,000 reels of microfilm to cartridges at the University of Pittsburgh Libraries, for example, estimated initial expenses for labor, cartridges, and required new readers and reader/printers at more than $60,000.[21] Partial conversion for very active materials, combined with the acquisition of micropublications in cartridges or cassettes whenever possible, can reduce conversion costs but may produce patron confusion over the introduction of another microform with different equipment requirements. As another alternative to the expense of full conversion to conventional cartridges, the Recordak (Kodak) Thread-Easy Magazine (Fig. 2-6) is an inexpensive plastic collar designed to hold a reel of 16mm or 35mm microfilm without leaders, trailers, or splicing tabs. The Thread-Easy Magazine eliminates manual film handling when used with appropriate Recordak readers and reader/ printers. The same results can be achieved with the 3M Easy-Load Cartridge, a leaderless 16mm reel microfilm container designed for use with the 3M 600 Dry Silver Reader/Printer. In both cases, prices are about one-third those of conventional Recordak or 3M cartridges. Reel microfilm can be converted to the Thread-Easy Magazine or Easy-Load Cartridge at the point of use without special equipment.

The lack of standardization has deterred the development of cartridge and cassette applications, while competition among the major suppliers has complicated the development of standards. Spreitzer estimated that, by 1969, about 32 different cartridges and cassettes were available for sale—all of them incompatible with one another.[22] Today, the two most popular cartridges, the 3M Cartridge and the Recordak Film Magazine, share common external dimensions but are otherwise incompatible. The choice of one cartridge necessarily limits future systems change and equipment selection, since the cartridges of one supplier cannot be used with readers or reader/printers manufactured by the other. Bell and Howell and Memorex cassettes are likewise incompatible. The National Micrographics Association standards for cartridges and cassettes, completed in 1975 after several years of work, are based on designs that are totally different from any existing products—a necessary precaution to avoid giving any one supplier an unfair advantage during the time required to develop and test new readers and reader/printers.[23] The extent

**Figure 2-6**

**Recordak Thread-Easy Magazine** (Courtesy: Eastman Kodak Company)

to which large cartridge and cassette collections will be converted to the new standard containers when they become available cannot now be determined. In the meantime, the Information Design Cartridge (Fig. 2-7), designed to operate on appropriately modified readers and reader/printers of several manufacturers, offers libraries a partial solution to the problem of incompatibility.

As an additional complication for libraries, the 3M Cartridge, the Recordak Film Magazine, the Bell and Howell Cassette, and the Memorex Cassette are designed exclusively for 16mm microfilm. Only the Information Design Cartridge and Recordak Thread-Easy Magazine will accept 35mm microfilm. There are no 35mm microfilm cassettes available in the United States.

Cartridges and cassette readers and reader/printers are mechanically complex and, hence, more expensive than reel microfilm equipment. The expense of providing a sufficient number of readers and reader/printers to encourage proper microform utilization must be a consideration in the decision to convert large reel microfilm collections to cartridges or cassettes. No portable cartridge or cassette readers are currently available.

While cartridges and cassettes protect film from smudges and fingerprints, the motorized film transport in some cartridge and cassette readers can scratch or otherwise damage film. Although cartridges are much easier to handle than reel microfilm, user instruction is still required. Uninstructed users may, for example, forget to rewind the microfilm before removing the cartridge from the reader. Cassettes eliminate this problem, but the number of cassette readers available in the United States is limited.

Finally, some disadvantages of reel microfilm—the inability to update a reel conveniently or to duplicate microimages selectively, for example—are actually compounded by conversion to cartridges or cassettes.


## FLAT MICROFORMS

### Microfiche

A microfiche is a sheet of film containing multiple microimages in a two-dimensional grid pattern of rows and columns (Fig. 2-8, p. 45). The term is used in both the singular and plural and is often simply abbreviated as *fiche*. While sheet microforms have been utilized extensively in Europe for making inexpensive reproductions of library materials since the 1950s,[24] microfiche are relatively new to the United States. The introduction of government technical reports on fiche during the 1960s put libraries in the forefront of applications development. Commercial applications were slow to follow.[25] As late as 1970, articles about micrographics in business periodicals described microfiche as an innovation, although the development of computer-output-microfilm and proprietary micro-publishing have led to a rapid expansion of fiche applications in the past five years. Seventy-three percent of the respondents to a 1977 survey of commercial and government micrographics users report the use of microfiche in one or more applications. In 1975, 57.2 percent reported microfiche use.[26] Much of this

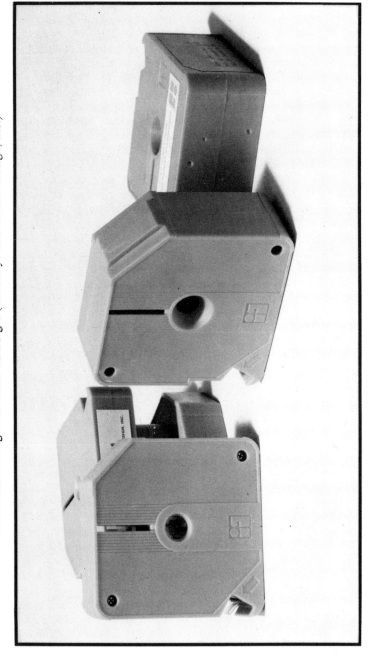

**Figure 2-7**

**Information Design Microfilm Cartridges** (Courtesy: Information Design, Inc.)

**Figure 2-8**

**Microfiche**

(Courtesy: Congressional Information Service)

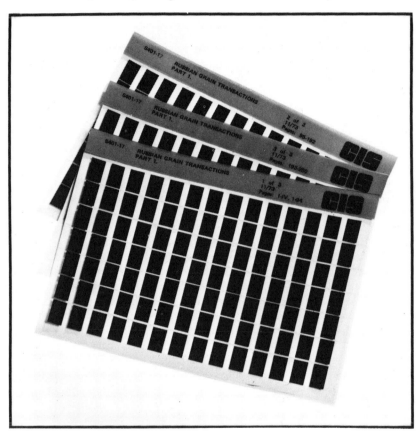

expansion has been at the expense of 16mm reel microfilm, reported use of which fell from 51.9 percent in 1975 to 40.2 percent in 1976 and 39.5 percent in 1977. Cartridge use rose only slightly, from 27.9 percent in 1975 to 29.7 percent in 1976, but dropped to 23.7 percent in 1977.

Users are generally attracted by the suitability of microfiche as a unit record for documents less than a few hundred pages in length and by the development of microfiche standards that have made possible the production of inexpensive, high-quality readers and reader/printers. Because of their high microimage capacity, reel microfilm, cartridges, and cassettes are often referred to as *non-unitized* microforms. A single reel, cartridge, or cassette may contain many, possibly unrelated, documents. The Xerox University Microfilm's *Early English Books Series*, for example, often groups discrete bibliographic units on 35mm microfilm reels without regard to the relationship of a given title to the one preceding or following it. Microfiche, on the other hand, are generally considered a *unitized* microform. Unitized microforms present a unit of information with no unrelated microimages. With their much lower microimage capacity, microfiche establish a one-to-one correspondence between a physical record (the microform) and a logical record (a file folder, technical report, periodical issue, or other multi-page document). This distinction between unitized and non-unitized microforms, while generally valid, must be made with caution. Roll microforms can effectively unitize large document collections, such as newspaper or periodical backfiles. The Roosevelt Library's edition of *The Press Conferences of Franklin D. Roosevelt, 1933-1945* groups transcripts by year on individual 35mm microfilm reels. On the other hand, many micropublishers offer very large document collections on microfiche without regard to unitization.

Although microfiche are available in several sizes, the 105 by 148mm (approximately four by six inch) microfiche is the American and international standard for both source documents and computer-output-microfilm. Libraries can thus purchase and exchange microfiche on a worldwide basis with reasonable assurance of size compatibility. There are exceptions, of course. Some European micropublishers continue to use non-standard sizes. The Inter Documentation Company, for example, offers its *Census of India, 1872-1952* on three by five inch fiche. Antiquariaat Junk, the Dutch micropublisher, offers the 39-volume set *Fauna und Flora des Golfes von Neapel und der angrenzenden Meiresabschnitte* on large nine by twelve inch fiche.[27] In the United States, departures from the standard size are sometimes made for particular systems. IBM chose tabcard size microfiche (3.25 by 7.375 inches) for its program of disseminating worldwide technical reports. The choice was based largely on the availability of significant amounts of tabcard filing equipment in the offices of IBM and its customers.[28] The 3M Library Processing System, described in detail in chapter five, uses a five by eight inch fiche. The standard size has, however, replaced the three by five inch and five by eight inch microfiche formerly used by the Atomic Energy Commission and National Aeronautics and Space Administration.[29]

Regardless of external dimensions, most microfiche produced in the United States employ a *uniform division* internal format consisting of a fixed grid pattern for microimages and a maximum practical reduction.[30] The National Micrographics Association Type 1 Standard for microfiche of source documents, for example, is designed for the reproduction of up to 98 letter size (8.5 by 11 inch) originals in seven rows and fourteen columns at 24X reduction. A fixed area is allotted to each microimage. Lower reductions are possible for smaller documents, such as five by seven inch book pages. Larger documents must be microfilmed in sections occupying several frames. Since 1971, the 98 microimage, uniform division format has been the standard for all United States government reports, replacing the 1965 COSATI standard of five rows and twelve columns at 18X reduction. Libraries with retrospective technical report collections will, however, continue to maintain COSATI microfiche. The COSATI format survives as the NMA Type 2 Standard, although the Type 1 Standard is designated *preferred*.[31] While commercially produced microfiche intended for the library market increasingly adhere to the preferred standard, the sixty-page format remains in use. Information Handling Services, for example, uses the COSATI format for its *Legislative History Current*

*Subscription Service*, as does Arcata Microfilm for its *Newsbank Urban Affairs Library*. The sixty-page format is also the standard for United Nations micropublications.[32]

Because of the rapid development of American and international microfiche standards, manufacturers have been able to build relatively inexpensive readers and reader/printers. As discussed in chapter six, the microfiche reader market is today very competitive. Even the lowest-priced models have features previously offered only on very expensive equipment. Portable readers enable microfiche to be used away from the library. At slightly more than one hundred dollars, these portable readers are priced within the budgets of many individual researchers. Because microfiche readers and reader/printers are less expensive than their roll microform counterparts, librarians can make more display equipment available, thereby overcoming one of the major objections of microform users.

Microfiche enjoy other substantial advantages. They can be quickly and easily duplicated on demand. Rather than circulate technical reports from the master fiche file, many special libraries make and distribute microfiche duplicates to be retained or discarded at the user's discretion. As noted in chapter one, the cost of microfiche duplication often compares favorably with the cost of either report circulation or full-size document reproduction.[33]

Unlike roll microforms, which are limited to serial access, microfiche permit semi-random retrieval. With the proper manual or automated filing system, a given microfiche can be accessed directly. Access to specific information within a fiche may, however, require serial examination of microimages.

An area on each microfiche is usually reserved for eye-legible bibliographic or other identifying information. This heading area can be color-coded for easier filing and retrieval. The microfiche itself can be corner-cut or edge-notched for protection against misfiling.

Like all microforms, fiche have limitations. While they are conveniently duplicated, master microfiche can be very expensive to create, often costing three to five times as much as reel microfilm in source document applications. Their ease of handling renders microfiche vulnerable to loss or theft. The micrographics industry supports microfiche systems so effectively with high-quality, inexpensive reading, printing, and duplicating equipment, that micropublishers are increasingly selecting fiche on that basis alone, in preference to other, potentially more suitable, microforms. Xerox University Microfilms' *Comprehensive Dissertation Index*, for example, is available on 800 microfiche, each containing sixty pages, but roll microforms would have more effectively unitized the micropublication and would have overcome problems of alphabetization that make the microfiche edition difficult to use. With such a large publication, the continuation of index keywords across several microfiche necessitates considerable insertion and removal of individual fiche to locate the desired entry.[34] In micrographics, as in all successful systems design, form must follow function.

## Updateable Microfiche and Microfilm Jackets

Conventional silver halide microfiche, like roll microforms, cannot be updated easily. A.B. Dick/Scott and the Microx Corporation are currently manufacturing and marketing updateable microfiche systems that employ unconventional microphotographic technologies. A third system, developed by Energy Conversion Devices, will be marketed by the 3M Company during 1978.

The most widely used of these systems, the A.B. Dick/Scott System 200 Record Processor (Fig. 2-9) is a self-contained, desk-size microfiche camera that creates microimages from source documents, using a special transparent electrophotographic (TEP) film.[35] The film, coated with light-sensitive photoconductors, is electrostatically charged and exposed to light reflected from a source document. As in conventional electrophotography, charges are dissipated in areas of the film corresponding to non-text areas of the document. The remaining electrostatic charges form a latent image that is rendered visible through the application of a toner containing carbon particles. Unlike silver halide microfilm, TEP film retains sensitivity through repeated exposure. Consequently, exposed TEP fiche can be re-inserted in the System 200 Record Processor, new microimages added, and superseded images overprinted.

The System 200 Record Processor is a files management tool for active record systems. Its principal intended application is the replacement of paper files containing documents up to ten by fourteen inches in size with four by six inch microfiche containing up to 98 microimages reduced 25X. Each microfiche is a miniature file folder, with a tab title area for eye-legible identifying information (Fig. 2-10, p. 50). Distribution duplicates of the master TEP microfiche can be created with the conventional diazo or vesicular equipment described in the next chapter. In the largest application to date, the Department of the Army is using eighteen System 200 Record Processors to convert 785,000 active files of officers and enlisted men to microfiche. The files contain over fifty million documents. Conversion is expected to take two and a half years.[36]

**Figure 2-9**

**System 200 Record Processor**
(Courtesy: A.B. Dick/Scott)

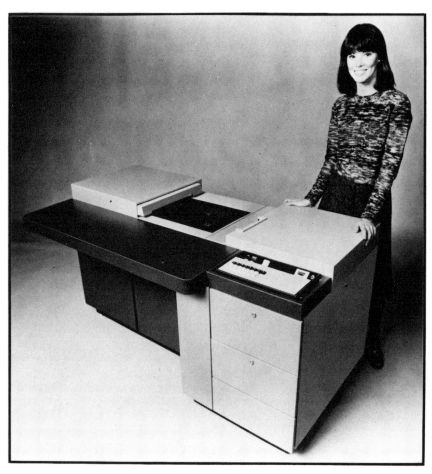

**Figure 2-10**

**Updateable Microfiche**
(Courtesy: A.B. Dick/Scott)

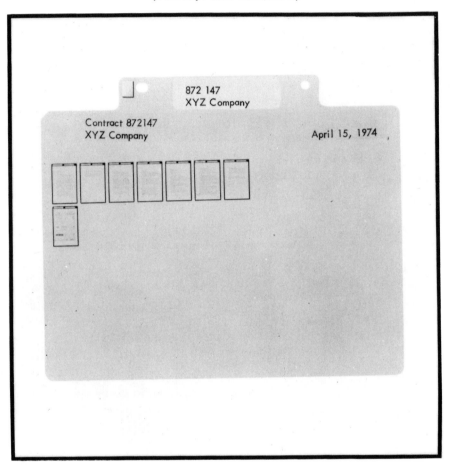

Priced at $30,000, the A.B. Dick/Scott System 200 Record Processor is beyond the budgets of most libraries. Pending the development of less expensive updateable microfiche systems, libraries with dynamic document collections will continue to rely on *microfilm jackets* for frequently updated file applications. The microfilm jacket (Fig. 2-11) is a transparent acetate or polyester carrier with one or more sleeves designed to hold 16mm or 35mm microfilm in flat strips. While microfilm strips can be cut from rolls and inserted in jackets by hand, a motorized cutter/inserter is usually used. New microimages can be added to the jacket, as long as space remains in the sleeves, and obsolete microimages removed. Jackets are avaialble in various sizes and sleeve configurations. The four by six inch jacket is size compatible with standard microfiche. Jackets with sleeves for both 16mm and 35mm microfilm strips are used to unitize files containing large drawings or maps with supporting letter-size textual documents. This unitization of 16mm and 35mm microimages is not possible with other microforms.

**Figure 2-11**

**Microfilm Jacket**
(Courtesy: NB Jackets)

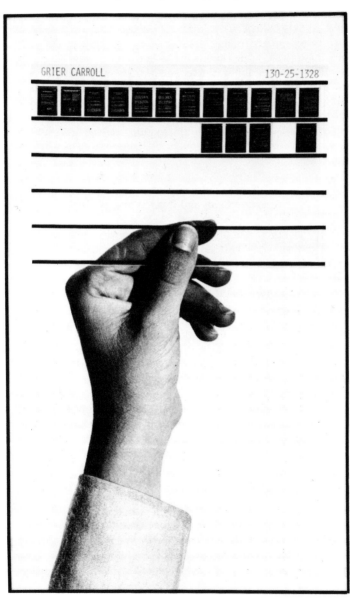

Each microfilm jacket typically includes a translucent, matte finish heading area for eye-legible identifying information entered by hand or typewriter. Jackets affixed to continuous forms carriers are available for high speed computer printing or to facilitate heading area alignment during conventional typing. Because microfilm jackets closely resemble miniaturized paper files, user resistance to the introduction of a well-designed jacket system is generally low. Extensive modifications of long-established filing procedures or other work patterns are generally not necessary. Only the file size is changed. Jackets themselves protect microimages from damage during heavy use. Like microfiche, they can be color-coded or edge-notched to prevent misfiling. Jackets can also be contact duplicated to create distribution microfiche. The excellent jacket application at the Consumer's Association Library in London was described in the previous chapter.[37]

Jackets, however, share certain of the disadvantages of microfiche. The creation of jackets from roll microfilm in applications involving large file conversions is a slow, labor-intensive, and expensive process. The microfilming of source documents for jacket applications requires care in image alignment. Like microfiche, jackets are vulnerable to loss or theft. Retention of a duplicate security roll is recommended.

### Aperture Cards and Related Microforms

The *aperture card* is one of several microforms that combine the space-saving advantages of microimages with human-eye-readable information in paper form (Fig. 2-12). The standard aperture card consists of a 35mm microfilm chip mounted in the rectangular aperture of a 3.25 by 7.375 inch tabcard. In an eighty-column card, the standard aperture spans columns 53 through 77 and measures 1.304 by 1.908 inches. It may contain one map, chart, or engineering drawing reduced 16X to 30X; up to four letter-size documents reduced 16X; or up to eight letter-size documents reduced 24X. Special card sizes, colors, and aperture positions are available. The face and reverse side of the card can be custom printed. The aperture card, or a slave card, can be keypunched for machine sorting. In some cases, the aperture is covered by a protective layer of optically clear mylar.

The aperture card is an excellent unit record for very large single-page documents or for files containing eight letter-size documents or less. The U.S. Bureau of Mines Map Repository in Pittsburgh, which serves as a reference center and archive for information about mines east of the Mississippi, converts maps acquired from state geologic surveys to aperture cards. The cards are filed in accession number order and retrieved, using computer-produced indexes, by state, county, and mine name.[38] The U.S. Patent Office maintains its numerical and classified search files on aperture cards, each containing up to eight microimages. Since 87 percent of U.S. patents are eight pages or less in length, the vast majority can be unitized on a single card, while 98 percent of U.S. patents will require two cards or less.[39] In addition to unitization, aperture cards were selected for ease of file maintenance, the availability of high speed card duplicators and enlarger/printers, and the possibility of using standard tabulating card equipment for automatic file manipulation.

Figure 2-12

Aperture Card, Jacket Cards and Card Jackets (Courtesy: Microseal Corporation)

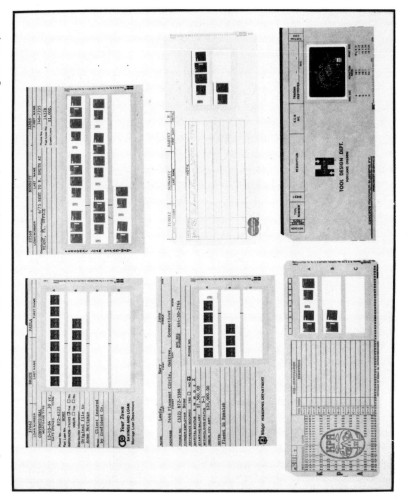

The *jacket card*, a variant of the conventional aperture card, has sleeves for the insertion of 16mm microfilm strips. As with microfilm jackets, various sleeve configurations and microimage capacities are available. The jacket card offers the advantage of updateability for dynamic document collections. Like aperture cards, jacket cards measure 3.25 by 7.375 inches.

The *card jacket* is a four by six inch card with sufficient sleeve space for up to 36 16mm or 35mm microimages. Although the card jacket is one of the newest microforms, the advantages of combining microimages with a note card for library materials were recognized as early as 1934.[40] The face and reverse side of the card can be used for eye-legible identifying information or annotations. Card jackets are size compatible and interfileable with standard microfiche and are available in a translucent version that can be contact duplicated in its entirety, including annotations, using conventional diazo microfiche duplicators.

## Ultra High Reduction Microforms

*Ultrafiche* and *ultrastrips* combine the ease of handling of flat microforms with sufficient microimage capacity to unitize books and other lengthy multi-page documents.[41] PCMI ultrafiche, produced by NCR, is a four by six inch transparency containing up to 3,100 microimages reduced up to 150X (Fig. 2-13). Ultrastrips containing microimages reduced 210X are produced by Microform Data Systems, primarily for telephone directory assistance and similar applications oriented toward retrieving a few lines of information from very large data bases. While ultra high reductions technically equal or exceed 90X, much of this section is relevant to the Microbook Fiche produced by Library Resources Incorporated at the very high reductions of 55X to 90X and to the 75X legal micropublications produced by West Publishing Company and Commerce Clearinghouse.

Although ultra high reductions were utilized in the earliest novelty applications of microphotography, modern ultrafiche technology developed out of research in optical computer memories.[42] The creation of ultra high reduction microimages is a complex, expensive process requiring a laboratory environment and unconventional microrecording materials and equipment. In a typical application, source documents are first microfilmed at low reductions of 9X to 12X on 35mm roll microfilm, using a planetary camera and conventional silver halide materials. Alternatively, 35mm microimages can be prepared from digital data via a computer-output-microfilm recorder. These microimages are then further reduced 10X, using photochromic microimaging materials and special cameras. Being grainless, photochromic materials will produce consistently high quality microimages at reductions exceeding the present capabilities of conventional silver halide microphotographic systems. These ultra high reduction microimages require no development and are inspected immediately following exposure. In the event of error, a microimage can be optically erased and re-exposed. When the master ultrafiche is complete, special printers, designed to achieve uniform contact at high speed, are used to produce intermediates and dissemination ultrafiche. The interrelationship of document characteristics, image contrast, exposure time, and other quality-control parameters is more complex than in conventional microphotography and must be carefully monitored. Because printed characters

**Figure 2-13**

**PCMI Ultrafiche**

(Courtesy: NCR Corporation)

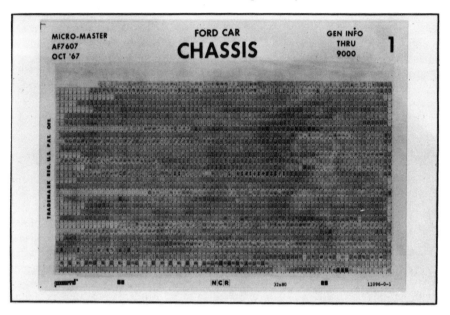

measuring 2mm to 3mm in full-size may be reduced to less than ten microns on ultrafiche, a clean room environment is necessary to control dust during production. In addition, dissemination ultrafiche are laminated to prevent scratches that could obscure or obliterate characters, lines, or even entire pages.

Because of the very high cost of creating the photochromic master, ultrafiche are an *edition-process* microform. Initial production costs must be recovered through the sale of a specific number of dissemination duplicates. The break-even point for edition size varies with the application. In commercial applications, ultrafiche are used primarily for catalog publication in microform. When many dissemination ultrafiche are required, the cost per microimage compares favorably with conventional microforms. In the library field, the British Library publishes *Books in English* on four by six inch ultrafiche, each containing 2,380 microimages reduced 150X. The ultrafiche are produced by NCR from COM-generated 35mm microfilm derived from combined LC and BNB MARC data bases. The British Library contends that the cost of ultrafiche micropublication compares favorably with 24X 16mm computer-output-microfilm at an edition size of 200 copies.[43]

Other ultrafiche publications produced for the library market include the *National Reporter System*, available from West Publishing Company, and the *Library of American Civilization*, a collection of 300,000 pre-1914 North American imprints produced by Library Resources Incorporated.[44]

Ultrafiche use requires a special and expensive high magnification display device with a powerful light source and short depth of focus. Although several recently introduced readers feature interchangeable high and low magnification lenses for alternate viewing of both ultrafiche and conventional flat microforms, the number of available ultrafiche readers and reader/printers remains limited.

Librarians should be aware that, unlike conventional microfiche, ultrafiche cannot be duplicated for demand distribution to patrons.

## Micro-Opaques

The opaque microforms–*Microprint, Microlex*, and *microcards*–are distinguished by paper rather than film microimage supports.[45] Of the three, only Microprint remains in production and in widespread use.

A proprietary product of the Readex Microprint Corporation, each Microprint consists of a six by nine inch card containing up to one hundred pages of text arranged in ten rows and ten columns (Fig. 2-14). Reductions range from 12X to 24X. Space at the top of each card is reserved for eye-legible bibliographic information. Like ultrafiche, Microprint is an edition-process microform employing unconventional technology. Microimages of source documents recorded on 35mm microfilm are stripped and mounted to create special plates that are used to produce Microprint cards. The microimages are actually printed by offset lithography onto one hundred percent rag content paper. Because photographic chemicals are not used during card production, Microprint can be stored under the same environmental conditions as books. Microprint ink and card stock conform to archival permanence requirements established by the National Bureau of Standards. Readex Microprint Corporation specializes in the micropublication of very large collections of significant scholarly works based on established bibliographies. Examples include the *Early American Imprints* series, a collection of almost 100,000 titles listed by Evans, Shaw, and Shoemaker; and *Great Works of American Literature*, which consists of 15,000 titles taken from Blanck's *Bibliography of American Literature*.[46]

Microlex and microcards are both defunct microforms. Microlex was a trade name used by the Microlex Corporation to denote an opaque card-type microform measuring 6.5 by 8.5 inches and containing up to 200 photographically produced microimages per side. Microlex cards were used primarily for legal publications.[47] As noted in chapter one, the microcard–a three by five inch card with up to forty photographically produced microimages–was first suggested by Fremont Rider in the 1940s as a solution to the space and expense problems associated with the exponential growth of research libraries. With full cataloging information on the reverse side, the microcard combined bibliographic description and text in a single unit record designed for filing in conventional card catalog trays. Although seventeen micropublishers were active in microcard production by 1952, microcards are no longer in production. Many large microcard sets—the collections of

Spanish and German plays produced by General Microfilm, for example—have been reissued on transparent microfiche. Microcards are of more than historical significance, however, since some research libraries will continue to maintain sizeable and important retrospective microcard collections.

**Figure 2-14**

**Microprint**

(Courtesy: Readex Microprint Corporation)

Church Catalogue.    Vol. 1.    p.190-276g.
Americana.    1482-1590.    Cat. nos. 82 (cont.)-120c. [1544-1578].

Courtesy New York Public Library.

Readex Microprint    1968    New York, N.Y.

## REFERENCES

[1] Microimages may also contain machine-readable information in the form of photo-optical binary codes used, for example, in the Kodak MIRAcode system discussed in chapter eight. Experimental holographic systems have stored both document images and their binary equivalents on film. See, for example, Fred N. Haritatos and John Mincieli, "Holographic Binary Data Storage on Microfilm," *Proceedings of the American Society for Information Science* 10 (1973): 81-82.

[2] Surveys of library applications of various microforms include: Hubbard W. Ballou and John Rather, "Microfilm and Microfacsimile Publication," *Library Trends* 4 (1955): 182-94; G. H. Davison, "Microcards and Microfiches: History and Possibilities," *Library Association Record* 63 (1961): 69-78; B. J. S. Williams, *Miniaturised Communications* (London: Library Association, 1970); Williams, "Microforms in Information Retrieval and Communication Systems," *Aslib Proceedings* 19 (1967): 223-31; Williams, "Progress in Documentation: Micrographics," *Journal of Documentation* 27 (1971): 295-304; P. R. P. Claridge, "What the User Needs from Microforms," in *Micropublishing for Learned Societies* (Hertis: National Reprographic Centre for Documentation, 1968), pp. 11-18; Fritz Veit, "Microforms, Microform Equipment and Microform Use in the Educational Environment," *Library Trends* 19 (1971): 444-66; Philip Rochlin, "Micro Media in the Library: A Once Over Lightly," *Journal of Micrographics* 6 (1973): 99-104; Peter New, *Reprography for Librarians* (Hamden, Conn.: Linnet Books, 1975), 41-50.

[3] Edward J. Forbes and Thomas C. Bagg, *Report of a Study of Requirements and Specifications for Serial and Monographic Microrecording for the National Library of Medicine* (Washington: National Bureau of Standards, Report No. 9446, August (1966).

[4] William R. Hawken, "Microform Standardization: The Problem of Research Materials and a Proposed Solution," *NMA Journal* 2 (1968): 14-27; see also Hawken's classic *Copying Methods Manual* (Chicago: American Library Association and Library Technology Project, 1966).

[5] John R. White, "Microfont—A New Letter Style for Microfilm," *NMA Journal* 2 (1968): 53-54; Don M. Avedon, "Typing and Lettering for Microreproduction," *Journal of Micrographics* 5 (1972): 153-54; "Draft British Standard Recommendations for the Preparation of Copy for Microfiche," *Microdoc* 14 (1975): 82-87. The idea of preparing library materials for eventual reproduction is not new. See, for example, Robert C. Binkley, "Typescript Formats for Blueprint Reproductions," *Journal of Documentary Reproduction* 1 (1938): 75-78.

[6] On standards, see F. Donker Duyvis, "Standardization as a Tool of Scientific Management," *Library Trends* 2 (1954): 410-27; William R. Hawken, "Microform Standardization: The Problem of Research Materials and a Proposed Solution," *NMA Journal* 2 (1968): 14-27; Carl E. Nelson, "Microfilm Standards, Their Creation and Impact on Design and Systems," *Proceedings of the National Microfilm Association* (Silver Spring, Md.: NMA, 1968), 346-54; Allen B. Veaner, "Microreproduction and Micropublication Technical Standards: What They Mean to You, the User," *Microform Review* 3 (1974): 80-84.

[7] Don M. Avedon, "The Development of Standards for Micrographics," *Journal of Micrographics* 6 (1973): 264-65; Hubbard W. Ballou, "American National Standards," *Journal of Micrographics* 4 (1971): 297-304; Avedon, "International Organization for Standardization," *Journal of Micrographics* 5 (1972): 311-13.

[8] Robert J. Morris, "Microfiche in the Automotive Aftermarket," *Proceedings of the National Micrographics Association* (Silver Spring, Md.: NMA, 1975), 371-76; John J. Napper, "Aerofiche," *Proceedings of the National Micrographics Association* (Silver Spring, Md.: NMA, 1975), 376-79; also, Russell E. Barkley, "Hardware Industry's Move to Microfiche," *Proceedings of the National Micrographics Association* (Silver Spring, Md.: NMA, 1975), 383-86.

[9] "CSUC Sets Library Standards for Microforms," *Advanced Technology/ Libraries* 2 (October 1973): 1-2; "CSUC Adopts its Microform Criteria as Official Writ," *Advanced Technology/Libraries* 3 (August 1974): 5; "Comment and News: Revised Microform Procurement Standards," *Microform Review* 4 (1975): 96-99. On the concept of a library microform standard, see Fremont Rider, "The Possible Correlation of All Forms of Microtext," *American Documentation* 2 (1951): 152-57.

[10] This usage is suggested in Daniel M. Costigan, "A Fresh Look at Micrographic Nomenclature," *Journal of Micrographics* 9 (1976): 291-93.

[11] Alex L. Baptie, "The 8mm Microfilm Concept," *Information and Records Management* 5 (April 1971): 57-60.

[12] Robert C. Olson, "VSMF—Billions in Low Cost Production," *Journal of Micrographics* 5 (1972): 221-27. On the use of the 8mm version in a library, see Ralph E. Swinburne, Jr., "Microfilmed Catalog Services," *Journal of Chemical Documentation* 10 (1970): 17-20.

[13] National Archives, *User Evaluations of Microfilm Readers for Archival and Manuscript Materials* (Washington: National Archives and Records Service, 1973).

[14] Ben H. Weil and Lee N. Starker, "Introduction to the Microfilm Forum: Experiences, Problems, and Plans of Microfilm Users," *Journal of Chemical Documentation* 19 (1970): 3-4.

[15] On the use of the various image placements, see the two Library of Congress publications already cited and *Recommended Practice for Microfilming Newspapers* (Silver Spring, Md.: National Micrographics Association, 1975).

[16] L. A. Brunelle, "The Impact of Magazine Film Use in the Microfilm Industry," *Proceedings of the National Microfilm Association* (Annapolis, Md.: NMA, 1962), 85-92; John M. Babb, "Implications of Cartridge-Load Microfilm," *Proceedings of the National Microfilm Association* (Silver Spring, Md.: NMA, 1968), 314-17.

[17] Examples include: Lee N. Starker, "User Experience with Primary Journals on 16mm Microfilm," *Journal of Chemical Documentation* 10 (1970): 5-6; Virginia L. Duncan and Francis E. Parsons, "Use of Microfilm in an Industrial Research Library," *Special Libraries* 61 (1970): 288-90; Joan M. Daghita, "A Core Collection of Journals on Microfilm in a Community Teaching Hospital Library," *Bulletin of the Medical Library Association* 64 (1976): 240-41; Ben H. Weil, et al., "Esso Research Experiences with Chemical Abstracts on Microfilm," *Journal of Chemical Documentation* 5 (1965): 193-200; C. Edward Carroll, "Microfilmed

Catalogs: A More Efficient Way to Share Library Resources," *Microform Review* 1 (1972): 274-78; O. P. Gillach and R. H. McDonaugh, "Spreading State Library Riches for Peanuts," *Wilson Library Bulletin* 45 (1970): 354-57.

[18] John J. Oliva, "Microfilm Cartridge System at Prince George Community College," *Journal of Micrographics* 6 (1972): 89-92.

[19] Graham Larkworthy and Cyril G. Brown, "A Microfilm Catalogue for Public Use," *NRCd Bulletin* 5 (1972): 78-80; D. G. R. Buckle and Thomas French, "The Application of Microform to Manual and Machine-Readable Catalogues," *Program* 5 (1971): 41-66; Jill C. Le Croisette, "Microfilm Catalogs in a British Public Library System," *Microform Review* 4 (1975): 104-107; Elizabeth Stecher, "RMIT Catalogue Study Results," *Australian Library Journal* 24 (1975): 384-89.

[20] William Saffady, "A Computer Output Microfilm List of Serials for Patron Use," *Journal of Library Automation* 7 (1974): 263-66.

[21] Homer I. Bernhardt, *A Report on the Role of Microforms in the University of Pittsburgh Library* (Pittsburgh: Graduate School of Library and Information Science, University of Pittsburgh, 1970).

[22] Francis F. Spreitzer, "Microfilm Cartridges and Cassettes," *Library Technology Reports* (May 1972).

[23] Donald R. Beeman, "Micrographic Standards for Containers (Cartridge and Cassette) for 16mm Roll Microfilm," *Journal of Micrographics* 9 (1975): 51-54.

[24] L. J. van der Wolk and J. C. Lannon, "The Microcopy on Flat Film as an Aid in Documentation," *Revue de la Documentation* 17 (1950): 134-41 and 8 (1951): 216-38; L. J. van der Wolk, "The Microfiche Foundation and the Availability of Information in Microfiche Form," *Aslib Proceedings* 20 (1968): 525-30; W. DeHaas, "The Microfiche," *American Documentation* 9 (1958): 99-106.

[25] William R. Hawken and Carl E. Nelson, "Microfiche Returns to Popularity," *IMC Journal* 1 (1967): 20-22; Hawken, "Microfiche, Microfilm, and Hard Copy— Problems and Prospects for the Research Worker," *National Micro-News* No. 73 (December 1964): 97-107; H. F. Versey, *The Use of Microfiche for Scientific and Technical Reports* (NATO, Advisory Group for Aerospace Research and Development, August 1970). Ralph Bennett, "Sheet Microfilm," *Journal of Documentary Reproduction* 3 (1940): 39-41 considered it unlikely that fiche would be tried in commercial applications.

[26] "Micrographics Survey '76," *Infosystems* 23 (April 1976): 34-37; "Micrographics '77: The Best is Yet to Come," *Infosystems* 24 (May 1977): 46-49.

[27] L. L. Ardern, "Microfiche," *Library Association Record* 60 (1958): 150-51 contains a still-applicable description of popular European fiche sizes.

[28] C. Allen Merritt, *Microfiche in an Information Retrieval System* (Armonk, N.Y.: IBM Technical Information Retrieval Center, April 1967).

[29] William R. Hawken, "Technical Reports on Microfiche—What Price Unitization?," *National Micro-News* No. 69 (April 1964): 195-207 demonstrated the superiority of the four by six inch fiche in achieving unitization with a minimum of wasted film space.

[30] Don M. Avedon, "International Microfiche Standards," *Journal of Micrographics* 7 (1974): 283-84 discusses the concept of uniform vs. variable division fiche formats.

[31] *Microfiche of Documents* (Silver Spring, Md.: National Micrographics Association, 1975). As noted in a preceding section, standards change to reflect the current state-of-the-art. The earliest NMA microfiche standards, for example, offered the user eight choices, including the 98-page format, the COSATI format, and a tab-size format. (See Don M. Avedon, *The User's Guide to Standard Microfiche Formats.* New York: Microfilm Publishing Corp., 1971.) The 1971 NMA standard prescribed the 98-page format only. On the history of fiche standards, see George B. Bernstein, "Why 24X/48X?," *Journal of Micrographics* 5 (1972): 295-300.

[32] Allan F. Windsor, "New UN Microfiche Service Augurs Large Storage Economies," *Special Libraries* 65 (1974): 234-36. Again, departures from either the Type 1 or Type 2 Standard are made for special systems. The National College Catalog Service, for example, uses a 42X, 288-page non-standard fiche for its micropublished academic catalogs.

[33] L. B. Heilprin, "The Economics of 'On Demand' Library Copying," *Proceedings of the National Microfilm Association* (Annapolis, Md.: NMA, 1962): 311-39.

[34] Murray S. Martin, "Review of 'Comprehensive Dissertation Index'," *Microform Review* 4 (1975): 36-39.

[35] David P. Habib and John D. Plumadore, "A New Microelectrophotographic System," *Journal of Micrographics* 7 (1974): 249-54; F. E. Dailey, Jr., and E. W. Bennett, "Some Considerations for a New Photorecording Technology," in Don Chenevert, ed., *Micrographics Science 1973: Winter Symposium* (Washington: Society of Photographic Scientists and Engineers, 1973), pp. 194-203.

[36] Leonard S. Lee, Charles E. Dexter, and Robert D. Legg, *Proposed Microform System for Administration of HQDA Military Personnel Records* (Alexandria, Va.: Department of the Army, 1975).

[37] Peter A. Thomas, "Microfiche in a Special Library," *New Library World* 76 (1975): 43-44; Marion Chinn, "A Microfiche System for Legal Materials at Consumers' Association Library," *Microdoc* 14 (1975): 109-111.

[38] Curtis Edgerton, "The Mine Map Repository—A Source of Mine Map Data," *Journal of Micrographics* 8 (1975): 235-40.

[39] Ethan A. Hurd, "The Patent Copy Document System," In *Proceedings of the National Microfilm Association* (Silver Spring, Md.: NMA, 1967): 117-23; William M. Lyons, "Microreproduction Systems within the U.S. Patent Office," In *Proceedings of the National Microfilm Association* (Silver Spring, Md.: NMA, 1972): II-105-106; Rolf E. Westgaard, "The Multi-Page Aperture Card: An Automated Microfiche," *Proceedings of the National Microfilm Association* (Annapolis, Md.: NMA, 1965): 222-26; Lester O. Kruger, "Patent Literature Information System Has Wide Application," *Journal of Micrographics* 7 (1973): 23-29; James G. Van Oot, "Patents and Patent Guides on Microforms," *Journal of Chemical Documentation* 10 (1970): 9-13.

[40] Atherton Seidell, "The Photomicrographic Reproduction of Documents," *Science* 80 (August 24, 1934): 184-85.

[41] On the concept of a book-length microform, see William R. Hawken, "Systems Instead of Standards," *Library Journal* 98 (September 15, 1973): 2515-25; Arthur Teplitz, "Library Fiche: An Introduction and Explanation," *Proceedings of the National Microfilm Association* (Silver Spring, Md.: NMA, 1968): 125-32; James G. Hodgson, "Microcopying Essentials (from a Librarian's Point of View)," *Journal of Documentary Reproduction* 1 (1938): 243-62; Norton F. Kristy, "System Design for Microbook Publishing," *Proceedings of the American Society for Information Science* 7 (1970): 221-23; Wynn D. Crew, "The Microaperture: A Design to Substitute for a Book," *Journal of Micrographics* 4 (1970): 3-11.

[42] Klaus W. Otten, "Ultrafiche Technology," *Journal of Micrographics* 4 (1971): 161-76; A. S. Tauber and W. C. Myers, "Photochromic Microimages: A Key to Practical Microdocument Storage and Dissemination," *Proceedings of the National Microfilm Association* (Annapolis: NMA, 1962): 257-67.

[43] J. E. Linford, "Books in English," *Canadian Library Journal* 30 (1973): 132-38, also in *Microform Review* 1 (1972): 207-213; S. J. Teague, "Books in English," *Microdoc* 15 (1976):38.

[44] On ultrafiche and libraries, see Norman Cousins, "UMF and the Future," *Saturday Review* 52 (April 19, 1969): 26; William R. Hawken, et al., "Microbook Publications—A New Approach for a New Decade," *Journal of Micrographics* 3 (1970): 188-93; Klaus W. Otten, "Ultramicrofiche Packages for Libraries: Pros and Cons of Different Approaches," *Proceedings of the National Microfilm Association* (Silver Spring, Md.: NMA, 1971): II-110-120; E. M. Greider, "Ultrafiche Libraries: A Librarian's View," *Microform Review* 1 (1972): 85-100; Paul Napier, et al.,"The Library Resources, Inc., Library of American Civilization Demonstration at the George Washington University Library," *Microform Review* 3 (1974): 158-76; C. W. Evans, "High Reduction Microfiche for Libraries: An Evaluation of Collections from the National Cash Register Company and Library Resources Incorporated," *Library Resources and Technical Services* 16 (1972): 33-47.

[45] A good survey is H. R. Verry, "Micro-Opaques," *Aslib Proceedings* 4 (1952): 153-62.

[46] Albert Boni, "Microprint," *American Documentation* 2 (1951): 150-52; Boni, "Readex Microprint—How It Began," *Microdoc* 11 (1972): 5-10; John Tennant, "Readex Microprints," *Journal of Documentary Reproduction* 3 (1940): 66-70. A related, and currently popular, technology is Miniprint, a book-type opaque microform employing low reductions of 4X to 10X in printing multiple microimages onto ordinary book pages. Miniprint images, while visible to the unaided eye, are typically read with an inexpensive hand-held magnifying lens. The success of the *Compact Oxford English Dictionary* indicates the potential of Miniprint in applications involving the retrieval of a few lines of information from multi-volume reference works that occupy much shelf space and are difficult to handle in full size. While its commercial application is recent, the concept of

Miniprint dates from the 1930s: see, for example, L. Bendikson, "When Filing Cards Take the Place of Books," *Library Journal* 58 (1933): 9†1-13. On one professional association's experience with user acceptance of Miniprint, see Gordon L. Dugger, Ruth F. Bryans, and William Morris, Jr., "AIAA Experiments and Results on SDD, Synoptics, Miniprints and Related Topics," *IEEE Transactions on Professional Communications* PC-16 (1973): 100-104, 178.

[47] Philip F. Cohen, "Use of Microform in Legal Publishing," *Law Librarian* 6 (1975): 9-10.

# CHAPTER 3

# SOURCE DOCUMENT MICROFILM

## MICROPHOTOGRAPHIC MEDIA

### Silver Halide Microfilms

As noted in the preceding chapter, microforms can be created from source documents—such as handwritten manuscripts, typed reports, or printed book pages—or from machine-readable digital data stored on magnetic media. This chapter describes the technology of source document microphotography and the equipment and supplies required to create and duplicate microforms from library source documents. The next chapter deals with the creation of computer-output-microfilm from machine-readable library data bases.

Despite recent interest in unconventional photographic technologies, the *silver halide* process remains the most important and widely used technique for the creation of microimages from source documents. Diazo and vesicular microfilms, described later in this chapter, are widely used for the duplication of existing microforms but lack the photographic speed required for original camera work. Silver halide microfilms are high-performance, fine grain photographic films. Three of their most important features are discussed in this section: 1) the emulsion, 2) the base material, and 3) the method of halation prevention.

Silver halide microfilms take their name from a light-sensitive emulsion of silver halide crystals suspended in gelatin.[1] When exposed to light reflected from a source document, the silver halide crystals are converted to silver nuclei in areas of the film corresponding to non-text (light) areas of the document. Being dark, the text areas of the source document absorb light. Little if any change occurs in the silver halide crystals corresponding to those areas. Following exposure, the microimage is complete but *latent* (invisible). Development reduces the altered silver halide crystals to visible black silver grains. The silver halide process is often described as *negative-working* or *sign-reversing* because normal development of microimages made from positive-appearing source documents produces a first-generation microform of negative polarity. *Polarity*, used in this context, indicates the change or retention of the dark-to-light relationship of corresponding areas of a microimage and the original source document from which the microimage was made. *Generation* is a measure of the remoteness of a particular microform from the original source document. Uninformed sources often erroneously equate first generation microforms with negative polarity and second generation duplicate microforms with positive polarity. As discussed later in this chapter, there is no necessary relationship between polarity and generation. Second, third, or succeeding microform generations may be negative or positive, depending on the duplicating process employed. Likewise, a special development technique called *reversal processing* can be used to create positive polarity first-generation microimages from positive-appearing source documents such as photographs, which depend on the maintenance of tonal values to be meaningful.[2]

On the microfilm itself, the silver halide emulsion typically rests on either a triacetate or polyester base.[3] *Cellulose triacetate* is the oldest and still most widely used microfilm base material. Triacetate camera microfilms for source document applications are supplied on spools in one hundred foot lengths and 16mm, 35mm, and 105mm widths. *Polyester* microfilms are thinner than their triacetate counterparts, allowing greater film capacity per reel, cartridge, or cassette. This can prove advantageous in reducing the number of roll microforms to be handled in such large-scale applications as library catalogs. Polyester microfilms for source document applications are supplied on spools in 215-foot lengths and in 16mm and 35mm widths. With the exception of several newer models, most source document cameras are designed for triacetate microfilm and must be modified to accept polyester stock. Polyester microfilms offer the further advantage of minimizing wasted camera preparation time by halving the number of required film loadings. Both cellulose triacetate and polyester are non-flammable, safety-base materials. The sale of non-safety-base microfilms is prohibited in the United States. When manufactured to current ANSI standards, and processed in a manner described later in this chapter, both types of base materials are suitable for archival storage.

Whatever the base material, light that passes through the emulsion can be reflected from the film base, causing ghost images—an undesirable effect known as *halation.* Methods of halation prevention vary. In some cases, the back of the base material is coated with light-absorbing dyes, which are ultimately removed during processing. These *dyeback* microfilms offer the advantage of daylight handling and loading. Kodak was the first microfilm manufacturer to introduce an *anti-halation undercoat* (AHU) between the emulsion and the base material. The undercoating is dissolved during processing. AHU microfilms are well suited to applications requiring very high image quality, but they must be handled and loaded in darkness. Anti-halation undercoated microfilms are now available from several manufacturers. In a similar technique, Agfa-Gevaert recently introduced an anti-halation incoating (AHI) microfilm, with a dye incorporated in the emulsion itself. The manufacturer claims excellent image quality.

In addition to their approach to halation prevention, silver halide microfilms differ in photographic speed, resolving power, and suitability for use in different cameras and with different types of source documents. Most camera microfilms for source document applications are of high contrast for recording textual materials. Lower contrast microfilms are available for recording photographs.[4] Generally, camera manufacturers specify the characteristics of the microfilm recommended for best results with their equipment. Librarians must be aware, however, of differences in base materials, methods of halation prevention, and other film characteristics that may ultimately influence the selection of cameras and processing equipment.

## Non-Silver Recording Processes

Despite the inconvenience of wet chemical processing, silver halide microfilms have remained the dominant microphotographic medium for the past century. The silver halide process is no longer, however, the sole microphotographic technology. Transparent electrophotographic (TEP) film, used in the A.B. Dick/Scott System 200 Record Processor, and photochromic microimaging (PCMI) materials, used by NCR to create ultrafiche, were described in the preceding chapter.[5] An updateable microfiche system recently developed by the Microx Corporation employs electrostatic charges and heat to form microimages on a special photoconductive surface coated on a layer of nickel-chronium. In early 1977, the 3M Company introduced its 1050 Step-and-Repeat Microfilm Camera, the first commercially available device capable of recording source document images on *dry silver* microfilm. Dry silver microfilms, which have been used successfully in 3M computer-output-microfilm recorders since 1969, are exposed by light but developed by heat alone, without wet chemicals.[6] The 3M 1050 Camera delivers developed microfiche ready for viewing or duplication. As noted in chapter two, the 3M Company also holds marketing rights to an updateable microfiche system developed by Energy Conversion Devices.

Acceptance of these, and future, alternative microrecording systems for the wide range of library applications will ultimately depend on demonstrations of archival potential at least comparable to that of silver halide microfilms. PCMI masters are not intended for archival storage. Preliminary tests of the archival potential of TEP film have been generally encouraging but inconclusive.[7] Dry silver films remain sensitive to light and heat. Analysis of dry silver films eight to ten years old supports predictions of a 25-year or longer life expectancy.[8] While this is adequate for many commerical applications, it is not acceptable for library materials of enduring value.

## MICROFILM CAMERAS

### Rotary Cameras

Source document microfilm cameras are precision reprographic devices with specially designed optical systems.[9] They are usually divided, by operation and application, into three groups: rotary cameras, planetary cameras, and step-and-repeat cameras. *Rotary* cameras are designed for applications where work throughput is the primary consideration. Kodak introduced the first rotary camera in 1928 for microfilming cancelled bank checks. Rotary cameras are now widely used for office records of all types and sizes. Special models are available for microfilming continuous forms. Available rotary cameras will accept only 16mm microfilm, in 100- or 215-foot lengths, depending on the model.

The Recordak Reliant 750 Microfilmer (Fig. 3-1) represents the current state-of-the-art in rotary cameras and illustrates many features found on equipment of other manufacturers. Documents fed into the camera manually or automatically are transported past a narrow slit aperture where they are photographed. Document width must not exceed 11.75 inches. There is no limitation on document length. Interior lamps provide the light necessary for exposure. Automatic exposure

## Figure 3-1

### Rotary Microfilmer
(Courtesy: Eastman Kodak Company)

control compensates for differences in document color by measuring reflected light and adjusting lamp intensity accordingly. Synchronization of film and document transports eliminates relative movement and permits very high speed operation. When equipped with the appropriate automatic feeder, the Reliant 750 will microfilm more than 600 check-size documents per minute. Four interchangeable reductions are available: 24X, 32X, 40X, and 50X. Depending on reduction, microimages can appear on film in one of three positions. The *simplex* position utilizes the full film width for a single microimage at 24X. In the *duplex* position, mirrors inside the camera permit simultaneous recording of the front and back, each occupying one-half the film width at reductions of 32X, 40X, or 50X. In the *duo* position, one-half the film width (8mm) is masked and the remainder exposed. When the full length of film has passed through the camera, it is removed and reloaded. The previously exposed portion is masked and the previously masked portion exposed. The duo position is sometimes called the *8mm filming principle*. It is used at higher reductions (32X, 40X, or 50X) to increase the microimage capacity of a single reel.

Optional accessories available for the Reliant 750 include automatic loading of cartridge film, a sequential document imprinter, and various indexing devices. Camera design is modular. The customer buys the basic unit and those accessories needed to accomplish present work. As new requirements arise, additional capabilities can be acquired.

The document transport mechanism gives the rotary camera the advantage of greater filming speed and consequently reduced labor costs. Without automatic feeding, rates of 800 to 1,000 documents per hour, sustained by a single operator throughout a work day, are realistic. At the New Jersey State Library, a rotary camera was used to microfilm 660 drawers of catalog cards in just 25 work days.[10] For microfilming research materials, however, this speed advantage is more than offset by the degraded image quality resulting from machine vibration and the necessity of photographing a moving document. Microimage quality is usually measured as the ability to resolve, or faithfully record, a specified number of lines per millimeter. Typical rotary camera resolutions of eighty to one hundred lines per millimeter, while suitable for many typewritten documents, are inadequate for footnotes and other printed text set in small type faces. The inability to accept bound volumes or fragile documents represents a further limitation for library applications. While the duplex positioning technique permits rapid, simultaneous microfilming of two-sided originals, significant amounts of show-through can occur. Finally, a fully equipped rotary camera like the Recordak Reliant 750 will cost well over $10,000 and can be justified only by intensive use. Portable units are available for less than $3,000, but their capabilities are necessarily limited.

### Planetary Cameras

*Planetary*, or *flat-bed*, cameras were developed for library applications in the 1930s and are used today to microfilm bound volumes, manuscripts, drawings, and other source documents requiring high resolution capabilities. Even the least expensive planetary camera will resolve more than 120 lines per millimeter. The Itek 1400 (Fig. 3-2) is typical of planetary cameras used in libraries. Source documents to be microfilmed are placed on a flat copyboard and remain stationary throughout exposure. The camera head, housing the lens and film supply, is positioned on a vertical column above the copyboard. Reductions are infinitely variable between 12X and 20X and are changed by moving the camera head closer to or away from the copyboard. The maximum acceptable document size is 25 by 32 inches. Standard output is 35mm microfilm. A 16mm conversion kit is available as a factory-installed option. Automatic exposure control is standard. Additional capabilities include a double-exposure device that allows microfilming of both sides of a document prior to film advance, a half-frame advance that eliminates wasteful gaps between small documents, and a built-in knife with detachable take-up magazine that facilitates the removal of short strips of exposed microfilm.

**Figure 3-2**

**Planetary Microfilm Camera**

(Courtesy: Itek Corporation)

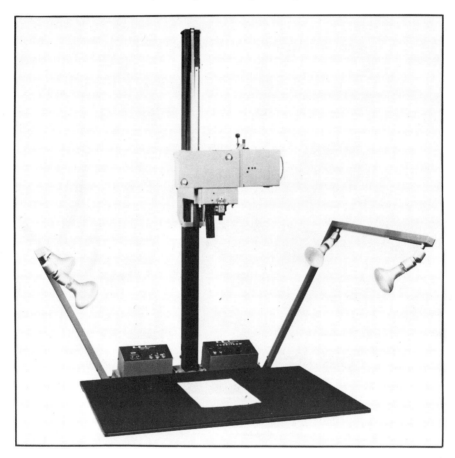

Since each document must be manually positioned on the copyboard, planetary camera throughput rates are usually much lower than those of rotary cameras. In the absence of automatic feeders, microfilming speed is a function of operator skill. An experienced operator microfilming single sheets in good condition may sustain an average of 300 documents per hour throughout the work day. Fragile documents or bound volumes may reduce this figure considerably. Librarians have long been interested in the development of an automatic feeding planetary camera that would provide high resolution at rotary camera speed. The DocuMate II (Fig. 3-3), developed by Terminal Data Corporation, is a high-volume, general-purpose planetary camera capable of continuous microfilming at the rate of 1.4 seconds per document. Documents inserted into the microfilmer manually or automatically are transported by belts past an exposure station. One or both sides

**Figure 3-3**

**Automated Planetary-Type Microfilmer**

(Courtesy: Terminal Data Corporation)

of the document can be exposed. The DocuMate II will produce 16mm or 35mm roll microforms and 105mm microfiche. List price is about $65,000. The recently developed Xerox Automated Catalog Cards Camera is a similar device, which utilizes a conveyer belt to transport catalog cards within camera range. Static electricity holds both the cards and film stationary as an exposure is made, thereby providing high resolution. University Microfilms International uses the camera, on a service bureau basis, to convert retrospective card catalogs in libraries maintaining a machine-readable record of recent acquisitions. The camera is not available for sale. The Automated Catalog Cards Camera was used by the New York State Library to convert its retrospective catalog of three million cards to microfiche.

Automatic feeding capability aside, planetary cameras are generally less expensive than comparably equipped rotary microfilmers. The Itek 1400, for example, is priced at around $5,000. A high quality 16mm planetary camera designed for the small office costs around $2,000.

## Step-and-Repeat Cameras

*Step-and-repeat* cameras, like the Dietzgen 4330 (Fig. 3-4), create microfiche by exposing source documents in a predetermined format of rows and columns on 105mm microfilm. The desired microfiche format must be specified at the time the camera is ordered. The Dietzgen 4330 is available in four formats and three reductions, including the NMA Type 1 Standard of 98 microimages reduced 24X. Special formats are available to order.

As with planetary cameras, the document to be microfilmed remains stationary on a flat copyboard. Following exposure, the document is removed, the camera automatically steps over to the next column position of film, another document is placed on the copyboard, and the process is repeated. At the end of a row, the camera advances the film and begins exposure again in the first column. When an entire microfiche is exposed, the film is again advanced to begin exposure of a new fiche. Most step-and-repeat cameras will also expose eye-legible typewritten or printed identifying information in the heading area of the microfiche. Unexposed 105mm microfilm is supplied in rolls. After processing, the developed roll must be cut to create individual microfiche. Because a roll is seldom exposed in its entirety prior to processing, the Dietzgen 4330 has a self-contained knife to facilitate removing short strips of film from the camera.

Like planetary microfilmers, step-and-repeat cameras feature high resolution suited to the wide variation in source document quality, but the absence of automatic document feeding slows work throughput. The Dietzgen 4330 does, however, incorporate a spring-loaded book holder to facilitate microfilming of bound volumes.

Step-and-repeat cameras are mechanically complex and, consequently, expensive. Priced at around $15,000, the Dietzgen 4330 can be cost-justified only in high volume operations. Although microfiche is functionally well-suited to the small office environment, step-and-repeat cameras priced within the budget of the small office and small library remain unavailable.

## Selecting a Microfilm Camera

Rotary cameras are selected for the high speed creation of 16mm microforms in applications where source documents are of uniformly good quality and work throughput is more important than resolution. In libraries, rotary cameras have been primarily used to microfilm catalog cards and office-type documents. Planetary cameras are preferred for applications requiring high quality 16mm or 35mm microimages for use on reels, in cartridges or cassettes, or for subsequent conversion to microfiche, microfilm jackets, or aperture cards. In libraries, the planetary camera is the camera of choice for microfilming research materials of

**Figure 3-4**

**Step-and-Repeat Camera**

(Courtesy: Dietzgen Corporation)

varied quality. Step-and-repeat cameras are used to create microfiche from 105mm roll microfilm. Regardless of type, the camera selected for library applications should be simple to operate without sacrificing quality or versatility.

Early microfilm cameras required many operator decisions that could only be made by trained technicians.[11] Most newer cameras are designed for operation by non-technical personnel, with a minimum of training, in an office environment. Simplified control panels and push-button operation are the rule. Warning lights and audible alarms signal the end of film, improper loading, burned-out lamps, and other sources of potential operator error. In most cases, the camera will not operate until the malfunction is corrected. Simplified controls are essential to step-and-repeat camera operators, who must be constantly aware of the row and column position under exposure. The operator must be able to skip an image, advance a row, or move quickly to the first or last frame.

All microfilm cameras offer some sort of exposure control to enable operators to compensate for variations in the color and texture of source documents. In manual systems, appropriate exposure settings for different types of documents are pre-determined by microfilming a representative group of samples. During actual work, the operator must make necessary exposure adjustments on a case-to-case basis, using a rheostat mounted on the camera. A number of microfilm cameras feature automatic exposure control systems as either a standard feature or an optional accessory. A photocell is used to determine the reflectance value of each document and make corresponding adjustments in either lamp intensity or shutter speed. Exposure errors resulting from operator misjudgment are thereby minimized. With high-speed rotary cameras, automatic exposure control is essential to maximum productivity and uniform image quality.

Microfilm loading and unloading are potentially wasteful and time-consuming tasks. As noted in a preceding section, the frequency of required film loading can be simply halved by selecting a camera that accepts polyester base microfilm in 215-foot lengths. Several cameras accept unexposed microfilm in a proprietary cartridge. Following exposure, the cartridge can be inserted directly into a microfilm processor. Processed film is then returned to the cartridge for use on readers and reader/printers. The 3M 3400 rotary camera is unique in allowing the operator to interrupt filming at any time by rewinding exposed microfilm into the cartridge and removing the cartridge from the camera. An odometer is used to identify the point on the film where work was interrupted. Later, the cartridge can be reloaded, the film advanced slightly beyond the point of interruption, and work continued. This ability to interrupt microfilming prior to exposure of an entire roll is crucial to optimum utilization of equipment in libraries where different groups of documents must be filmed daily or where several departments must share the same camera.

Versatility has long been a great strength of microfilm cameras. Despite complaints that the ability to microfilm source documents of different sizes at varying reductions and in different formats has complicated the development of both standards and inexpensive readers,[12] interchangeable reductions remain a major selling point for currently available equipment. Rotary cameras change reductions by interchanging film units. Planetary cameras usually change reductions by moving the camera head closer to or away from the copyboard. Planetary camera reductions may be pre-selected or infinitely variable between two extremes.

Step-and-repeat cameras are engineered at the factory to produce microfiche in a specified format and at a specified reduction. Field modifications to alter format and reduction are generally difficult to accomplish.

The ability to encode, or otherwise index, images during microfilming is essential to later retrieval from 16mm roll microforms. The significance of such camera-generated microfilm codes as sequential frame or document numbering, bar code lines, and image count marks is discussed in chapter eight.

Other features worth considering in selecting microfilm cameras for library applications include the ability to expose two rolls of film simultaneously for applications requiring both a working and a security copy of microfilmed documents; the ability to vary frame size and film advance to avoid waste in microfilming smaller documents; and the availability of spring-loaded book holders to keep bound volumes flat and correctly positioned during microfilming.[13] Careful attention should be given to the nature and extent of the manufacturer's warranty, provisions for operator training, and the availability and quality of maintenance service.[14]

## Microfilming Practice

While there are no standards that deal specifically and exclusively with the microfilming of library materials, several sources provide valuable practical guidelines. *Specifications for the Microfilming of Books and Pamphlets in the Library of Congress* (Washington: Library of Congress, 1973) presents current procedures employed by the LC Photoduplication Service in microfilming monographs. Individual sections deal with the preparation of books and pamphlets for filming; preparation and placement of bibliographic and technical targets; image placements and reductions; processing, inspection, and duplication. Guidelines for the microfilming of newspapers can be found in *Recommended Practice for Microfilming Newspapers* (Silver Spring, Md.: National Micrographics Association, 1975) and *Specifications for the Microfilming of Newspapers in the Library of Congress* (Washington: Library of Congress, 1972). *The Selection and Preparation of Records for Publication on Microfilm* (Washington: National Archives, 1970) provides detailed guidelines for the arrangement, processing, and description of archives and manuscripts to be microfilmed.

## MICROFILM PROCESSING

### Conventional Processing

A microfilm processor is the mechanical device that provides the physical and chemical treatments required to produce a visible microimage from exposed microfilm.[15] The processing of silver halide microfilm usually requires five steps. Exposed microfilm is first immersed in an alkaline developing agent that reduces exposed silver halide grains to black metallic silver. Brief immersion in an acid solution stops the development process. The developed microfilm is next immersed in a fixing solution to dissolve unexposed silver halide grains which, if unremoved, would gradually darken when exposed to light. A clear wash removes these dissolved grains. Finally, the processed microfilm is dried. Microfilm processors perform these steps automatically and in succession. Normal development produces a negative microimage from a positive source document. If *reversal processing* is required, exposed silver grains are dissolved prior to fixing. Silver grains remaining in areas corresponding to dark areas of the source document are then re-exposed and developed. The result is a positive microimage from a positive source document.

Microfilm processors vary in size, speed, and capability. Some equipment designed for high volume applications will process up to 100 feet of microfilm per minute, accept several film sizes simultaneously, and permit normal or reversal processing. These high volume units are widely used by micropublishers and microfilm service bureaus; they are usually operated by photographic technicians.

For the lower volumes characteristic of most library applications, the Cordell 240 Varifilm Processor (Fig. 3-5) is an example of a table-top unit designed for operation by non-technical personnel in an office environment. The Cordell 240 will automatically thread and process 16mm, 35mm, or 105mm microfilm at a speed of 2.5 feet per minute. An optional multi-strand kit permits simultaneous processing of three rolls of 16mm or two rolls of 35mm microfilm, thereby greatly enhancing effective throughput. Pre-mixed chemicals are provided in disposable containers. The processor will operate with or without external plumbing. These table-top processors form a relatively new but increasingly competitive product group. Prices now range between $2,500 and $6,000.

### Camera/Processors

Regardless of their convenient features, stand-alone conventional processors still require additional film handling. Camera/processors are integrated units designed to expose and develop microimages as one continuous operation. They are intended for applications where exposed microimages must be used immediately or where the user wants to avoid the inconvenience of external processing.

The Canon 161G (Fig. 3-6, p. 77) is a planetary camera/processor designed for the small office. It will expose and process 16mm roll microfilm at reductions between 24X and 29X. Camera operation and capabilities resemble those of other planetary microfilmers. Exposed microfilm passes through an integrated processing chamber at seven inches per minute. A special film buffer compensates for differences between processor and camera speeds. Developed microfilm is delivered on a 16mm reel, ready for use. The 161G is priced around $3,000. Other, more expensive, camera-processors are available for the high volume creation of microfiche or aperture cards.

### Microfilm Inspection

Processed microfilm must be inspected for image quality and stability. Required inspection equipment includes a light box, a pair of film rewinds, lint-free globes, a densitometer, a microscope, and editing and splicing equipment. Recommended inspection practice is outlined in NMA publication MS 104-1972,

**Figure 3-5**

**Table-Top Microfilm Processor**

(Courtesy: Cordell Engineering, Incorporated)

Figure 3-6

16mm Microfilm Camera/Processor (Courtesy: Canon, U.S.A.)

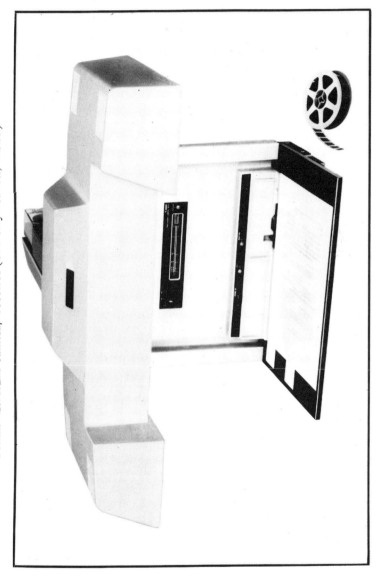

*Inspection and Quality Control of First Generation Silver Halide Microfilm* (Silver Spring, Md.: National Microfilm Association, 1972).

The purpose of image quality inspection is to insure legibility equal to or greater than an acceptable minimum standard and to insure duplicability through the required number of generations.[16] Inspection for legibility generally takes the form of a resolution test. Resolution, as noted in a preceding section, is a measure of the ability of optical systems and photographic materials to render fine detail visible. Resolution is expressed as the number of lines per millimeter discernible in a microimage. At 24X reduction, the minimum acceptable reduction for research materials is 120 lines per millimeter. In processed microfilm, resolution is a function of the emulsion, exposure, camera lens, camera vibration, and processing method. Resolution is most often measured by examining a microfilmed test chart under a microscope. All resolution test charts consist of a series of similar elements which progressively decrease in size and spacing. The National Bureau of Standards Microcopy 101a resolution target is the most widely used in the United States. In examining the processed microfilm, the observer must determine the set of numbered lines within the microimage that is just barely distinguishable. Resolvable lines per millimeter are computed by multiplying the number of the smallest discernible line set by the reduction. Thus, if the 5.0 line set is discernible in microimages reduced 24X, the resolution is at least 120 lines per millimeter. As critics of this method of microimage evaluation point out, the determination is necessarily subjective and agreement among observers is poor.[17]

The legibility and duplicability of processed microfilm is strongly influenced by image contrast. Contrast is an expression of the relationship between high and low density areas of a photographic image. Densities in the range 1.0 to 1.4, as measured by a densitometer, are generally acceptable for most library materials, although individual source documents may require special attention to produce sufficient contrast for viewing or duplication. Recommended densities for various types of source documents are given in the NMA *Inspection and Quality Control* publication.

The stability of processed microforms is affected by a number of factors, including the composition of the microfilm base material, the extent to which residual thiosulfate chemicals are removed during processing, and, ultimately, temperature and humidity conditions in the storage area. With respect to image stability, NMA *Inspection and Quality Control* guidelines differentiate expendable, commercial, and archival processing requirements.

*Expendable* microfilm is to be used and discarded in a very short time and, consequently, requires no special processing procedures beyond those necessary to develop legible and duplicable microimages. A computer-output-microfilm library catalog, updated weekly or monthly, is an example of an expendable microform.

*Commercial* microfilm is to be used for a limited period of time—typically less than ten years—and is not intended as a permanent record. Following processing, commercial microfilm must be inspected for residual thiosulfate concentration. Thiosulfate is the agent used to remove unexposed silver grains from microfilm during the fixing stage of development. Residual thiosulfate in excess of a prescribed amount will react with metallic silver, causing image fading and discoloration. American National Standard PH 4.8-1971 defines two procedures for determining the amount of residual thiosulfate on processed microfilm. The methylene blue method, the preferred test, measures the concentration of a blue dye formed during the analytical procedure. The silver densitometric method measures a density stain produced by residual thiosulfate. A residual thiosulfate test should be performed whenever film, chemicals, or the processor are changed.[18] Residual thiosulfate concentration on commercial microfilm must not exceed four micrograms per square centimeter of developed microform. Storage conditions for commercial microfilm must provide temperatures of less than ninety degrees Fahrenheit and relative humidity of less than sixty percent. Library purchasing records, microfilmed to save storage space during the period of required legal retention, are an example of an application for commercial microfilm.

Most processed microforms intended for inclusion in library collections must be of *archival* quality. Archival quality refers to the ability of an entire processed microform to retain its original characteristics and resist deterioration over time.[19] Silver halide microfilms for applications requiring archival quality must be manufactured to specifications presented in American National Standard PH 1.28-1969 (for triacetate base materials) and PH 1.41-1971 (for polyester base materials). Manufacturers complying with these specifications place a small triangle on the film edge to signify archival potential.[20] Archival quality microfilm processing must leave no more than one microgram of residual thiosulfate per square centimeter of developed microform.[21] Temperature in the storage area must not exceed seventy degrees Fahrenheit, with forty percent relative humidity. A humid atmosphere encourages the development of a chemical reaction between metallic silver and residual thiosulfate and promotes the growth of fungus on silver halide microfilms. Rapid cycling of temperature and humidity—any change greater than five degrees or percent in 24 hours—may result in condensation within microform containers and should be avoided. The discovery in 1963 of redox blemishes resulting from the displacement of image silver by oxidation in improperly stored library microforms underscores the significant interplay of materials, processing procedures, and storage conditions in a total archival preservation system.[22]

## PRODUCTION SUPPORT EQUIPMENT

As noted in the preceding chapter, an increasing amount of reel microfilm is converted to other microforms following processing and inspection. Special production equipment supports such conversion. Manual or motorized loaders, for example, are used to convert 16mm reel microfilm to cartridges or cassettes. Special leader and trailer must be spliced to the film and to the cartridge. A jacket viewer/inserter (Fig. 3-7) is used to convert 16mm reel microfilm to microfilm jackets. Microimages are viewed on a screen, cut into strips, and automatically inserted in jacket channels. Similar devices are available for aperture cards, jacket cards, and card jackets (Fig. 3-8, p. 81). While microfiche can be created directly on 105mm microfilm using a step-and-repeat camera, they can also be formed from strips of 16mm or 35mm microfilm, using a special composing station. The resulting microfiche master is contact duplicated to create use copies.

**Figure 3-7**

**Automated Jacket Viewer/Inserter**
(Courtesy: Motion Technology Corporation)

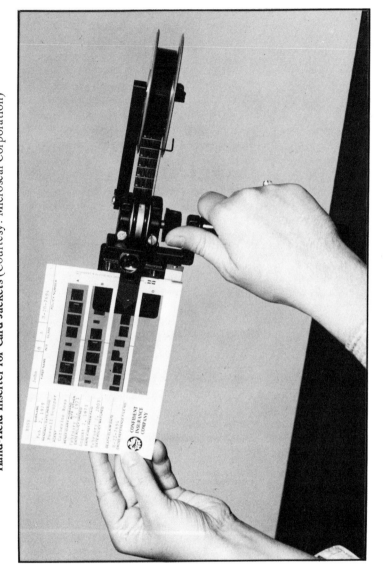

Figure 3-8

Hand-Held Inserter for Card Jackets (Courtesy: Microseal Corporation)

## MICROFORM DUPLICATION

### Silver Halide Print Films

Microform duplication is the production of a single or multiple microform copies from a master microform. The master microform may be either the original camera microform or a duplicate that is one or more generations removed from it.[23] Unlike original microphotography, which is an optical process, duplicate microforms are usually made by contact printing onto silver, diazo, or vesicular film stock. Silver microform duplication can be complicated, expensive, and time-consuming. Silver halide *print* films, like silver halide camera films, must be exposed and processed in separate operations. They must be handled in darkness and require wet development. They are used primarily in applications requiring duplicates of archival quality. This is typically the case with micropublications produced for the library market.

Silver halide print films are of two types: reversing and direct-duplicating. *Reversing* silver halide print films change the polarity of the master microform, making a positive duplicate of a negative master. They are particularly useful in producing positive duplicates for archival storage. Because they contain fewer potentially unstable silver grains, positive microforms are preferred for long-term preservation. *Direct-duplicating* silver halide print films maintain the polarity of the master microform, producing a negative duplicate of a negative master. They are used to make archival quality negative duplicates without first making a positive intermediate.[24]

### The Diazo Process

*Diazo* microfilms feature an emulsion of diazonium salts. When exposed to ultraviolet light transmitted through a master microform, these salts are dispersed in areas of the microfilm corresponding to light areas of the original microimage. Areas on the diazo microfilm that correspond to dark areas of the master microform are protected from exposure and remain unchanged, forming a latent image that is developed with ammonia fumes. The ammonia couples with the remaining diazonium salts to produce deeply colored azo dyes. The diazo process maintains the polarity of the master microform. Thus, it will make a negative duplicate from a negative master. Depending on the dye employed, the microimages will appear black, blue, or sepia. Blue diazo microfilms are especially suitable for viewing. Sepia diazo microfilms are used to make printing intermediates.[25]

The diazo process holds several advantages over silver halide print films. Because diazo microfilms are grainless, high resolution can be maintained through several generations. Diazo dyes are embedded in the film and resist abrasion during heavy use, an important consideration in many library applications. Because of their low speed, unexposed diazo microfilms can be handled in daylight. The diazo process itself is simple and continuous, requiring minimal film handling or operator intervention.

Diazo microfilms are used in applications where the polarity of the master microform must be maintained and archival quality is not required. Although some diazo microforms created twenty years ago remain in good condition, standards for manufacturing, processing, and storing archival quality diazo microfilm do not exist. A committee of the American National Standards Institute has been formed to study the archival potential of diazo microfilm, but its work has been slowed by the lack of available published information on the behavior of diazo materials.[26] There is considerable concern about the possible fading of diazo images exposed to strong light over time. A recent study by the National Reprographic Centre for documentation reports that diazo microimages fade slowly when exposed to actual or simulated ambient light but relatively quickly when exposed to light in reader projection systems. Significant information loss may occur in as little as eight hours of constant exposure. In a library, a reader accidentally left on during a weekend could render part of a diazo microform totally illegible.[27] Silver halide microimages, however, absorb heat as well and such prolonged exposure to intense light is not recommended for microforms of any type.

## The Vesicular Process

The vesicular process is a system of dry photography involving exposure to ultraviolet light and development by heat alone. Vesicular microfilms feature a light-sensitive emulsion suspended in a thermoplastic resin on a polyester base. The emulsion is hard and stable in an office environment, but exposure to ultraviolet light transmitted through a master microform creates pressure pockets within it that form a latent image. Rapid application of heat deforms the emulsion, developing the image. The removal of heat results in re-hardening of the emulsion and image fixation. Subsequent applications of heat must be avoided. The vesicular process requires no chemicals and is convenient, fast, and odorless.[28] Vesicular microforms are readily identified by their distinctive beige, grey, or light blue color.

Although non-reversing vesicular microfilms are available, the vesicular process normally reverses the polarity of the master microform. Vesicular microfilms are most widely used to duplicate microforms produced by computer-output-microfilm recording. Original COM-generated microforms are usually of positive polarity. Negative COM microimages are generally preferred for viewing and for use in reader/printers. Because the vesicular microimage is formed by a physical rather than a chemical process, it is particularly resistant to rough handling. Although vesicular microforms stored for many years under semi-tropical conditions show no significant changes in photometric characteristics,[29] standards for determining the archival properties of vesicular microforms do not exist. A committee of the American National Standards Institute is examining the archival potential of vesicular microfilms, but much work remains to be done.[30]

## Duplicating Equipment

A wide range of equipment is available for the duplication of roll and flat microforms. Duplicators for micropublishers, microfilm service bureaus, and other high-volume users are designed for the rapid production of multiple silver, diazo, or vesicular copies from individual roll or flat microform masters.[31] Of greater significance for libraries, however, is the increasing number of low-volume, desk-top diazo and vesicular duplicators designed specifically for the production of copies of master microfiche, microfilm jackets, or aperture cards in the small office. Rather than permit the use of master microforms in readers and reader/printers, a growing number of research libraries are using desk-top duplicators to produce single microfiche duplicates for the personal use and retention of patrons.

The desk-top microfiche duplicator product group is developing rapidly in terms of both economy and convenience. Hardware prices range between $1,000 and $5,000. The more expensive models are faster, provide multiple copy capability, and permit semi-automatic operation. There is considerable variety in equipment configuration and operation at all prices. Some units, like the Micobra MS-2 Duplicator and D-Series Developers (Fig. 3-9), expose and develop microfiche

**Figure 3-9**

**Microfiche Duplicator with Separate Developing Unit**
(Courtesy: Micobra Corporation)

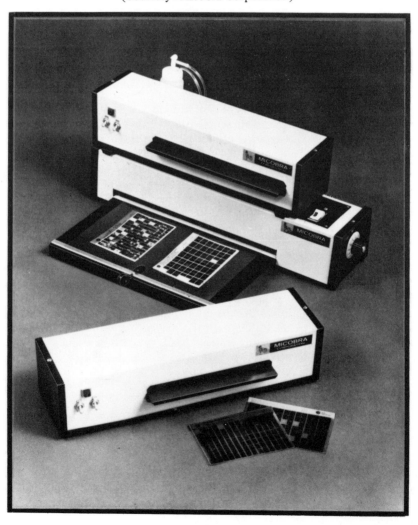

in separate steps. Others—the Dietzgen Mini-Dupe (Fig. 3-10), for example—integrate the exposure and developer units within a single machine. Integrated units tend to be more compact. Separate units may be more flexible, since the duplicator will expose either diazo or vesicular film and can be used with the developers of other manufacturers.

Most available desk-top duplicators produce developed microfiche copies in less than thirty seconds. Some units expose and develop two or more fiche simultaneously, thereby enhancing throughput. All available desk-top duplicators are designed for operation by non-technical personnel in an office environment. Operator controls are simplified. Vesicular development requires no chemicals. Chemical replenishment in diazo duplicators is easily accomplished. External venting is rarely required.

**Figure 3-10**

**Integrated Microfiche Duplicator**
(Courtesy: Dietzgen Corporation)

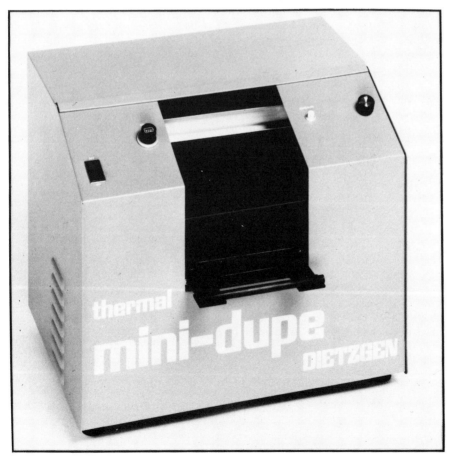

## MICROFILM SERVICE BUREAUS

A microfilm service bureau is an organization—usually a private business—that provides micrographic services using a customer's own material. The range of service bureau activities includes source document microfilming, computer-output-microfilming, microfilm processing, microfilm inspection, microform duplication, and microimage enlarging. Generally, customers take their work to the service bureau's facilities. For an extra fee, some service bureaus bring their equipment to the customer's site.

Forty percent of the academic libraries that provide microforms in response to interlibrary loan requests contract at least one phase of their microform production to an outside source.[32] Libraries without sufficient volume to justify the purchase of even an inexpensive microfilm camera may elect to employ a service bureau to create microforms for them. Even libraries with extensive microfilming facilities use service bureaus to supplement or enhance their own capabilities for high-volume work that must be completed in a short time, or for applications requiring special equipment or technical expertise. Some libraries with very high volumes send exposed microfilm to service bureaus for processing and inspection, thereby freeing themselves of the quality control precautions required in these two steps of microform production. Libraries without in-house processing facilities can also purchase microfilm with processing provided by the manufacturer.

The nature and acceptability of services to be rendered is a matter for individual negotiation between the library and the service bureau. In selecting a microfilm service bureau, libraries should look especially for demonstrated understanding of the requirements of their application, ability to provide high-quality services within the time allotted, and a record of satisfactory performance, preferably in library-related applications. A tour of the service bureau's facilities prior to the award of any contract is essential to knowledgeable selection.[33]

## COLOR MICROFORMS

Color microforms have been used successfully to miniaturize art works, navigational charts, interior design samples, and anatomical displays.[34] Thirty-five millimeter color microfilm is used at the Earth Resources Observation System Data Center, an archival repository for photographs of remotely sensed data.[35] The University of California at Santa Cruz has microfilmed a number of valuable land maps in color.[36] Despite their attractiveness for these and other applications, color microforms have many significant limitations.[37] Color film resolution is generally limited to eighty lines per millimeter. Reductions in excess of 24X are not recommended. The microfilm camera lens must be color-corrected. Color dyes are inherently unstable. For long-term preservation, color negatives must be stored in a deep-freeze in archival packaging. Because the microfilm base supports three emulsions, duplication of color microforms can result in serious loss of color rendition, resolution, and contrast. Since the microform reader also affects color rendition, it should have high illumination and a gray screen. Available reader/ printers are not suited to use with color microforms. Finally, the cost of color microforms—often ten times the cost of black-and-white—significantly restricts their use to those source documents requiring color to convey information content.

## REFERENCES

[1] The best discussion of the strenghts of the silver halide process in document reproduction is in William R. Hawken's *Copying Methods Manual* (Chicago: American Library Association, 1966). On silver halide microfilms, see G. W. W. Stevens, *Microphotography: Photography and Photofabrication at Extreme Resolution*, 2nd ed. (New York: John Wiley, 1968); Stevens, "Grainless Emulsions and Their Technical Applications," *Journal of Micrographics* 7 (1973): 9-20; D. G. West, "An Introduction to Microfilms and Their Properties," *Proceedings of the National Microfilm Association* (Silver Spring, Md.: NMA, 1969), 336-45.

[2] On microfilm polarity, see Don M. Avedon, "Standards: Microfilm Generation and Polarity Terminology," *Journal of Micrographics* 5 (1972): 261-64. Reversal processing is often used to avoid the loss of resolution inherent in duplication. See, for example, Langhorne D. Francis, "Microfilming Negative Photostats for Reproduction by Xerox Copyflo," *Journal of Micrographics* 8 (1975): 177-82.

[3] Harold J. Fromm, "Basic Microfilm Technology," *Proceedings of the National Micrographics Association* (Silver Spring, Md.: NMA, 1975), 95-109; Fred W. Hoyt and D. B. Thompson, "The New Kodak Thin Microfilm Program," *NMA Journal* 2 (1968):52.

[4] William Saffady, "Microfilm Equipment and Retrieval Systems for Library Picture Collections," *Special Libraries* 65 (1974): 440-44.

[5] On unconventional recording technologies, see Carl E. Nelson, "Microimaging Materials," *Proceedings of the National Microfilm Association* (Annapolis, Md.: NMA, 1967), 75-86; William E. Bixby, "Applications of Microxerographic Techniques to Information Recording," *Proceedings of the National Microfilm Association* (Annapolis, Md.: NMA, 1962), 229-47; Martin Leibert, "Legible Microcopy: The Middle Road in Microforms," *Proceedings of the National Microfilm Association* (Silver Spring, Md.: NMA, 1968), 167-73; R. J. Cox, ed., *Non-Silver Photographic Processes* (New York: Academic Press, 1975).

[6] Joseph W. Shepard, "Dry Silver Film Technology," *Proceedings of the National Microfilm Association* (Silver Spring, Md.: NMA, 1972), II-74-85; Shepard, "Dry Silver Films," *Proceedings of the National Microfilm Association* (Silver Spring, Md.: NMA, 1973), II-237-40.

[7] T. C. Bagg, *Evaluation of Transparent Electro-Photographic Film and Camera System* (Washington: National Bureau of Standards, 1976).

[8] Kenneth R. Kurttila, "Dry Silver Film Stability," *Journal of Micrographics* 10 (1977): 113-19.

[9] On camera design, see Carl Nelson, *Microfilm Technology: Engineering and Related Fields* (New York: McGraw-Hill, 1965), esp. pp. 11-58; Walter Mandler, "Survey of Microfilm Lenses," *Proceedings of the National Microfilm Association* (Annapolis, Md.: NMA, 1963), 23-37.

[10] O. P. Gillack and R. H. McDonough, "Spreading State Library Riches for Peanuts," *Wilson Library Bulletin* 45 (1970): 354-55.

[11] See the descriptions in Herman H. Fussler, *Photographic Reproduction for Libraries* (Chicago: University of Chicago Press, 1942); M. L. Raney, "The Microphotographic Camera," *ALA Bulletin* 31 (1937): 211-13; Raney, "First Steps in Microphotography," *ALA Bulletin* 32 (1938): 164-66; Charles Bishop, "Problems in the Production and Utilization of Microfiche," *American Documentation* 12 (1961): 53-55. For a more detailed discussion of cameras currently available, see William Saffady, "Microfilm Cameras: A Survey of Features and Functions," *Special Libraries* 68 (1977): 1-6.

[12] William R. Hawken, "Microform Standardization: The Problem of Research Materials and a Propsoed Solution," *NMA Journal* 2 (1968): 14-27.

[13] For a possible solution to the problem of copying from bound volumes, see "The Prismascope—A Device to Facilitate the Recording of Books, Especially Those Fragile or Tightly Bound," *NRCd Bulletin* 5 (1972): 47-48.

[14] For an excellent discussion of service contract provisions, see Richard A. Lidstad, "Customer Service and Support," *Proceedings of the National Micrographics Association* (Silver Spring, Md.: NMA, 1975), 406.

[15] Milton L. Schreiber, "Microfilm Processing Equipment," *Proceedings of the National Microfilm Association* (Silver Spring, Md.: NMA, 1971), II-58-62; Maynard Short, "Development Mechanism of Silver Halide Emulsions," *Proceedings of the National Micrographic Association* (Silver Spring, Md.: NMA, 1971), II-17-19.

[16] Harold J. Fromm, "Methods for Controlling the Quality of Microimages in Microproduction Systems," *Proceedings of the National Microfilm Association* (Annapolis, Md.: NMA, 1965), 103-115; T. J. Morgan, "Microfilm Procedures and Quality Control." In *Micropublishing for Learned Societies* (Hatfield, Herts, Eng., National Reprographic Centre for Documentation, 1968), pp. 19-23; H. G. Morse, "Microfilm Inspection Equipment," *Proceedings of the National Microfilm Association* (Silver Spring, Md.: NMA, 1971), II-63-66.

[17] G. W. W. Stevens, "Application of Different Methods of Image Evaluation in the Microfilm Industry," *Proceedings of the National Microfilm Association* (Silver Spring, Md.: NMA, 1970), 5-24; Gilbert S. Cranwell, "Problems of Establishing an International Standard for Microcopying Resolution Testing," *Journal of Micrographics* 7 (1974): 257-65; H. B. Archer, "The RIT Alphanumeric Resolution Test Object," *Journal of Micrographics* 7 (1974): 205-209; Harold Dorfman, "Quality Criteria," *Microfilm Techniques* 5 (March/April 1976): 9-10, 13, 28.

[18] R. Mottice and M. Schreiber, "New Method for Residual Thiosulfate Analysis," *Journal of Micrographics* 3 (1969): 38-45; Milton L. Schreiber, "Technical Note: New Residual Thiosulfate Test Methods," *Journal of Micrographics* 5 (1971), 53.

[19] Don M. Avedon, "Microfilm Permanence and Archival Quality: Standards," *Special Libraries* 63 (1972): 586-88.

[20] *Specifications for Photographic Film for Archival Records, Silver-Gelatin Type on Cellulose Ester Base* (New York: American Standards Institute, 1969); *Specifications for Photographic Film for Archival Records, Silver-Gelatin Type on Polyester Base* (New York: American National Standards Institute, 1973);

P. Z. Adelstein, "A Review of Proposed USA Standard for Archival Film on Polyester Base," *NMA Journal 2* (1969): 134-42.

[21] *Methylene Blue Method for Measuring Thiosulfate, and Silver Densito-metric Method for Measuring Residual Chemicals in Films, Plates, and Paper* (New York: American National Standards Institute, 1971).

[22] C. S. McCamy and C. I. Pope, "Redox Blemishes—Their Causes and Prevention," *Journal of Micrographics* 3 (1970): 165-70; Vernon D. Tate, "Microscopic Blemishes and the Storage of Permanent Record Microfilm in Perspective," *National Micro-News* No. 70 (June 1964): 243-48.

[23] If many duplicates of a camera original microform are required, a printing intermediate is usually made to save wear and tear. Most micropublications sold to libraries are third generation microforms, produced from such a printing intermediate.

[24] Harold J. Fromm, "Microfilm Duplication with Silver Halide Print Films," *Proceedings of the National Microfilm Association* (Silver Spring, Md.: NMA, 1968), 250-56; Fromm and Stephen C. Insolaco, "A New Direct Duplication Silver Halide Film," *Proceedings of the National Microfilm Association* (Annapolis, Md.: NMA, 1966), 30-40; W. S. Suydam, "Updated Film Copying," *Proceedings of the National Microfilm Association* (Silver Spring, Mc.: NMA, 1971), 21-24; Charles G. LaHood, Jr., "Film Stock—Some Considerations on the Purchase of Different Types for Library Use," *Library Technology Reports* (March 1975).

[25] G. W. Smith, "Diazo for Microfilm," *Microdoc* 10 (1971): 2-4; Smith, "Reply to R. I. H. Charlton," *Microdoc* 10 (1971): 83-84; Alfred H. Stuart, "Technology of Diazo Microfilm," *Proceedings of the National Microfilm Association* (Silver Spring, Md.: NMA, 1973), II-24-248; M. S. Dinaburg, *Photosensitive Diazo Compounds and Their Uses* (London: Focal Press, 1964); John P. Deley and John S. Dejer, "A Review of Federal Specification L-F-3156," *NMA Journal* 1 (1968): 49-51.

[26] P. Z. Adelstein, "A Progress Report: ANSI Activities on Stability of Processed Diazo and Vesicular Films," *Journal of Micrographics* 9 (1976): 99-101.

[27] R. N. Broadhurst, *An Investigation of the Effects of Exposure to Light on Diazo Microfilm* (Hatfield, Herts, Eng., National Reprographic Centre for Documentation, 1976).

[28] H. H. McGregor, "Vesicular Photography—An Overview," *Journal of Micrographics* 9 (1975): 13-20; Bert L. Zaccaria, "Vesicular Film," *Proceedings of the National Microfilm Association* (Silver Spring, Md.: NMA, 1973), II-248-52; M. G. Anderson, "What's New in Vesicular Film Technology?," *Proceedings of the National Microfilm Association* (Silver Spring, Md.: NMA, 1972), II-86-87.

[29] M. G. Anderson and V. L. Wagner, "Stability of Vesicular Microfilm Images," *Photographic Science and Engineering* 8 (1964): 353-58; A. Tulsi Rom and Elvin W. Potter, "Stability of Vesicular Microfilm Images—II," *Photographic Science and Engineering* 14 (1970): 283-88.

[30] Kalvar Type 16 vesicular microfilm, used between 1967 and 1970 by Microfilming Corporation of America for its microform edition of the *New York Times*, proved unstable in storage, emitting hydrogen chloride gas which produced hydrochloric acid when mixed with chloride in the air. Several libraries storing these microfilms reported the rotting of cardboard containers and rusting of metal cabinets. Manufacturers of vesicular microfilms now recommend that they be stored in plastic containers on open shelves. ANSI PH. 1.43 and 1.54 strongly oppose the interfiling of microfilms of different chemistry in order to avoid possible interaction.

[31] See, for example, James Metzger and William Callaghan, "Duplicating Third Generation 48X COM Output on Vesicular Film for Large Scale Distribution: Problems and Quality Control," in Don Chenevert, ed., *Micrographics Science 1973: Winter Symposium* (Washington: Society of Photographic Scientists and Engineers, 1973), pp. 133-36; Robert C. Olson, "Proprietary Microprinting," *Proceedings of the National Micrographics Association* (Silver Spring, Md.: NMA, 1975), 259-61.

[32] Joseph Z. Nitecki, *Directory of Library Reprographic Services: A World Guide* (Weston, Conn.: Microform Review, 1976).

[33] For general guidelines, see George H. Harmon, "A Service Bureau—How to Select One," *Journal of Micrographics* 8 (1975): 135-37.

[34] Lawrence M. Aleomoni, *The Effects of Using Color Microfiche upon Achievement in a Course on Interior Home Design* (Urbana, Ill.: Office of Instructional Resources, University of Illinois, 1971); Wilber E. Renner, "Color Microfiche as a Self-Instructional Medium," *Proceedings of the National Microfilm Association* (Silver Spring, Md.: NMA, 1974), II-295-99; Renner and Richard F. Walters, "The Use of Color Microfiche in Medical School Instruction," In Chenevert, pp. 120-24; Chandler Smith, "Color Microfiche for Teaching Anatomic Pathology," *Journal of Micrographics* 4 (1971): 83-89.

[35] Keith A. Maas, "Earth Resources Browse Microfilm—A Challenge for the Microfilm Industry," *Proceedings of the National Micrographics Association* (Silver Spring, Md.: NMA, 1975), 322-27.

[36] Stanley D. Stevens, "Microfilming Maps in Color," *Proceedings of the National Microfilm Association* (Silver Spring, Md.: NMA, 1971), II-48-50.

[37] Harold H. Dorfman, "Color Microfilm Program," *Proceedings of the National Microfilm Association* (Silver Spring, Md.: NMA, 1974), II-303-305; Ralph A. Sickles, "A Look at Color Microfilming," *Proceedings of the National Micrographics Association* (Silver Spring, Md.: NMA, 1975), 320-22.

# CHAPTER 4

## COMPUTER-OUTPUT-MICROFILM (COM)

### COM TECHNOLOGY

#### Overview

Since the nineteenth century, microphotographic technology has permitted the creation of microimages from bound volumes, technical reports, office correspondence, and other source documents, using the high-precision cameras described in the previous chapter. By definition, source document microfilming requires the prior existence of information in paper form. The acronym COM denotes the product (*computer-output-microfilm*), the process (*computer-output-microfilming*), and the device (*computer-output-microfilmer*) that converts machine-readable, computer-processable digital data to human-readable textual or graphic information in microform *without first creating paper documents.*

Computer-output-microfilmers, or COM recorders, were introduced in the late 1950s as high speed output devices for computer programs generating complex scientific graphics.[1] With the proliferation of computer-generated paper reports during the 1960s, COM developed as a powerful records management tool for business applications.[2] The first library application—a computer-produced catalog—was reported in 1967 by the Lockheed Technical Information Center.[3] The early 1970s saw increased user acceptance in non-scientific applications, due largely to the introduction of new equipment capabilities and increased customer confidence resulting from beginning standardization.[4] The total volume of COM viewing equipment—estimated at 10,000 to 15,000 units in the late 1960s—had more than doubled by the end of 1971.[5] Today, COM holds an increasingly large share of the total micrographics market and is the focus of industry and user interest. One COM manufacturer estimates that the installed base of non-scientific recorders will triple during the period from 1975 through 1980.[6] Microfilm's share of the total computer output market—which also includes paper printers and display devices—is expected to approach 25 percent by 1980, up from 16 percent in 1974 and an estimated 4 percent in 1972.[7]

Libraries, as noted in chapter one, have recently demonstrated considerable interest in the development of COM applications. This chapter discusses COM technology and systems design as it relates to libraries. Any discussion of COM requires the use of computer science and data processing terminology, which may not be familiar to all readers. Such terms are defined in the notes as they appear in the text.

### The COM Recorder

A COM recorder (Fig. 4-1) is both a computer peripheral device and a high-speed microfilmer.[8] As a computer peripheral, on-line or off-line operation is possible. On-line COM recorders are connected to a computer and operate under its direct control. Digital data to be recorded on microfilm are received directly from the computer. All available on-line COM recorders are designed for operation with IBM System 360/370 computers only.[9] Interface to the central processor is through a selector or multiplexor channel. The computer recognizes the on-line COM recorder as the equivalent of an IBM 1403 line printer.

**Figure 4-1**

**A COM Recorder**
(Courtesy: Eastman Kodak Company)

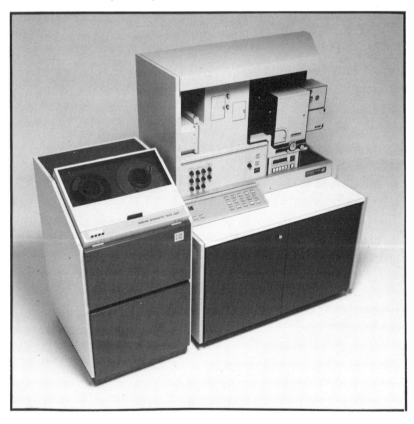

Most COM recorders operate *off-line*. The off-line COM recorder is a stand-alone device that reads digital data from an appropriately formatted magentic tape. The tape, resulting from the execution of a computer program, must be brought to the COM recorder and mounted on an internal or attached tape drive. The tape may be formatted on a host computer, using one of several software techniques described later in this chapter. Alternatively, the off-line COM recorder may incorporate a programmable minicomputer designed to accept and reformat tapes prepared for conventional paper printers.

The cost of the required magnetic tape drive makes the off-line COM recorder substantially more expensive than on-line models. Off-line recorders are more versatile, however. Most available units will accept input tapes prepared on a wide range of general-purpose computers. On-line recorders, as already noted, are limited to the IBM System 360/370 environment. Because the off-line COM recorder is not connected to a computer, availability and productivity are not limited by computer malfunction. Off-line COM recorders may be located at some distance from the computer on which the input tape is prepared and are widely used by microfilm service bureaus and other vendors offering COM services to libraries.[10]

## Recording Methods

Regardless of mode of operation, logical circuits within the COM recorder translate digital input into a combination of information and instructions, determining what data are to be recorded and in what size and position. The data are then recorded on microfilm in one of four ways: by photographing a cathode-ray-tube (CRT) display; by exposing a light-emitting diode (LED) display; by an electron beam; or by a laser beam.

*Cathode-ray-tube (CRT) photography* is the oldest and most prevalent COM recording technology. Data from magnetic tape or, in the case of on-line COM recorders, from the computer itself, are displayed as a page of information on the screen of a CRT located inside the COM recorder.[11] The CRT display is then photographed by a high-speed microfilm camera, the film advanced, the display erased, a new page displayed, and the process repeated (Fig. 4-2). Recording speeds range from two to five pages per second, depending on the recorder and the way in which the data are presented.

The method of character generation on the CRT screen varies with the manufacturer. Some COM recorders use electron beam *strokes* to define characters. Others shape individual characters by selectively illuminating light points in a *dot matrix* on the CRT screen. COM recorders manufactured by Stromberg Data-graphiX use a *Charactron*[TM] *shaped beam tube* which forms individual characters by directing a stream of electrons through a small template located in the neck of the CRT. For library applications, the method of character generation in CRT-type COM recorders is of particular importance because of its relationship to possible character set expansion. This relationship is discussed in a later section of this chapter.

Regardless of the method of character generation, the recording medium in CRT photography is typically a blue-sensitive, low-contrast, black-and-white silver halide microfilm designed for rapid processing.[12] In most cases, the exposed silver

**Figure 4-2**

## COM Recording by CRT Photography (Courtesy: Bell and Howell)

*Bell & Howell 3700 COM Recorder Simplified Data Flow*

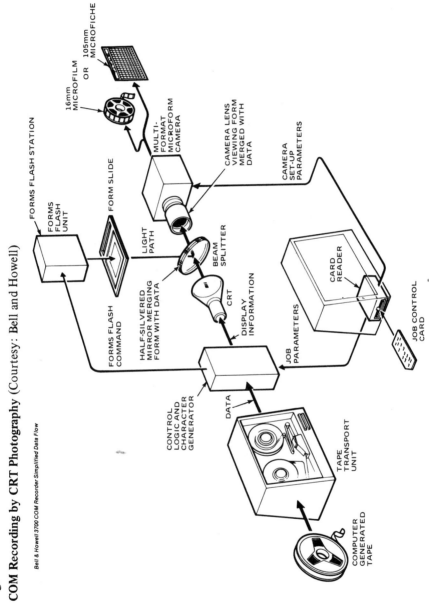

halide microfilm is removed from the recorder and taken to a separate processor. The Quantor 115 (Fig. 4-3) is an example of an integrated COM recorder/processor that will expose, develop, and deliver cut, dry microfiche in one continuous operation. Throughput speed is about one microfiche per minute. Chemicals are furnished in pre-mixed containers for ease of replenishment. External plumbing is not required. These integrated recorder/processors are well-suited to computer room installations where operating personnel lack microphotographic expertise.[13]

Because the CRT display consists of light characters on a dark background, normal development of COM original film will result in a first generation microform of positive polarity. Negative duplicates, generally considered preferable for viewing or use in reader/printers, are usually made by the vesicular process. As noted in the previous chapter, vesicular duplication reverses the polarity of the master microform. Alternatively, reversal processing can be used to produce a negative original microform for diazo duplication.

The Memorex 1603 COM Printer is currently the only COM recorder using light-emitting diode (LED) technology.[14] Inside the Memorex 1603, a bank of *light-emitting-diodes* is used to create and record a line of up to 132 characters. Each character is formed from a five by seven matrix of very fine glass rods. These rods are selectively illuminated to shape the desired characters. The completed line is then exposed to a special silver halide microfilm that is sensitive to infrared energy. Following exposure, the film is advanced, a new line formed, and the process repeated. Recording speed is approximately 10,000 lines per minute, or two to three pages per second. Exposed microfilm is processed and duplicated in a conventional manner. Normal development results in a positive microform master.

In both CRT photography and LED recording, the total energy at the film plane is relatively low. The recording medium is consequently restricted to silver halide photographic materials with the attendant inconvenience of wet chemical processing. Microrecording onto vesicular, diazo, or other unconventional dry-processed photographic materials would require an order-of-magnitude increase in CRT or LED energy output that does not now appear feasible. It is expected, therefore, that future COM systems will employ alternative recording technologies.[15] Two such technologies are now available in the United States.[16]

The 3M Electron Beam Recorder (EBR) reads digital data from magnetic tape and deflects an *electron beam* that strokes latent character images directly onto 3M brand dry silver microfilm at the rate of two to five pages per second.[17] As noted in the previous chapter, dry silver microfilm is a light-sensitive recording medium that is developed by the application of heat alone. The dry silver processor can be attached directly to the 3M EBR for continuous operation and delivery of developed, immediately readable microimages. Polarity of the developed dry silver microform is positive. Vesicular duplication is typically used to make second generation negatives for viewing or use in reader/printers. Because the archival potential of dry silver microfilm has not been demonstrated, those COM applications requiring archival quality for long-term preservation must employ silver halide duplicates made from dry silver masters.

**Figure 4-3**

**COM Recorder/Processor** (Courtesy: Quantor Corporation)

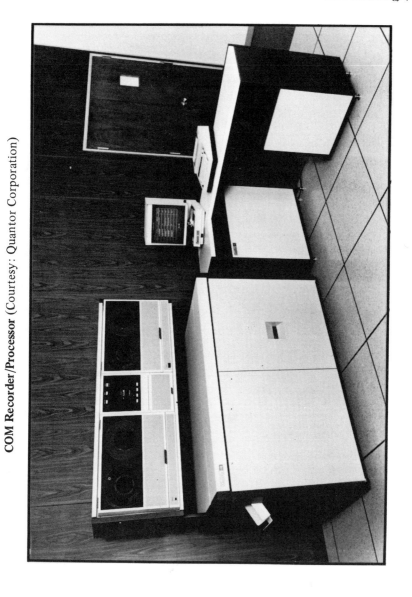

In *laser beam recording*, a low-power laser is used to activate and expose points in a dot matrix on film (Fig. 4-4). Laser beams can be directed with great precision and turned on and off at very high speeds. When the laser scans a matrix on film, the beam exposes only those points necessary to shape individual characters. Mirrors are used to move the laser from line to line and across pages. Effective recording speed is 10,000 lines per minute or two to three pages per second. Unlike conventional light which consists of a mixture of wavelengths or colors, laser light is concentrated and much more powerful. Consequently, lasers, like electron beams, can generate the energy required to expose unconventional photographic media. The 3M Laser Beam Recorder (LBR), for example, utilizes 3M brand dry silver film. The Kodak Komstar Microimage Processor records onto Dacomatic DL film, a fine-grain silver halide microfilm with embedded processing chemicals. Both films are dry-processed.

## Forms Recording

To emulate report production on pre-printed paper stock, all COM recorders will merge dynamic digital data with a static form. This is typically accomplished with a *forms slide*, a transparent piece of glass or film bearing the image of a business form with blank spaces for variable information to be filled in by the COM recorder from the user's input.[18] The form slide image is superimposed on the data during recording, using a mirror. Form slide artwork must be designed for optimum reproducibility at high reductions. Line placement accuracy is crucial to proper registration of the form image and data. Standard form slides—consisting of lines, shading, and frame borders—are used to establish frame limits and speed retrieval of columnar data. Special form slides can be designed for particular applications. Some COM recorders will store several form slides and interchange them, as required, within the same microform.

## PREPARING DATA FOR COM RECORDING

### Tapes Accepted by Off-Line Recorders

As noted in a preceding section, off-line COM recorders read digital data from magnetic tape. Librarians considering the conversion of one or more reports to COM must determine which tape sizes, recording densities, and coding formats are acceptable to the recorder to be used.

Most off-line COM recorders used by microfilm service bureaus incorporate a universal tape drive which will accept seven or nine track, NRZI or PE tapes at recording densities of 200, 556, 800, or 1,600 bits per inch.[19] Less versatile units, often used by corporate or institutional data processing centers equipped with computers of a single manufacturer, will accept only specific tape sizes recorded at specific densities. In terms of tape coding, all available off-line COM recorders will read EBCDIC code, the internal system code of IBM System 360/370 computers.[20]

Most off-line COM recorders will also read ASCII code, used widely by non-IBM computers,[21] and BCD code, used by the IBM 1401, a second generation computer that remains in use.[22] A few off-line COM recorders will accept tapes prepared by Honeywell, NCR, and other computers with special code structures.

**Figure 4-4**

**Laser-Beam COM Recording**
(Courtesy: Eastman Kodak)

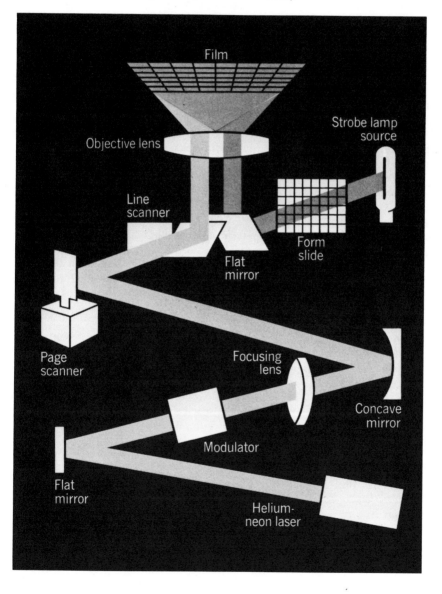

## Tape Preparation

Off-line COM recorders require a specially-formatted magnetic tape containing both the data to be recorded on microfilm and embedded machine commands. These machine commands instruct the COM recorder to begin a new line, frame, or fiche; change type font, size, or intensity; indent to present information in columns; and so on. Magnetic tapes containing data to be recorded on microfiche must also include instructions for the content and placement of eye-legible titling and for the derivation of index information from the data itself. Machine commands are generally unique to each COM recorder. The repertoire of interpretable commands varies with the capabilities of the recorder. Libraries can create appropriately-formatted COM tapes in one of three ways: by modifying existing paper-oriented application programs to call special formatting subroutines; by using translator programs to reformat line printer records for COM; or by using a minicomputer-controlled COM recorder with self-contained reformatting software.[23] All three alternatives require special software capable of generating the necessary instructions for control of the COM recorder by appending special control characters to print-data generated by the library's application program. The three alternatives differ significantly in the relative involvement of programmer time, the host computer, and the COM recorder itself.

The subroutine method is flexible and efficient but requires programmer involvement. When linked to the library's existing paper-oriented application program, COM formatting subroutines restructure output normally intended for a line printer, making it acceptable for COM recording. The result is a formatted COM tape created in a single computer run. While all COM recorder manufacturers make one or more pre-written and pre-tested subroutine packages available to customers, the services of a programmer will generally be required to adapt these vendor-supplied subroutines to the library's application. As a rule, such subroutines will prove easiest to implement in the IBM System 360/370 computer environment. The level of required programmer involvement will typically be greater with computers of other manufacturers.[24]

The print-tape translation method is well-suited to libraries without access to the services of a programmer capable of handling COM formatting subroutines. In most general-purpose computer environments, the output resulting from execution of an application program is written onto a tape, or occasionally a disk, from which it is later printed onto paper. This technique, called *spooling*, is designed to minimize inefficiencies resulting from the speed differential between the computer and its output devices, notably the line printer. The file of print-records created in this way is variously called a spool-tape, a print-tape, or a print-file. COM print-tape translator software is designed to read and reconstruct these records, producing a COM tape with appropriate embedded machine commands. Most COM recorder manufacturers provide print-tape translators for a wide-range of general-purpose computers. Unlike the subroutine method, the library using print-tape translation to convert its printer-oriented applications to COM will not require the services of a programmer. Separate computer runs are necessary, however, to first produce, then translate, the print tape. For library programs executed frequently, host computer time and charges may increase significantly.[25]

For libraries without access to the additional computer time required for print-tape translation, an increasing number of COM recorders incorporate minicomputers with self-contained software designed to reformat print-tapes prepared on a wide range of general-purpose computers.[26] The minicomputer software eliminates the need for an intermediate COM tape. Minicomputer-controlled COM recorders produce microform output directly from a library-supplied print-tape. By using a service bureau equipped with a minicomputer-controlled COM recorder, a library can quickly and easily convert any printer-oriented report to COM. In converting its computer-generated serials holdings list from paper to 16mm microfilm cassettes, the Wayne State University Libraries selected a COM service bureau equipped with a minicomputer-controlled Gould Beta COM 700L. Following each execution of the holdings list updating program, the library gives the service bureau a print-tape containing records suitable for an IBM 1403 line printer. A DEC PDP-8/E minicomputer attached to the Beta COM automatically performs the print-tape translation necessary for COM output.[27]

## Data Preparation for On-Line Recording

On-line recorders, as already noted, will accept digital input only from IBM System 360/370 computers. Because these computers recognize the on-line COM recorder as the equivalent of an IBM 1403 line printer, the production of printed page-images on unindexed 16mm roll microfilm usually requires no modification of application programs designed for paper output. To produce microfiche or indexed roll microfilm, however, application programs must be modified to call formatting subroutines. These subroutines, which are available from COM recorder manu-facturers, are virtually identical with those used to prepare COM tapes for off-line recording.

## COM OUTPUT CAPABILITIES

### Microforms Produced

Most available COM recorders will produce both 16mm roll microfilm and standard 105 by 148mm microfiche. A few older COM recorders will produce only 16mm roll microfilm, for use on reels, in cartridges and cassettes, or in jackets. Several newer recorders, reflecting changes in the popularity of the various microforms discussed in chapter two, will produce only microfiche.[28] The use of 35mm microfilm, the most popular microform for library source document applications, is generally limited to COM-generated graphics, engineering drawings, and multi-page alphanumeric records intended for insertion in aperture cards. The significant exception, described more fully in chapter five, is *Books in English*, the British Library micropublication which is first recorded via COM on 35mm roll microfilm, then further reduced by NCR to create ultrafiche masters. A few COM recorders will produce the tab-size microfiche used by IBM for its technical publications.

## Effective Reductions and Internal Formats

Microforms, by definition, present information in reduced size. As discussed in chapter two, reduction in source document microfilming represents a measure of the number of times a given linear dimension of a document is reduced through microphotography. Because full-size documents are not involved in COM recording, COM reductions are termed *effective* reductions. Effective reduction is a measure of the number of times a given linear dimension of an *imaginary* document would have to be reduced to equal the size of the corresponding linear dimension of a COM microimage. In most cases, the imaginary document is an eleven by fourteen inch computer printout page.[29]

The most widely-used effective reductions for 16mm roll microfilm and microfiche are 24X, 42X, and 48X. On 16mm roll microfilm, a COM recorder will record the equivalent of one computer printout page per frame at 24X, two computer printout pages per frame at 42X, or four computer printout pages per frame at 48X. Depending on the effective reduction, the total capacity of a 100 foot roll ranges from about 2,000 to about 8,000 microimages. In most cases, microimages may be oriented in comic or cine mode. The three most popular COM microfiche formats provide for 63 computer printout pages in seven rows and nine columns at 24X reduction; 208 computer printout pages in thirteen rows and sixteen columns at 42X; and 270 computer printout pages in fifteen rows and eighteen columns at 48X.[30]

Within the COM recorder, careful control of type face, size, and image density permit the use of reductions well in excess of those suitable for source document microphotography. From the systems design standpoint, higher reductions are attractive because they increase microform image capacity, thereby reducing duplication costs and minimizing microform handling for the very large data bases typical of library applications. While 48X is the maximum effective reduction for most currently available COM recorders, it is expected that improvements in microfilm emulsions will eventually permit high-quality, single-step reductions in excess of 100X.[31] U.S. Datacorp, the world's largest COM service bureau, has customized recorders capable of producing high-quality microfiche with 690 frames reduced 72X. The 3M Beta COM 800, a CRT-type recorder, can reduce its display size by fifty percent for microfilming with a 48X lens, thereby achieving an effective reduction of 96X. Unfortunately, the required capital investment in readers and reader/printers for reductions in the 100X remains prohibitively high for the many use-points required in a typical library COM application such as a public catalog or serials holdings list.

Within a COM microfiche, pagination typically proceeds vertically–down columns and across rows. Most COM recorders will also paginate horizontally, the standard for source documents, or in zig-zag fashion, a convenient but little-used format that minimizes microfiche carrier movements during viewing by paginating down one column and up the next.

## Alphanumeric vs. Graphic Recording

COM recorders have historically served two broad application areas: *alphanumeric* (business) and *graphic* (scientific). As the name implies, alphanumeric COM units will record only alphabetic characters, numeric digits, punctuation marks, and other symbols commonly used in textual documents. Graphic COM recorders have full alphanumeric capability and can also construct complex charts, graphs, plots, network diagrams, and circuit drawings. In scientific and technical applications, graphic COM recorders serve as high-speed replacements for mechanical digital plotters. Although the earliest COM recorders had graphics capability, the majority of currently available units are alphanumeric. Of potential significance for library applications is the small number of essentially alphanumeric COM recorders with limited *business graphics* capability.[32] Such recorders will construct line charts, bar charts, pie charts, labelled axes, histograms, and other graphic presentations useful in management summary reports.

## COM Character Sets

The basic character set of most available COM recorders totals sixty to seventy characters, including the upper-case alphabet, numeric digits, and frequently-used punctuation symbols. Most alphanumeric COM recorders offer an optional extended set of 90 to 150 characters, including the lower-case alphabet and additional special punctuation and mathematical symbols. A few COM recorders offer foreign alphabetic characters essential to COM applications in large research libraries. The optional extended character set available with the DatagraphiX 4500 COM recorders (Fig. 4-5) includes the upper and lower case alphabet, diacritical marks, special characters, and European characters.[33]

Many COM recorder manufacturers will create one or more special symbols to customer order. The ease with which this can be accomplished, as noted in a preceding section, depends on the method of character generation during the recording process. Character set changes or additions in DatagraphiX COM recorders, for example, require modification or replacement of the character-forming matrix located in the neck of the Charactron CRT. Charactron matrices are currently available for Cyrillic and Japanese Katakana alphabets. Character set expansion in dot matrix recorders is necessarily limited by matrix size—the greater the number of available light points, the greater the character-forming capability. Character set expansion in stroke-generation COM recorders is technically simple, requiring only a minor modification of character-generating circuitry. Graphic COM recorders invariably employ stroke-generation and can be programmed to create virtually any character. At the present time, however, most COM service bureaus employ recorders equipped with character sets designed to satisfy ordinary business applications rather than the more complex library requirements. Where extended character sets are available, costs tend to be high.[34]

**Figure 4-5**

**Extended COM Character Set**
(Courtesy: Stromberg DatagraphiX, Inc.)

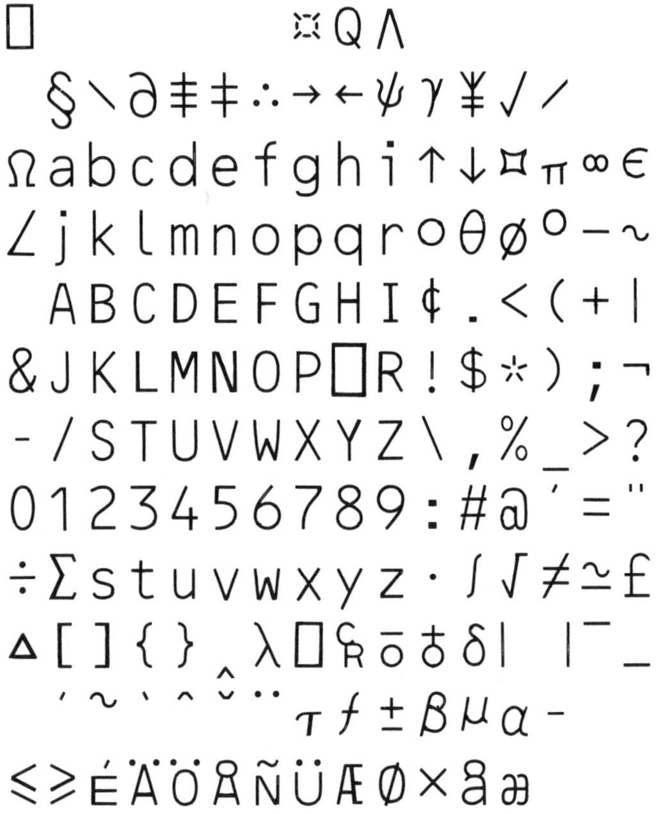

**Type Face, Size, and Intensity**

The goal of most COM type faces is to preserve legibility, often through several generations of duplicates, while striving for eventual compatibility with optical character recognition (OCR) input devices.[35] While there is no standard COM type face, the National Micrographics Association recommends the European Computer Manufacturers Association's OCR-B Alphanumeric Character Set, which is also available in an IBM Selectric element for typing source documents. Where typographic quality is essential, the Information International COMp80 recorder, will print a wide selection of utility and graphic arts type faces. The COMp80 system is designed for the rapid and economical photocompositions of catalogs and lists subject to frequent change.[36]

Several alphanumeric, and all graphic, COM recorders offer a choice of several character sizes and intensities. In some cases, sizes and intensities can be varied within a microimage—an important feature that permits, for example, the printing of the main entry portion of catalog data in one size and the collation and tracings portions in a smaller size.

## Page Formatting

As noted in the section on effective reductions, the most prevalent COM page format emulates an eleven by fourteen inch computer printout sheet consisting of 64 lines of up to 132 characters each. Some COM recorders permit other formats. For greater information compaction, the number of lines per page can be increased to 88, and the number of characters per line increased to 172.[40] Alternatively, line lengths can be reduced to eighty characters, producing the equivalent of a letter-size document image and increasing the number of images on a standard microfiche to ninety-eight (in seven rows and fourteen columns) at 24X effective reduction; 325 (in thirteen rows and twenty-five columns) at 42X; and 420 (in fifteen rows and twenty-eight columns) at 48X. At 24X, the letter-size imaginary document results in a COM microfiche format that is compatible with the NMA Type 1 Standard for source documents.

For 16mm roll microfilm applications, several COM recorders feature a variable frame advance that allows users to significantly increase information compaction by reducing the gap between frames. In the comic mode, for example, the width of frames can be reduced to accommodate catalog card images and other bibliographic data formatted in lines of less than 132 characters. This flexibility permits the expansion of library catalogs and other dynamic data bases without unduly increasing the number of reels, cartridges, or cassettes the user must handle.

On roll microfilm or microfiche, several COM recorders will enhance information compaction by eliminating frames altogether. This technique, called *scrolling*, presents information on cine mode 16mm microfilm or in microfiche columns as a series of continuous lines. Scrolling is used in several COM-generated bibliographic products including the Georgia Tech Library's LENDS microfiche catalog, described in chapter one, and MARCFICHE, a MARC-derivative biblio-graphic service discussed in the next chapter.

## MICROFILM AS A COMPUTER OUTPUT ALTERNATIVE

### COM as a Line Printer Replacement

As computer output devices, COM recorders compete with paper printers and on-line screen displays. For the production of catalogs, holdings lists, and batch reports from machine-readable library data bases, COM recorders are invariably faster, generally more versatile, and often more economical than line printers or non-impact paper output devices.[37] Computer manufacturers and users have long been troubled by the increasingly great disparity between computing speed and the relative slowness of output devices, especially line printers. While even early computers could output data at rates exceeding one thousand lines per second, the rated or maximum speeds of the fastest available line printers seldom exceed two thousand lines per minute. Actual speeds vary with the size of the printable character set and may prove to be significantly lower than rated speeds. The resulting output bottleneck can be significant in the production of library circulation lists and similar reports involving straightforward computer processing with large amounts of printing. For example, a 500-page computer-processed list of items in circulation, to be distributed to twenty use points in an academic library, will require five printer runs on four-ply interleaved carbon forms to produce the desired number of copies. Using an IBM 1403 line printer with a standard sixty character print chain, each run would require about half an hour with two and a half hours of printing time necessary to complete the entire job. By way of contrast, COM recorder rated speeds range between 10,000 and 30,000 lines per minute. Although actual speeds vary with page lengths and the method of input preparation, rates of 15,000 to 20,000 lines per minute are realistic. A Kodak KOM-80 or Bell and Howell 3700 COM recorder will convert circulation data on an appropriately-formatted magnetic tape to five hundred pages of human-readable information on three 42X microfiche in less than three minutes. Allowing time for microfilm processing and diazo or vesicular duplication, complete microfiche sets can be ready for distribution to twenty service points in less than half an hour. A single COM recorder, like the KOM-80, has output capacity equivalent to about a dozen line printers. COM recorder speeds greatly exceed the capabilities of the Xerox 1200 Computer Printing System, an electrostatic printer rated at 4,000 lines per minute, and compare favorably with the IBM 3800 and Honeywell Page Printing System, two non-impact paper-output devices with printing speeds in excess of 12,000 lines per minute.

For library catalogs and other public-use products derived from machine-readable bibliographic data bases, COM offers improved typographical quality and versatility unobtainable with line printers. Line printer quality is typically fair-to-good for the first few copies in a carbon form set and fair-to-poor for the last few. COM duplicates, however, are all made directly from the master microform and are of uniform quality. Although line printers can be equipped with an ALA print chain, output speed is thereby drastically reduced.[38] Even with the extended character set, type face, size, and intensity remain fixed. As noted in a preceding section, COM recorders are available with extended character sets, special symbols to customer order, and entire foreign alphabets. Some alphanumeric COM recorders permit type face, size, and intensity changes with a frame or line, and offer underlining, proportional spacing, columnar printing, and other text formatting facilities. Graphic COM recorders have essentially unlimited character set and page formatting capabilities.

Several libraries report substantial cost reductions in the conversion from line printer output to COM. At Los Angeles Public Library, where a 22,000-page patron directory required twelve printer runs to produce 71 distribution copies, conversion to COM saves $100,000 annually.[39] Proportional savings have been realized in smaller applications in British and Australian libraries.[40] To set the potential economic advantages of COM in perspective, Table 4-1 compares typical COM and line printer costs for a five hundred page library circulation report to be distributed six times weekly to twenty use points. While the application is hypothetical, the costs given are realistic, subject to situational variation. It is assumed that the paper version of the report will be produced on an IBM 1403 or equivalent line printer in

**Table 4-1**

**Cost Comparison
COM v. Line Printer Output**

Application Parameters:

    Report Length: 500 pages
    Number of Distribution Points: 20
    Frequency of Issue: 24 times per month

| Paper System | | Microfiche System | |
|---|---|---|---|
| Printer time: 2.5 hrs @ $50 per hour | 125.00 | Production of COM Tape | 25.00 |
| Paper @ .05 per page of 5-part Interleaved carbon forms (2,000 pages required) | 100.00 | Production of 42X COM master fiche @ .05 frame | 25.00 |
| | | Production of 60 vesicular duplicates (20 sets) @ .25 per fiche | 15.00 |
| Cost per Run | 225.00 | | |
| Monthly Cost | 5,400.00 | Cost per Run | 65.00 |
| | | Monthly Cost of fiche production | 1,560.00 |
| | | 20 Readers @ $225 each; amortized over 36 months | 125.00 |
| | | Monthly reader maintenance allowance | 35.00 |
| | | Monthly Cost | 1,720.00 |
| | | Monthly Savings | 3,680.00 |
| | | Annual Savings | 44,160.00 |

a university computer center that charges all costs back to the library. COM costs assume the use of a microfilm service bureau equipped with a minicomputer-controlled COM recorder capable of creating 42X microfiche from a library-supplied magnetic tape containing print records prepared on a general-purpose computer. The cost analysis includes the full purchase price of required microfiche readers, dedicated to this application and amortized over a three year period, with a generous allowance for repair and bulb replacement. In this example, COM's substantial cost advantage is a function of report length, frequency of updating, and the number of distribution copies. _As a general rule, COM will be more economical than line printer output for long or frequently updated reports distributed to many use points._ For the hypothetical circulation list, reductions in the number of required copies or frequency of issue would make COM less attractive in terms of cost.

## COM vs. On-Line Systems

In library circulation control, as in all transaction-oriented applications, there is a direct relationship between the value of information in a computer-produced report and the frequency of report updating. Because of the relative slowness of line printers, computer centers may not be able to schedule and guarantee the regular and timely production of the very long reports characteristic of many library applications.[41] In such cases, the library requiring access to circulation data that is no more than a specified number of hours old, may turn to an on-line, real-time computer system. In such a system, a machine-readable circulation file is maintained on magnetic disk, drum, or other direct access storage device. Unlike off-line systems which batch circulation transactions for processing against a master tape or disk file at pre-determined intervals, on-line, real-time systems record transactions in the circulation file as they occur. Using a remote display or printing terminal, the file can be queried with assurance that the information it contains reflects the most recent circulation activity.[42] In a batch processing system, line printer or COM-produced reports do not reflect circulation transactions occuring in the interval between file updates.

While on-line, real-time systems offer many benefits—in circulation control, the ability to easily identify returned library materials to be held for another patron or to identify delinquent borrowers are two important examples—they can be prohibitively expensive. Although prices are dropping steadily, disk and drum storage still cost more than the magnetic tape used in batch-processing systems. On-line access requires a terminal at every use point. Programming requirements for on-line systems are complex, with long development times. Printed reports may still be required to provide information during times when the computer is unavailable.[43] The role of COM as an interim technology in library applications for which on-line, real-time access is desirable but not presently economically feasible was introduced in chapter one. To minimize costs in applications where currency of information is important but access to up-to-the-minute information is not essential, COM recording speed can facilitate report production at frequent intervals—several times a day, if necessary—often at lower costs than either on-line systems or batch-processed paper reports printed less frequently.[44]

For library applications with some real-time requirement, COM can interface with on-line access in an economical hybrid system.[45] In circulation control, for example, transactions are recorded on disk or drum as they occur. At regular and frequent intervals, these transactions are batch-processed against a master circulation file on magnetic tape and a COM circulation list is produced, duplicated, and distributed. Information reflecting transactions occurring in the interval between report updates—together with a list of delinquent borrowers and items on hold, if desired—are fully accessible on disk via a remote terminal, but the required amount of expensive on-line storage is markedly reduced. A minicomputer located in the library could be used for this purpose with batch-processing and COM report production occurring at a remote computing center.[46]

## Limitations of COM

Well-designed computer output systems take advantage of the strengths of particular technologies while minimizing their weaknesses.[47] COM itself shares limitations common to all microform-based information systems: microimages cannot be annotated; special viewing equipment is required; user resistance is likely. As already indicated, COM is generally not a cost-effective production method for short or infrequently updated reports distributed to few use points. Likewise, reports that are divided into separate parts for the use of various individuals may be best produced in paper form. The extent to which any or all of these factors will limit the applicability of COM is situational-dependent and must be carefully analyzed. Where the ability to write on report pages is essential, for example, COM should be avoided. Where the potential for significant cost reduction exists, however, the librarian responsible for systems design should closely examine the necessity of stated requirements that constrain change.

## COM SERVICE BUREAUS

Because of the sizeable volume of microform production necessary to justify the high cost of an in-house COM recorder, many COM users rely on service bureau facilities. For libraries, service bureaus provide an easy way to develop COM applications quickly. Many of the criteria employed in the evaluation and selection of microfilming services for source documents apply to COM: the availability of suitable equipment, the ability to offer the required range of services, assurance of quality control, reasonable cost, and a record of satisfactory performance, preferably in similar applications. Other parameters that are especially meaningful in evaluating and selecting COM services include the ability to meet critical deadlines, the availability of back-up recorders, the level of software support provided to customers, and the availability of staff expertise in both data processing and micrographics.[48]

In addition to conventional service bureaus that produce computer-output-microfilm or microfiche from library-supplied magnetic tapes, Autographics, Blackwell North America, Brodart, and other organizations specializing in the processing of library materials will create and/or maintain machine-readable data bases for eventual COM production. Blackwell North America, for example, will produce

COM catalogs from the history file of cardsets previously sold to its customers. Alternatively, a library can supply Blackwell with machine-readable records in MARC or non-MARC formats. The University of Texas-Dallas, for example, sends Blackwell its OCLC archival tape for conversion to bi-weekly cumulating microfiche. Blackwell supports COM production with a wide range of bibliographic services. For the conversion of retrospective shelf lists or the creation of union catalogs from data obtained from several libraries, Blackwell offers extensive editing services. The form of entries can be reviewed to insure filing consistency. Using its own machine-readable files, Blackwell will undertake subject or name authority work, revising syntax and inserting appropriate cross-references. Blackwell will alphabetically sort edited records into a dictionary or divided arrangement for COM catalog production. Standard output is 42X microfiche. Other formats and reductions can be created to customer specifications. For libraries preferring to procure COM services locally, Blackwell will furnish a sorted print tape.

# REFERENCES

[1] The best history of COM is Sherman H. Boyd, "Technology of Computer Output Microfilm: Past, Present, and Future," *TAPPI* 56 (1973): 107-10.

[2] Stromberg DatagraphiX developed the first business-application COM recorder, a specially designed device, for the Social Security Administration in 1958. Production models for commercial applications appeared in the early 1960s, but applications developed slowly. Although an estimated 300 COM recorders were installed by 1968, an NMA survey of 74 users indicated that 33 percent of their applications were scientific. See Don M. Avedon, "Computer Output Microfilm: An NMA Survey of the Field," *Journal of Micrographics* 3 (1969): 7-12.

[3] W. A. Kozumplik and R. T. Lange, "Computer-Produced Microfilm Library Catalog,"*American Documentation* 18 (1967): 67-80.

[4] W. D. Robinson, "Today's Marketplace—A Guide to COM Development." In Don Chenevert, ed., *Micrographics Science, 1973: Winter Symposium* (Washington: Society of Photographic Scientists and Engineers, 1973), pp. 141-49.

[5] Dick Enders, "COM Viewers—A Generalized Overview of Their History, Growht, and Future Direction." In *Proceedings of the National Micrographics Association* (Silver Spring, Md.: NMA, 1975), pp. 165-69.

[6] *Facts on Film* (Mountain View, California: Quantor Corporation, 1975).

[7] Joan Ross, "The Great Output Race: COM Joins the Winner's Circle," *Journal of Micrographics* 10 (1976): 11-15; Douglas B. Smith, "It's Still a Paper World," *Journal of Micrographics* 6 (1972): 21-25; Tom McCusker, "Paper vs. Film: It's All in How You View It," *Datamation* 21 (May 1975): 157-58 reports the Predicasts projection that, by 1985, COM will account for one-half of the estimated $6 billion micrographics market.

[8] Peripheral devices are machines that are used in combination or conjunction with a computer but are not a part of the computer itself. In addition to COM recorders, the list of peripherals include card readers, terminals, printers, magnetic disk devices, and magnetic tape units. For an overview of COM technology, see Don M. Avedon, *Computer-Output-Microfilm* (Silver Spring, Md.: National Micrographics Association, 1971); Avedon, "Fundamentals of COM," *Proceedings of the National Microfilm Association* (Silver Spring, Md.: NMA, 1973), II-83-88; J. R. Antal, "A Potential Buyer Looks at COM," *Journal of Micrographics* 3 (1969): 79-84; Alfred L. Clarke, "ABC's of COM," *Journal of Micrographics* 5 (1972): 205-206; A. E. Kingett, "COM: An Assessment," *Microdoc* 10 (1971): 50-57; F. Robinson, "The Uses of OCR and COM in Information Work," *Program* 8 (1974): 137-48; *Computer-Output-Microfilm* (Washington: National Archives and Records Service, 1975); Robert F. Gildenberg, *Computer-Output-Microfilm Systems* (Los Angeles: Melville Publishing Co., 1974); *A Guide to Computer-Output-Microfilm* (Pennsauken, N.J.: Auerbach Publishers, 1976); William Saffady, *Computer-Output-Microfilm (COM) Hardware and Software: The State of the Art*. In the RLMS Microfile Series (Washington: Library of Congress, 1977).

[9] The IBM System 360 and 370 in their various models are the most widely used series of third-generation digital computers. On-line COM recorders will generally operate with a System 360, model 25 or above, or any System 370.

[10] For additional points of comparison, see Franklin I. Bolnick, "On-Line Versus Off-Line COM Systems," *Journal of Micrographics* 4 (1971): 123-31.

[11] A cathode-ray-tube (CRT) is an electronic vacuum tube containing a luminescent screen on which information is displayed by a focused beam of electrons.

[12] Sherman H. Boyd, "Film Requirements for Computer Output Microfilm." In *Proceedings of the National Microfilm Association* (Silver Spring, Md.: NMA, 1972), III-35-49.

[13] Arthur C. Titus, "On-Line Processing in a COM System." In *Proceedings of the National Microfilm Association* (Silver Spring, Md.: NMA, 1972), III-21-32.

[14] P. H. Herbert, "A New Concept in COM Printers," *Microdoc* 10 (1971): 66-71.

[15] J. A. Norcross and P. I. Sampath, "Non-Silver Photographic Materials and Lasers in the Micrographics Industry." In Chenevert, pp. 187-93; W. C. Meyers, "Non-Silver Halide Laser Micrographic Recording Systems and Applications." In *Proceedings of the Third International Congress on Reprography* (London: IPC Science and Technology Press, 1971), pp. 39-47.

[16] I. M. MacLeod, "COM with a Difference," *Microdoc* 15 (1976): 4-9 describes a laser plotter that records on diazo microfiche. The device is not available in the United States.

[17] Rolf E. Westgaard, "Electron Beam Recording—Microfilm's New Method for Conversing with Computers." In *Proceedings of the National Microfilm Association* (Silver Spring, Md.: NMA, 1967), 124-30; J. M. Firisen, "Series F. Electron Beam Recording System," *Microdoc* 10 (1971): 45-49. Image Graphics, Inc. has developed a carographic electron beam recorder for the U. S. Army Topographic Laboratories. The recorder, now offered commercially as the Series 2000 Electron Beam Recorder, is described in P. F. Grosso and A. A. Tarnowski, "Electron Beam Recording on Film—Applications and Performance," *Electro-Optical Systems Design* (August 1976): 56-61.

[18] Tom R. Pauer, "Formslides: Information for the User," *Journal of Micrographics* 9 (1976): 161-63.

[19] Tape recording density is a measure of the number of characters that can be stored per unit of tape length. Tape densities are typically expressed in bits per inch, with the total of bits across the tape width forming one character. Characters are normally encoded in tracks that are seven or nine bits wide.

[20] The Extended Binary Coded Binary Interchange Code (EBCDIC) is an eight bit code that can represent up to 256 distinct characters.

[21] The American Standard Code for Information Interchange (ASCII) is a seven bit code adopted to facilitate the interchange of data among various types of data processing and data communications equipment.

²²The Binary Coded Decimal (BCD) code represents each of the decimal digits by a distinct group of binary digits. BCD code has been replaced in third-generation IBM computers by EBCDIC code.

²³For a discussion of this important but neglected subject, see Bobby R. Peoples, "COM Software—State of the Art," *Proceedings of the National Microfilm Association* (Silver Spring, Md.: NMA, 1972), II-84-90. COM software can be obtained in several ways. The primary source is the equipment manufacturer. Such manufacturer-supplied software packages are typically written in assembler language for IBM system 360/370 computers and in ANSI COBOL for computers of other manufacturers. Some COM manufacturers offer extensive software libraries to customers, usually without charge. Alternatively, users may create their own software—as Boeing did for its library catalog—or obtain it from service bureaus or other third parties. The COMDEX package offered by Wright Data Systems is an example of a COM indexing program that can be used to create titled, indexed microfiche in a variety of formats and reductions on any recorder with microfiche output capability. U. S. Datacorp, the world's largest COM service bureau, maintains a software library of more than 400 programs. On the Boeing catalog mentioned above, see Kenneth A. Rogers and Earl C. Vogt, "Cost Benefits of Computer Output Microfilm Library Catalogs," *Proceedings of the American Society for Information Science* 10 (1973): 199-200.

²⁴Two further limitations apply to the subroutine method. There is a minimum core requirement that varies with the software package. The host computer must also support the programming language in which the subroutines are written. In the general-purpose computer environment, this is rarely a limitation, but some of the minicomputers that are increasingly used by libraries will not support an ANSI COBOL compiler.

²⁵Several COM manufacturers have recently introduced report-generator software packages as an alternative to conventional print-tape translators. These report-generators significantly reduce the software effort necessary for conversion to COM by creating full-titled, indexed, and formatted microfiche directly from raw data files without an application program. The user typically supplies application parameters on cards at run time.

²⁶The minicomputer used varies with the COM manufacturer but is generally on the order of a DEC PDP-11/04. User's application parameters are typically stored on tape cartridges, cassettes, or diskettes. A Teletype ASR-33 or equivalent terminal permits communication between the operator and the system. In addition to tape translation, most minicomputer software will provide job statistics. In some cases, the minicomputer can be programmed to perform additional manipulation of input data prior to recording on microfilm.

²⁷William Saffady, "A Computer Output Microfilm Serials List for Patron Use," *Journal of Library Automation* 7 (1974): 263-66.

[28] A 1969 NMA survey indicated that 55 percent of COM applications involved roll microforms. Twenty-one percent utilized microfiche. The remaining 24 percent was evenly divided between aperture cards and microfilm jackets. Don M. Avedon, "Computer Output Microfilm: An NMA Survey of the Field," *Journal of Micrographics* 3 (1969): 7-12. "Micrographics '77," *Infosystems* 24 (May 1977): 46-49 reports that over seventy percent of microforms users employ fiche for one or more applications.

[29] In CRT-type COM recorders, the display that is microfilmed is typically smaller than the imaginary document it represents. In the Cal Comp 2100 Series COM recorders, for example, the CRT display measure 2.2 by 1.833 inches–a 6X reduction from computer printout size.

[30] For a discussion of COM microfiche reductions, see George B. Bernstein, "Why 24X/48X?," *Journal of Micrographics* 5 (1972): 295-300; Don M. Avedon, "Proposed ISO Standard 'Computer Output Microfiche'," *Journal of Micrographics* 9 (1976): 309-14.

[31] James F. Heacock, "The Evolution and New Developments in Films for the Micrographics Industry." In *Proceedings of the National Micrographics Association* (Silver Spring, Md.: NMA, 1975), pp. 73-75. Any space savings derived from conversion to microforms is satisfactorily achieved at low reductions. The extra expense associated with high or ultra high reduction is generally justified by ease of handling and consequently faster retrieval. See Klaus W. Otten, "Ultrafiche Technology," *Journal of Micrographics* 4 (1971): 161-76. On possible systems advantages of lower reductions, see Douglas J. Greenwold, "Rethinking 24X COM from a New Perspective," *Journal of Micrographics* 10 (1976): 55-56.

[32] Thomas S. Doran, "Micrographic Reports, a New Dimension for Management," *Journal of Micrographics* 4 (1971): 133-41; Richard A. Wells, "What is COM Business Graphics?," *Proceedings of the National Microfilm Association* (Silver Spring, Md.: NMA, 1972), 92-95; Robert P. Horst, "COM in Business Graphics: A Better Way to Present Management Reports," *Proceedings of the National Microfilm Association* (Silver Spring, Md.: NMA, 1974), 96-99.

[33] There is a trend toward extended character sets in newer alphanumeric COM recorders. The DatagraphiX 4550 and 4560, for example, feature a standard set of 128 characters expandable to 160 and 190 characters respectively. By way of contrast, the older DatagraphiX 4360 could print only 64 characters.

[34] S. Michael Malinconico, "The Display Medium and the Price of the Message," *Library Journal* 101 (Ocrober 15, 1976): 2144-50 cites frame prices in the range 1.4 to 9.3 cents for extended character set work.

[35] *Format and Coding for Computer Output Microfilm* (Silver Spring, Md.: National Micrographics Association, 1976). An optical character recognition (OCR) device converts human-readable information to machine-readable, computer-processible data by scanning rather than keystroking. The most effective and economical OCR devices employ special recognizable fonts. Computer-Input-Microfilm (CIM), the micrographic component of OCR, is discussed in chapter nine.

[36] On photocomposed quality and COM recorders, see Donald G. Gerlich, "Micro-Composition for Utility Printing," *Journal of Micrographics* 5 (1971): 83-89; Brett Butler and John Van Pelt, "Microphotocomposition–a New Publishing Resource," *Journal of Micrographics* 6 (1972): 7-13; Larry Schrieber, "Photocomposition on a COM Recorder," *Journal of Micrographics* 8 (1975): 251-54. A line printer is a computer output device that utilizes print characters mounted on a chain which moves horizontally in front of paper. The chain may contain several sets of characters. As the character to be printed passes in front of each position on the paper where it is to be printed, a magnetically-controlled hammer impacts the paper against the type face, thereby printing the character. Line printer speed is such that it appears that an entire line is being printed at one time. On the various types of computer printers, see Susan Wooldridge, *Computer Output Design* (New York: Petrocelli/Charter, 1975).

[37] James G. Massie and Jay Smink, "COM Operation–is COM a Better Way?," *Proceedings of the National Microfilm Association* (Silver Spring, Md.: NMA, 1973), 164-76; Dwight C. Burnham and James A. Hernon, "COM Applications and Future Trends," *Proceedings of the National Microfilm Association* 186-219; John R. Robertson, "A Rational Approach to COM," *Journal of Micrographics* 3 (1969): 73-77; J. Woods, "Micromation Printers and Auxiliary Equipment and Examples of Their Applications," *Microdoc* 10 (1971): 39-45; R. J. Zoch, "Computer Output Microfilm and On-Line Cathode Ray Tube Display Devices as Information Retrieval Tools," *Proceedings of the National Microfilm Association* (Silver Spring, Md.: NMA, 1969), 118-28; Isaac L. Auerbach, "Strategies for the Management of Computer Output," *Journal of Micrographics* 10 (1977): 127-29.

[38] The IBM 1403 line printer, for example, is rated at 1100 lines per minute with a sixty character print chain but will print only 563 lines per minute with a 120 character chain.

[39] Barbara J. Anderson, "COM Restores Calm to the Los Angeles Public Library," *Information and Records Management* 7 (May 1973): 40-42.

[40] David Buckle, "The Cost of a COM Catalogue System at Birmingham University Library," *Microdoc* 13 (1974): 15-18; Buckle and Thomas French, "The Application of Microform to Manual and Machine Readable Catalogues," *Program* 5 (1971): 41-66; John R. Spencer, *An Appraisal of Computer Output Microfilm for Library Catalogues* (Hatfield, Herts, England: National Reprographic Centre for Documentation, 1973); Elizabeth Stecker, "RMIT COM Catalogue Study Results," *Australian Library Journal* 24 (1975): 383-89.

[41] Library applications are rarely accorded high priority by institutional computer centers. See Allen B. Veaner, "Institutional, Political, and Fiscal Factors in the Development of Library Automation, 1969-1971," *Journal of Library Automation* 7 (1974): 5-26.

[42] It is important to note that *real-time* systems are not synonymous with *on-line* access via remote terminal. A data base may be queried on-line but transactions may be collected in a separate file and processed in periodic batches.

This is the case with some library circulation systems. See, for example, James S. Aagaard, "An Interactive Computer-Based Circulation System: Design and Development," *Journal of Library Automation* 5 (1972): 3-11.

[43] This is especially true in life support applications where constant access to information is mandatory and computer downtime cannot be tolerated. See, for example, Barry H. Rumack, M.D., "Poisonindex: An Emergency Poison Management System," *Proceedings of the National Micrographics Association* (Silver Spring, Md.: NMA, 1975): 359-69; Sidney N. Smock, "Microfiche Poison Index and Management Saves Lives," *Journal of Micrographics* 8 (1975): 127-30.

[44] Frank Malabarba, "Microfilm Information Systems (MIS): A Data Base Alternative," *Journal of Micrographics* 9 (1975): 3-11; Tom L. Harrison, "COM: The Information Form that Fits the EDP Environment," *Journal of Micrographics* 7 (1974): 199-203.

[45] Tom L. Harrison, "CRT vs. COM–Real Time vs. Real-Time Enough," *Journal of Micrographics* 7 (1973): 37-44; William L. Corya, "The Integration of Formats to Provide Catalog Access Services." In Frances G. Spigai, et al., eds., *Information Roundup: Proceedings of the 4th ASIS Mid-Year Meeting* (Washington: American Society for Information Science, 1975), 96-104.

[46] Michael K. Buckland and Bernard Gallivan, "Circulation Control: Off-Line, On-Line, or Hybrid," *Journal of Library Automation* 5 (1972): 30-38 describes such a hybrid system with which COM could be used.

[47] See Truett Airhart, "Computer Output Microfilm: A Powerful Systems Tool," *Journal of Micrographics* 7 (1974): 99-105.

[48] S. Arnold Kober, "What to Look for in a COM Service Bureau," *Journal of Micrographics* 9 (1976): 187-90; Roger E. Blue, "Why a COM Service Bureau?," *Proceedings of the National Micrographics Association* (Silver Spring, Md.: NMA, 1975), 175-78.

# CHAPTER 5

# MICROPUBLISHING

## OVERVIEW

### Types of Micropublishers

The important role of micropublishers as the dominant producers of microforms for the library market was introduced in chapter one. Micropublishers are producers of information in multiple-copy microform for sale or distribution to the public.[1] As noted in chapter one, the library market is served by both institutional and commercial micropublishers. *Institutional* micropublishers include government agencies, libraries, archives, historical societies, professional associations, universities, and other non-profit organizations. As a group, institutional micropublishers attempt to make significant research materials available to scholars, scientists, and other interested persons at the lowest possible cost. While some items offered by institutional micropublishers may prove popular enough to generate significant revenue, profit is not their primary objective. The National Archives' extensive micropublishing program, for example, is financed by a trust fund that restricts the selling price of individual 35mm microfilm reels to a flat rate of cost plus ten percent, regardless of an item's market value. Any profits realized through sales are used to expand the Archives' microfilming facilities.[2] The National Archives views its micropublications, with their accompanying finding aids, as extensions of reference service to researchers in remote geographical locations.[3]

The micropublishing programs of some libraries have developed out of preservation microfilming or inter-library loan request fulfillment. The Library of Congress, which microfilms many items in response to customer requests or internal preservation orders, offers duplicate microforms for sale to interested libraries at reasonable cost. LC routinely distributes circulars announcing the availability of these micropublications as they are created. The National Archives likewise distinguishes its "M" Series micropublications, consisting of record series pre-selected by the Archives staff for their high research value, from its "T" Series micropublications, which are created to customer order and subsequently offered for sale to the public. The Hoover Institution, which began microfilming its holdings in response to inter-library loan requests in the 1950s, now has an extensive micropublishing program designed to make its rare or unique research materials more widely available.[4]

*Commercial* micropublishers are for-profit businesses. This in no way implies that their prices are necessarily higher than those of institutional micropublishers, or that their products are less responsive to the needs of scholarship. If anything, the successful commercial micropublisher must meet demonstrated library needs at attractive prices. Unlike institutional micropublishers, however, commercial micropublishers tend to avoid significant research materials with only limited market appeal. While the Library of Congress publishes microform versions of the *Philippine Congressional Record, 1945-61*; the *Ottoman Official Gazette, 1835-54*; and the stenographic minutes of the Latvian National Council, 1918-20, few commercial micropublishers could risk offering such esoteric items.[5] On the other hand, commercial micropublishers enjoy the flexibility of selecting items from many repositories. Libraries, archives, and other institutional micropublishers generally rely exclusively on their own holdings.

Commercial micropublishers include large diversified corporations (Xerox, Bell and Howell), conventional book publishers (Pergamon Press, Oxford University Press), microfilm service bureaus (Dakota Microfilms, General Microfilm Company), and very small companies (Creative Micro-Libraries, Barry Shurlock and Company) offering only a few titles.[6]

## The Economics of Micropublishing

Because current printing technologies do not permit the economical production of single copies to order, the conventional book publisher must make a decision on edition size prior to the actual printing of a book. There is a minimum edition size necessary to recover editorial, design, advertising, and plant costs. Large editions permit lower book prices, but unsold copies must be warehoused, thereby incurring storage costs. Money invested in unsold stock cannot be used for other purposes or invested at interest. If unsold copies must be liquidated, additional advertising and distribution costs will be incurred. While various formulae can be used to assist in the determination of optimum edition size, the results must still be analyzed and modified by judgment. Risk is unavoidable.[7]

With two exceptions to be noted below, micropublishing is a *demand* rather than an *edition* publishing process. In most types of micropublishing, duplicate microfilm reels or microfiche are produced from the master microform only when an order is received. To establish a price, the cost of producing the microform master is typically amortized over the sale of a few duplicates. There is no need to estimate edition size. Warehousing and unsold stock are eliminated. Money previously invested in inventory is freed to meet other expenses or for reinvestment at interest. In addition, the required capital investment in a microfilm camera, film, processing, and duplicating equipment is generally much lower than the cost of print shop equipment and supplies.[8] Thus, micropublishing is well-suited to items in limited demand, for which the cost of a full paper edition cannot be justified. From the librarian's point of view, the on-demand nature of micropublishing offers the additional advantage of keeping a publisher's back-list forever in print.[9]

The foregoing analysis applies only to roll microforms and microfiche. Ultrafiche and Microprint, as indicated in chapter two, are edition process microforms. As in conventional publishing, the very high cost of creating an ultrafiche or Microprint master must be recovered through the sale of a specified number of copies. The break-even point is, however, generally lower than the edition size required to recover costs in conventional printing. The investment in unsold inventory is correspondingly reduced. Readex Microprint Corporation, for example, has produced editions as small as fifty copies.[10] Such small editions are not economically possible in paper form. Because these edition process microforms are physically smaller than full-size books, savings in warehousing costs can still be realized.

Critics of micropublishing point out that, while significant savings can be realized in the micropublication of out-of-print books and such voluminous materials as archives and manuscript collections, the micropublication of new titles will result in a reduction of only those costs associated with printing and edition maintenance.[11] These together, they contend, account for perhaps fifteen to twenty percent of total book production costs. If demand micropublishing reduced these costs by fifty percent, the cost of producing a ten dollar book would only be reduced by about one dollar. For research materials in limited demand, however, even this small cost reduction may well make publication feasible. Representative examples are discussed in the next sections of this chapter.

## ORIGINAL MICROPUBLICATIONS

### Monographs and Technical Reports

As defined in chapter one, original micropublications contain information published for the first time in any form. This definition includes micropublications like the computer-output-microfilm version of *Library of Congress Subject Headings*, 8th edition, issued first in microform and later, with a different appearance, in printed form. The definition excludes publications of identical appearance and content issued simultaneously in paper and microform. These simultaneous micropublications are discussed in a subsequent section of this chapter.

Original micropublishing for the library market is an activity of increasing significance. Original micropublication can be an economical alternative to conventional printing for materials in limited or unpredictable demand, or for monographs, technical reports, and other research materials containing significant amounts of graphic material. Doctoral dissertations provide the earliest example of the original micropublication of scholarly monographs in limited demand. University Microfilms has made dissertations available on 35mm reel microfilm since 1939. Over 325 North American universities now submit their doctoral dissertations for filming on a regular basis. *Dissertation Abstracts International* and the *Comprehensive Dissertation Index* provide both bibliographic control and ordering information.[12]

The Educational Resources Information Clearinghouse (ERIC) and the National Technical Information Service (NTIS) are the largest producers of original micropublications for the library market. NTIS, an agency within the United States Department of Commerce, is the central source for the dissemination of reports resulting from federally-sponsored research. NTIS acquires about 250 reports daily from the Department of Defense, the National Aeronautics and Space Administration, the Energy Research and Development Administration, and other government agencies. These reports are analyzed for subject content and reproduced on NMA Type 1 Standard microfiche for sale to libraries, research organizations, or other interested parties. Bibliographic control and ordering information are provided by the NTIS summary publications, *Government Reports Announcements and Index* and *Weekly Government Abstracts*, both described more fully in chapter seven. Microfiche can be ordered individually or through the Selected Research in Microfiche (SRIM) program which uses pre-established interest profiles to provide subscribers with the full texts of reports in designated subject areas on a bi-weekly basis.[13] The NTIS retrospective file includes about 300,000 titles. The limited and unpredictable demand for technical reports is reflected in the fact that NTIS never receives a single order for one-third of its 60,000 annual accessions.[14]

ERIC, an agency within the Office of Education of the Department of Health, Education and Welfare, relies on a network of geographically-dispersed clearinghouses that identify, acquire, and analyze relevant materials in assigned subject areas within the broad field of education. These materials, which are often of a fugitive nature, are indexed and abstracted in the ERIC publication *Resources in Education*, described in chapter seven. The ERIC Document Reproduction Service (EDRS)—currently operated by the Computer Microfilm International Corporation of Arlington, Virginia—records the indexed source documents on NMA Type 1 Standard Microfiche. Libraries can purchase entire sets, subsets in a given subject area, or individual microfiche on demand.[15]

Several university presses are using microfiche for the original publication of highly specialized monographs in such fields as literary criticism, classics, art, philosophy, philology, and regional history. The State University of New York Press, for example, has published several titles exclusively on microfiche, including Brian Regan's *The Gothic Word*, a detailed study of the semantics of medieval vocabulary.[16] Similarly, the University of Kansas Press offers J. Neal Carmon's *Foreign Language Units of Kansas* on forty microfiche. As with dissertations and technical reports, the market for these specialized scholarly monographs is both limited and difficult to estimate.[17]

When the work to be published contains many illustrations, the cost advantages of micropublishing can prove to be the decisive factor in the decision to utilize microforms rather than paper as the original publication medium. The Institut d'Ethnologie of the Musée de l'Homme relies heavily on microforms for the publication of profusely illustrated research studies which are too large to produce economically in book form. The Institut's recent micropublication, *Cave Art*, for example, is a lengthy textual and pictorial survey of archaeological sites. The Institut recognizes microforms and print as complementary, rather than competing, publishing media, each with strengths suited to particular applications. In 1972, the University of Chicago Press published Sue Allen's *Victorian Bookbinding: A Pictorial Survey* on four color microfiche, each with sixty frames. The fiche are sold for one dollar each, a price impossible to achieve in a printed edition containing color plates. The University of Chicago recently announced an innovative *Text/Fiche* micropublishing program that combines black-and-white and color photographic reproductions of illustrative material on microfiche with text and captions printed in an accompanying paper booklet. The first *Text/Fiche* publication list includes 1,062 photographs of the 1905-1907 Breasted Expeditions to Egypt and the Sudan (twenty-nine pages of text/thirteen black-and-white fiche); 419 French Impressionist and modern American paintings from the private collection of Duncan Phillips (sixty pages of text/five color fiche); and 996 photographs of Persepolis and ancient Iran taken during the Oriental Institute expedition of 1931-1939 (forty-nine pages of text/twelve fiche, one in color).[18]

## Journals and Proceedings

Several scholarly journals, unable to meet the information needs of limited readerships in paper form, are published exclusively in microfiche.[19] *Wildlife Disease*, an irregular serial publication of the Wildlife Disease Association, has been an original micropublication since 1959. Each issue is devoted to a specific topic and contains one or more important research papers that, for reasons of length or quantity of illustrative material, could not be published in the *Journal of Wildlife Diseases*, the association's printed journal. Other journals published exclusively in microform include *Aesthetic, Reconstructive, and Facial Plastic Surgery* (New York: The Educational and Research Foundation of the American Academy of Facial, Plastic, and Reconstructive Surgery, Inc.); the *International Microform Journal of Legal Medicine* (Ann Arbor: Xerox University Microfilms for the Milton Heilprin Library of Legal Medicine, New York); *Architectual Psychology News-letter* (London: Architectural Press Ltd.); and *La Revue Internationale d'Histoire du Cinema* (Paris: L'Avant-Scene). The *American Journal of Computational Linguistics* (Buffalo, N.Y.: The American Association for Computational Linguistics) is an original micropublication issued in two units: NMA Type 1 Standard microfiche containing research papers; and four by six inch cards containing abstracts, announcements, and advertisements. Each unit contains a file heading pre-printed at the top. An annual subscription includes index guide cards with appropriate subject tabs.[20]

Microfiche is an increasingly popular medium for the publication of papers presented at meetings of professional and scholarly associations. One-third of all papers and certain proceedings of the American Astronautical Society are published only in microform.[21] The American Institute of Aeronautics and Astronautics makes all the meeting papers and other documents listed in *International Aerospace Abstracts* available on microfiche. Microfiche Publications Incorporated does the same for the 5,000 items listed annually in *Environment Abstracts*. The Society of Automotive Engineers publishes only selected papers in full in *SAE Transactions*. The remainder are noted in an abstract and are available on microfiche from the Society. The 1976 *Proceedings* of the American Society for Information Science are in two parts: abstracts in printed form, and full papers on microfiche.[22]

The National Auxiliary Publication Service (NAPS)—operated for the American Society for Information Science by Microfiche Publications Incorporated—is a repository and micropublishing service for original works and supplemental materials relating to papers published in scholarly and technical journals but which, for reasons of space, cannot be published in paper form. Over two hundred journals regularly deposit material with NAPS. Footnotes in the published article indicate the NAPS accession number. Individual microfiche copies may be ordered on demand. The microform editions of many American Chemical Society journals contain original supplemental material such as spectra, structure tables, and extended calculations not available in printed copies. Footnotes in the original printed article indicate the existence of such supplemental material.

## Bibliographies and Reference Works

An increasing number of original micropublications are created by computer-output-microfilm (COM) from machine-readable bibliographic data bases. A few of these rely on COM for the production of economical subject bibliographies. The *American Studies Bibliography*, produced by the Institute of United States Studies at the University of London, is an example.[23] Most of them, however, are MARC-derivative products designed to provide more current bibliographic verification and cataloging data than can be obtained through the *National Union Catalog* or other printed sources, at costs much lower than on-line access through OCLC or other computerized bibliographic data bases. Because of their significance in a wide range of library applications, these MARC-based bibliographies are discussed in detail below.

*Books in English* (BIE), mentioned briefly in other chapters is an ultrafiche micropublication produced by the British Library from combined LC and UK MARC data bases.[24] BIE is a bi-monthly alphabetical author-title list of English-language books cataloged by the Library of Congress or the British Library. Each ultrafiche contains up to 2,380 microimages reduced 150X. The total number of entries per ultrafiche exceeds 10,000. Unlike the NUC, which cumulates at quarterly and annual intervals, the economy of ultrafiche publishing allows BIE to cumulate continuously through year end. Previous issues in a given year can, thus, be discarded on receipt of the bi-monthly replacement. Each entry gives full cataloging data, including the LC and Dewey class numbers, LC card number, and tracings. Information is current through the month preceding dispatch. In a study of the utility of various sources for bibliographic verification at the University of Bradford, BIE was found to offer "the most chance of success for the least effort" when compared to the *British National Bibliography*, *Whitaker's*, *British Books in Print*, *Books in Print*, *Books of the Month*, and the *Cumulative Book Index*. BIE was judged far more effective than the NUC, receipt of which at Bradford has proven too erratic to be useful.[25] The subscription price of £125 per year is low when considered against the extensive coverage provided.

*MARCFICHE*, a product of the MARC Applied Research Company, is a COM-generated microfiche bibliographic data base derived from MARC tapes.[26] Primary coverage includes MARC cataloging, 1967 to date, plus 90,000 additional twentieth century imprints. The total data base exceeds 800,000 entries. Customers receive new cataloging data weekly. MARC Applied Research claims that microfiche updates are completed and mailed within one day of the receipt of MARC tapes from the Library of Congress. Entries, following the traditional main entry format, are in random order within the data base. Access to desired entries is obtained through indexes to main entry/title, LC card number, LC class number, and ISBN. Index entries indicate the microfiche number within the data base and entry locations within the particular fiche (Fig. 5-1). The indexes themselves are on COM-produced fiche and cumulate quarterly. Weekly index updates cumulate between quarters. Quarterly subject and phrase indexes are optionally available. At $276 per year for the weekly data base and four standard indexes, *MARCFICHE* is the lowest-priced source of current MARC cataloging data. The entire retrospective backfile can be purchased for $295. Various other *MARCFICHE* packages are available to meet individual library needs.

## Figure 5-1

## MARCFICHE Index Keyed to Fiche Look-Up Coordinates
(Courtesy: MARC Applied Research, Inc.)

```
Dusinberre, Juliet.        *Shakespeare and    522v09
Dusseldorf. Kunstmuseum*Master drawings        524i21
Dussourd, Henriette.     *Le Bourbonnais /      516d17
Dust of the earth / Vera and Bill Cleaver      521i31
Duthie, Enid Lowry.       *The foreign visio    521f09
Duthnot.                   *Shockers from a      512j39
Dutt, Nripendra Kumar,  *The Aryanisation       510a34
Duvakin, V. D.            *Rostafenster : Ma     513v41
Duval, Claude, 1913-     *L'imprime outil       526c17
Duval, Pierre, 1618-168*La Suisse, par P.*527z03
Duver, Frank.             *Gold und Sonderzi    513u40
Duverger, Maurice, 1917*Modern democracie      524f06
Duvignaud, Jean.          *Le theatre contem    526e31
Duvigneau, Michel, 1939*Jeune cinema, 19       526i40
Duwaerts, Leon.          *Notions fondament    523430
Dybdekart i syv blad over de norske kystf*527u21
Dye, Allan.              *Gestalt approache    510m39
Dyer, Brian.             *Without regrets       521e26
The Dyer County population and economic        515t29
Dyer, Wayne W.           *Your erroneous zo-525j20
Dyer, William G.         *The sensitive man    524b21
Dyes from your garden / by Berenice Gille-521y10
Dyestuffs and fibers market trends [by]        510231
Dyfed (south part), administrative areas       519237
A dying business / Evelyn Dewar.               522m34
The dying of the light : a searching look     511g18
Dykstra, Gail Sullivan,*A bibliography of     522o43
Dylan Thomas: the legend and the poet; a       507416
Dyment, Alan R.          *The literature of    522j14
Dynamic development in todays sports info     522o22
Dynamic economics : a system theoretic ap-525c14
Dynamic maturity. [Motion picture]            *528127
  LA230.A57      Alternative education : a    -524f27
  LA230.5.W48L43 1973      Issues and needs    512i14
  LA258.W48      Florida's crisis in public    515j18
  LA259.D3D32 1973      Proposed planning gu   512h15
  LA267.5.D38      Data book on Illinois hig*527p21
  LA292.K38 1968      The view from the clas   512h17
  LA302.M6M57a      Annual report - Montgome*527c42
  LA316.A54      Innovative and exemplary pr   514h32
  LA319.5.M9 1975      Commission recommenda   508u30
  LA320.D38S35      A history of the rural     508i26
  LA330.M54H86      A brief history of the     515u35
  LA333.T4D3      Triumph in a white suburb;   520224
  LA333.5.N53 1970      New Jersey master pl   517320
  LA379.A34      The Virginia plan for highe*529244
  LA412.C14      Student progress through th   524c41
  LA418.N5N46 1970      Lectures complementa   513p04
  LA418.N8N68a      Higher education in Nova   518l12
  LA505.V5C63      Institutional consequence   525u05
  LA541.E28      Educational alternatives in   523m29
  LA556.F27      Educacao, a nova ideologia    526i35
  LA621.H57      The History of education in   512415
  LA622.J36      For a Community policy on      522w01
  LA627.C57      The medieval universities     522105
  LA631.4.B7 1972      Elizabethan schoolday   524i40
  LA631.7.W47 1975b      Education and the     513219
  LA632.B552      Black paper 1975 : the fig   508w13
  LA633.S48      Primary experiences / Rolan   512s19
  LA635.B43      We must choose which we wan   525w19
  LA635.C28 1972      A concise description    513218
  LA635.N34 1952      The curriculum of the    512h02
  LA635.S42      The Secondary school timeta   522w35
  LA682.P82      Public education in Hungary   508f08
  LA692.O74 1972      Educational policy and   520i12
```

The *Micrographic Catalog Retrieval System* (MCRS), developed by the defunct Information Dynamics Corporation and now maintained and marketed by the Library Systems division of the 3M Company, offers access to a wide range of bibliographic data in microform.[27] The full system, designated MCRS-540, includes all Library of Congress cataloging for English and foreign-language books, audio-visual materials, music, and items cataloged in publication; the *National Union Catalog*; and original cataloging prepared by selected North American libraries. Original cataloging for common law titles, prepared by the Harvard Law Library, is available as an option. Various subsets of the full system are available for smaller libraries or for customers requiring only a particular type of cataloging data. With the exception of Cataloging-in-Publication data, which is derived from MARC tapes and recorded on fiche via COM, all MCRS microimages are created by planetary cameras from catalog cards or printed NUC pages. Entries prepared by the Library of Congress appear on special five by eight inch fiche to differentiate them from the standard four by six inch fiche containing cataloging obtained from other sources or through the CIP program. The reduction is 24X throughout. Subscribing libraries receive additional microfiche weekly. There is, however, a two to three week delay between the receipt of cataloging data from LC and the mailing of new fiche to customers. As with *MARCFICHE*, entries are in random order within the data base. Indexes permit access to a desired card image by main entry, title, or LC card number. The indexes indicate the location of a desired entry within the data base by fiche number, row, column, and position. Weekly indexes cumulate within each month and subsequently cumulate monthly from January through June and bi-monthly in August and October. The December index is cumulative from the beginning of the present quinquennium. The main-entry and title index are on microfiche. The LC card number index is in paper form. The MCRS system is priced on a sliding scale based on the customer's total expenditure for library materials.

*CARDSET*, a product of Information Design Incorporated, differs from other microform bibliographic data bases in two important respects: 1) the data base is contained on 20X COM-generated, 16mm roll microfilm loaded in Information Design cartridges, six entries per microfilm frame; and 2) the data base includes not merely main entries but fully formatted catalog card sets with call numbers in place and overprinted headings for each added entry indicated in the tracings.[28] Finished card sets can be produced on card stock directly from the data base, using a Xerox Microprinter modified to accept Information Design cartridges. Alternatively, information from microfilm can be copied onto paper using other reader/printers; typed onto card stock; or converted, via key stroking, to machine-readable form. As with *MARCFICHE* and the MCRS, the data base is in random order and is accessed through indexes to title, series, and LC card number. Customers receive additional cartridges and indexes twice per month. The COM-generated indexes are continuously cumulative and are delivered on a special 16mm reel reduced 42X for use with the Information Design ROM II reader. A Xerox Microprinter is not included. Information Design supplements *CARDSET* with a 35mm microfilm version of the *National Union Catalog*, prepared from the printed version and supplied in Information Design cartridges.

A growing number of library and union catalogs are available as original micropublications. The Georgia Tech LENDS catalog, mentioned in previous chapters, was one of the first COM catalogs published from locally-maintained machine-readable bibliographic data. The LENDS catalog is intended for both internal use and sale to libraries wanting to expedite loan requests from Georgia Tech's holdings. The *California Union List of Periodicals*, published by the California State Library on microfiche, lists 31,000 titles in the holdings of 216 public and community college libraries.[29] Library of Congress catalogs available on reel microfilm include the Union Card File of Oriental Vernacular Serials, which contains titles omitted from the *Union List of Serials*, and the *Hebraic and Yiddish Title Catalog*. World Microfilms offers the title, personality, and subject card indexes of the British Film Institute. Greenwood Press has microfilmed the *Author-Title Index to the Library of the State Historical Society of Wisconsin* to supplement its cloth edition of the Society's subject catalog. The Inter Documentation Company, which offers the card catalog of the Economische-Historische Bibliotheek of Amsterdam on microfiche, has also microfilmed the unpublished inventories, indexes, and other finding aids listed in the published guides to foreign archives prepared by the International Council on Archives and UNESCO.

As mentioned earlier in this chapter, the LC Cataloging Distribution Service now offers *Library of Congress Subject Headings*, 8th edition, with supplements, on 45 24X COM-generated microfiche or 4,508 frames of 16mm reel microfilm. The LCSH in microform, which developed out of a successful pilot project to test the acceptance and utility of microform bibliographic products in technical services applications, is distributed in advance of the printed version. The Library of Congress also offers the *Register of Additional Locations* on COM-generated fiche or film. The first microform edition contains location reports for approximately 1.75 million titles through 1975. The economy of COM production permits subsequent issues to be continuously cumulative. Because of the rapid production capability of COM and the importance of the *Register* in inter-library loan, the Library of Congress is attempting to determine the optimum frequency of publication and the extent to which the COM version could supplant the printed edition.[30]

Following the lead of national bibliography, an increasing number of trade bibliographies are issued as original micropublications. Ingram's, the Nashville-based book jobber, offers its customers a weekly microfiche catalog and reader for a nominal monthly charge. The *B/NA Title Index*, an alphabetical listing produced by Blackwell/North America, is a 1.2 million entry microfiche data base designed to facilitate bibliographic verification and order preparation for Blackwell customers. The COM-produced index cumulates quarterly with weekly supplements within each quarter. A weekly cumulative microfiche list indicates whether a given LC card number appears in the title index and gives the B/NA master order number. Brodart's *Book Information System* is a million item 16mm COM-generated data base reflecting virtually every title available for sale through normal trade channels. Designed to expedite order processing for Brodart customers, entries consist of author, title, publisher, date of publication, publication status, LC card number, type of binding, price, and ISBN. Monthly updates are continuously cumulative. The system also serves as a complete title index to the cumulative LC MARC file.

Abstracting and indexing publications, such as *Chemical Abstracts* and *Engineering Index*, have been available in microform for many years. In most cases, however, such micropublications were made from the printed pages of the paper editions. The availability of abstracting and indexing data in machine-readable form has given rise to several original micropublications produced via COM. *Biofiche V*, for example, is a microfiche edition of *Biological Abstracts* for the period 1970 through 1974. While the abstract sections are identical with those in the printed version, the index sections have been entirely reprocessed and differ from the successive annual index cumulations. For users of the DIALOG Information Retrieval Service, the DIALIST, produced by Lockheed Information Systems, is a COM-generated microfiche listing of subject terms and their frequencies of occurrence in various DIALOG data bases. DIALIST is designed to assist in the determination of the utility of data base search strategies prior to an actual on-line search, enabling the user to save connect charges through advance preparation. The System Development Corporation supports its ORBIT search service with a similar microform listing.

Microforms are rarely the original publication medium for general reference works, although several important works have been produced on COM fiche from machine-readable data bases. The *Import/Export Microtables*, offered by Micro-editions Hachette, is a COM-generated microfiche listing of information regarding the trade activities of the members of the Organization for Economic Cooperation and Development. The fiche, created from data supplied by the OECD, are updated and cumulated quarterly. COM has served as the original publication medium for several concordances. Examples include S. C. Jacobson, et al., *Concordance to Joseph Conrad's Heart of Darkness* (Carbondale: Southern Illinois University Press, 1972) and Aldo S. Bernardo, *Concordance to the Familiari of S. Francisco Petrarca* (Albany: State University of New York Press, 1977), both available exclusively in microfiche.

## Archives and Manuscripts

Because of their great volume and highly specialized nature, micropublishing represents an economical alternative to letterpress editions for previously unpublished archival record series and manuscript collections.[31] The extensive micropublishing program of the National Archives has already been described. The Library of Congress has microfilmed a number of manuscript collections from its holdings, including the papers of twenty-three United States presidents.[32] Since 1964, the National Historic Publications and Records Commission (NHPRC) has provided financial assistance to archives, manuscript libraries, historical societies, and other agencies for purposes of arranging, organizing, and otherwise preparing significant primary source materials for micropublication.[33] Projects funded by the NHPRC have resulted in the greater availability of personal papers of important Americans for which the cost of extensively-edited letterpress publication could not be justified. An NHPRC grant, for example, assisted the Buffalo and Erie County Historical Society in locating, preparing, microfilming, and indexing the papers of Millard Filmore. Other grant recipients have included Cornell University, Dartmouth College, the Minnesota Historical Society, and the Academy of Natural Sciences of Philadelphia.

For very significant, but large, collections, microforms can serve as an adjunct to letterpress publication. Selections from the Adams Family Papers, for example, are available in an extensively-edited letterpress edition prepared by the Massachusetts Historical Society. Items omitted from the letterpress edition are published on microfilm.[34]

Several commercial micropublishers offer important archival and manuscript collections in microform. Examples include the *Socialist Party of America Papers*, produced by Microfilming Corporation of America from the holdings of the Duke University Library; Princeton Datafilm's microfiche version of *Dr. Humphrey Osmond's Indexed Notes*, a collection of personal papers dealing with conceptual models in psychiatry; and Chadwyk-Healey's series of *Archives of British Publishers*, which makes private materials from the files of George Allen and Company, George Routledge, Cambridge University Press, Longmans, and other organizations widely available for the first time.

Verbatim transcripts of oral interviews, radio broadcasts and television programs represent an increasingly important area of original micropublishing. Microfilming Corporation of America, for example, offers the *New York Times Oral History Program*, the *Columbia University Oral History Program*, *CBS News Broadcasts*, and transcripts of *Sixty Minutes* and other regular and special CBS public affairs programs.

## SIMULTANEOUS MICROPUBLISHING

### Concept

As the name implies, simultaneous micropublications are issued at the same time as their paper edition counterparts. Generally, the microform edition is created after the paper version by filming printed pages.

Since their introduction in the early 1970s, simultaneous micropublications have had to struggle for acceptance. In 1972, Pergamon Press offered simultaneous microfiche editions of a number of its journal publications. The program was cancelled for lack of interest. It was revived as an experiment in 1975 when Pergamon offered eight consecutive microfiche issues of the chemistry journal *Tetrahedron Letters* free of charge to libraries subscribing to the paper edition. Only 100 of 5,000 subscribers considered the offer attractive enough to respond to it.[35] Despite this discouraging result, Pergamon now offers over 250 scholarly journals and 65 United States government serial publications, including *Index Medicus*, in simultaneous microfiche editions. Recent sales are reported to have improved, with over two-thirds of the microfiche titles having at least one subscriber by June 1976.[36] The Institute of Electrical and Electronic Engineers offers all of its journals in simultaneous micropublications, but only 1.5 percent of its subscribers choose them over paper. When the American Biological Chemists proposed a simultaneous microfiche publication to reduce journal delivery time to foreign countries, less than five percent of United Kingdom subscribers indicated an interest. Less than one percent of American Chemical Society subscribers select journals in simultaneous microfiche editions. Interestingly, most of these are individuals rather than libraries.[37]

## Pricing

There is some indication that lower prices may motivate libraries to select a microform in preference to paper, either as a first or a duplicate copy. A 1972 survey of British and North American librarians by the Butterworth Group confirmed the general lack of enthusiasm for simultaneous micropublications but indicated that 75 percent of 125 responding North American libraries would consider acquiring duplicate copies in microform if the price were at least fifteen percent lower than the paper edition. Actual pricing policies vary considerably, however. The American Chemical Society and the Optical Society of America do not discount their simultaneous microfiche journals. Pergamon Press, however, charges eighty percent of the paper price for subscribers who elect a microfiche edition only. With a combined subscription to both microfiche and paper editions, the microfiche is sold at fifty percent of the paper price. *Physics Bulletin, Physics Education*, and other Institute of Physics (UK) publications are available in simultaneous microfiche editions at a thirty percent discount. While paper editions are shipped to New York by air freight and mailed to United States subscribers, the microfiche edition is dispatched by air directly to subscribers from London. The University of Washington Press offers its simultaneous micropublications at a flat rate of two dollars per fiche. Thus, Geza Roheim's *Hungarian and Vogul Mythology*, which is ninety pages long, will cost two dollars in microform or five dollars in cloth binding. Howard C. Payne's *The Police State of Louis Napoleon Bonaparte* at 352 pages requires four fiche for a total of eight dollars. The cloth edition is $7.50. Academic Press Library Editions are a unique series of simultaneous micropublications consisting of both a hardcover book and an accompanying second copy in microfiche, delivered in an envelope in the book's back cover. The microfiche is intended for inclusion in the library's microform collection. The price for the combined publication is only thirty percent higher than the price of the hardcover edition alone.

## RETROSPECTIVE MICROPUBLISHING

### Newspapers

As defined in chapter one, retrospective micropublishing is the re-issuing, in multiple-copy microform, of material previously published in paper form. As such, retrospective micropublishing is a form of reprinting.[38] Despite much recent interest in original and simultaneous micropublishing, retrospective micropublishing dominates the library market. The earliest retrospective micropublishing programs concentrated on newspaper backfiles and grew out of a concern for the research value and ephemeral nature of information in newsprint. Today, a wide range of North American and Western European newspapers are available in microform.

In the United States, commercial micropublishers have been generally attracted to leading newspapers reflecting various geographical and political viewpoints. Microfilming Corporation of America is the micropublisher for the *New York Times*. Bell and Howell, the micropublisher with the largest number of newspapers in regular production, offers the *Washington Post, Chicago Tribune, Wall Street Journal, Newsday, Christian Science Monitor, Village Voice*, and many other titles. Several commercial micropublishers offer newspapers reflective of ethnic life or selected historical periods. Examples include Bell and Howell's collections of *Black Community Newspapers* and *North American Indian Contemporary Newspapers*, and the Readex Microprint edition of *Early American Newspapers, 1704-1820*, produced from the holdings of the American Antiquarian Society. Institutional micropublishers have generally concentrated on local newspapers of insufficient market appeal to attract commercial firms. The Ohio Historical Society, for example, has microfilmed nineteenth and twentieth century newspapers of Ohio towns. Although most micropublished newspapers are reproduced in their entirely, the *Los Angeles Times* is available in a special library edition that omits whole-page advertisements and community news sections.

Canadian newspapers are available from several micropublishers, including Maclean-Hunter and the Canadian Library Association. Commonwealth Microfilm Library, Ltd. specializes in western Canadian newspapers including the *Vancouver Sun*, *Vancouver Province*, and *Victoria Daily Times*.

Turning to Western Europe, Newspaper Archive Development Ltd. is the micropublisher for the *London Times* and its related newspapers. L'Association pour la Conservation et la Reproduction Photographique de la Presse (ACRPP) is a non-profit organization dedicated to the reconstruction and microfilming of complete backfiles of French newspapers. The ACRPP micropublications also include French-language Algerian newspapers, Arabic newspapers published in France, ephemeral publications of the Revolution and nineteenth century, and resistance newspapers. The preservation of German language newspapers on microfilm, long a concern of the Association of German Archivists and similar groups, is now coordinated by the Mikrofilm-Archiv der Deutschsprachigen Presse at the Institut für Zeitungsforschung in Dortmund. To date, the Mikrofilm-Archiv has filmed a number of anti-Nazi newspapers as well as national and local papers of the nineteenth and twentieth centuries. The German Jewish newspapers preserved in the Leo Baeck Institute are available from Princeton Datafilm.[39]

Responsibility for microfilming Eastern European, Asian, and Third World newspapers is not well established. The Association for Research Libraries, in cooperation with the Library of Congress, has steadily assumed leadership in this important area. The Library of Congress is also microfilming foreign official gazettes, as is KTO Microform.[40] A few commercial micropublishers offer the most important titles. Bell and Howell, for example, has microfilmed *Pravda* and *Izvestiya*. The Four Continents Book Shop markets several Soviet newspapers filmed under the aegis of the Lenin Library. Many of the Russian republican newspapers needed for research remain unavailable, however.[41]

Microform clipping services, offered by several commercial firms, are a special variant of newspaper micropublishing. The *Newsbank Library*, for example, presents news reports on selected subjects from over 150 papers in 130 cities in fifty states. The 9,000 articles selected each month reflect local rather than national opinion. Maclean-Hunter offers a microfiche clipping service in sixteen subject areas of Canadiana.[42] Bell and Howell offers several clipping collections on special topics, including the *Assassination of John F. Kennedy*, which contains relevant news reports from 175 papers in eighty cities, and the *LBJ Clipping File*, a selection of news items from the *Houston Post*, 1948-1969.

## Serials

As discussed in chapter one, a number of libraries acquire backfiles of popular, technical, and scholarly journals and magazines in microform, primarily to save space and binding costs. Xerox University Microfilms, the leader in this area of retrospective micropublishing, offers more than 10,000 titles on film and fiche. A number of professional associations also offer their serial publications in microform, usually at year end. Considerable attention has been given to defunct serials of significant research value. Chadwyk-Healey, for example, offers the irregular serial publications of the various English Record Societies on microfiche. These serials, while invaluable for research, are available in paper editions only in older libraries. Lost Cause Press likewise offers the important Parker Society publications, 1841-1855. Clearwater Publishers offers the *Bulletin of the Taylor Society*, 1914-1934, an important landmark in the history of scientific management. The *Union List of Serials* indicates that only thirteen research libraries own a complete paper set. Many have no issues at all.

Several micropublishers offer serial backfiles in special subject areas. Examples include the Greenwood Press collections of Black journals (50 titles), women's rights periodicals (24 titles), U.S. radical periodicals (125 titles), and science-fiction magazines (15 titles). Plenum Publishing Company offers microform versions of significant Russian serials in cover-to-cover translations. Xerox University Microfilms' *Early British Periodicals* contains 3.5 million pages from 168 eighteenth and nineteenth century titles. The same micropublisher also offers *Early British Literary Periodicals* and *British Periodicals on the Creative Arts*. Rothman Reprints offers both contemporary law reviews and historical legal periodicals in microform.

## Out-of-Print Books

Micropublishing can be an economical form of reprinting for out-of-print titles, especially those in limited demand. Xerox University Microfilms, again the leader in this field, maintains a backlist of over 120,000 out-of-print titles available in microform. Through its *Books on Demand* program, University Microfilms will attempt to locate and microfilm any title to customer order. A number of smaller micropublishers specialize in out-of-print titles in selected subject areas: Dakota Microfilms in rare musical works, Helios Microfilms in the history of photography, Micrographics II in nineteenth century Virginia imprints, Andronicus Publishing Company in colonialism, slavery, and women's rights. Oxford University Press offers selected out-of-print titles from its history and literature backlists in microfiche. Although micropublication usually serves as a facsimile reprint technique for out-of-print titles, new material is occasionally included. The microfiche version of Kuhn's 1821-1823 edition of Galen's *Opera Omnia*, done by Oxford Microform Publications, features an introduction by Dr. Vivian Nutton critically examining the Kuhn edition. The micropublication of the defunct serial *Central Asian Review, 1953-71* by the Central Asian Research Centre includes a new introduction by Geoffrey Wheeler.

Because editorial, design, and author royalty costs were typically absorbed by the printing of the original paper edition, micropublications of out-of-print books tend to be reasonably priced. The eleven Daumier volumes of Henri Loys Deteil's *Le Peintre-Graveur Illustre*, for example, are available in an offset reprinting for $980. The same volumes are available on microfiche from Chadwyk-Healey for $148. New University Press, a micropublisher specializing in medieval studies, offers Buckle's *History of Civilization in England*, three volumes, for a total of $9.00. A paper reprint of volume one alone is priced at $24.50.

## Large Microform Sets

In addition to the re-issuing of individual out-of-print titles, large microform sets are available for in-depth collection augmentation. The role of these microform sets in the development of library collections was introduced in chapter one. Newer academic libraries are the principle market for large microform collections of basic out-of-print titles. The *Opening Day Collection*, offered by Xerox University Microfilms, consists of 2,000 such titles selected for undergraduate libraries by the editors of *Choice*, enhanced by 4,700 additional titles selected by Xerox University Microfilms from reviews in *Choice*. Information Handling Services offers titles listed in *Books for College Libraries*, divided into twelve separate packages by broad subject area. The Library of American Civilization, developed by Library Resources, Incorporated, consists of selected pre-1914 imprints on three by five inch Microbook transparencies described in chapter two. Total collection size approaches 20,000 titles. Information Handling Services' *Learning Resource System*, developed by NCR as the *PCMI Library*, is an ultrafiche collection of significant titles from standard titles in each of several broad subject areas, including American civilization, literature, science, and the social sciences. Using four by six inch transparencies with up to 3,200 microimages reduced 150X, the *Learning Resource System* groups seven to ten related titles on a single ultrafiche, thereby minimizing microform handling and permitting some subject browsing.[43]

As discussed in chapter one, libraries have long relied on microforms for the acquisition of rare imprints available only in very distinguished research collections. To meet the need for research materials to support faculty and doctoral research, several commercial micropublishers offer large microform sets consisting of all available titles listed in standard retrospective bibliographies. The best known examples of such rare imprint collections—Xerox University Microfilm's offering of titles listed in the *Short-Title Catalogue*, both Pollard and Redgrave and Wing, and the Readex Microprint edition of *Early American Imprints*, based on titles listed by Evans, Shaw, and Shoemaker—were mentioned in chapter two. Other representative offerings include selections from Kaplan's *Bibliography of American Autobiographies*, available from Northern Micrographics; titles from Staton and Tremaine, *A Bibliography of Canadiana*, offered by Information Handling Services; *The Kentucky Thousand*, one thousand items listed in J. Winston Coleman, Jr., *A Bibliography of Kentucky History*, microfilmed by Lost Cause Press; and General Microfilm Company's *Scandanavian Culture Series*, a collection of pre-1600 Swedish imprints, ninety percent of which are unavailable outside of Scandanavia. The collection is based on Isak Gustaf Collijn, *Sveriges Bibliografi intill ar 1600*.

Similar large microform sets are available for libraries associated with professional schools. The Inter Documentation Company's *History of Medicine* collection consists of 261 rare monographs and 68 scarce serials selected from the *Garrison-Morton Medical Bibliography*. Research Publications' *Early American Medical Imprints, 1668-1820* is based on the bibliography of the same title by R. B. Austin. Rothman Reprints has microfilmed public domain titles from *Law Books Recommended for Libraries*, a list compiled by the Association of American Law Schools. World Microfilm Publications offers rare books on accounting and related subjects selected by the British Institute of Chartered Accountants.

## Subject Collections in Microform

Subject collections are an interesting variant of the large microform set. Subject collections in microform have been compared to huge anthologies, containing not merely selections but whole books and related materials on broad or narrow topics.[44] In some cases, the editors of such collections base their selections on the holdings of distinguished existing repositories. Microfilming Corporation of America's *Crime and Juvenile Delinquency* collection, for example, consists of 2,200 titles from the library of the National Council on Crime and Delinquency. Research Publications *Social Problems and the Churches* is based on the Harlan Paul Douglass Collection of the National Council of Churches of Christ. Bell and Howell has filmed the *Cornell University Collection of Women's Rights Pamphlets,* while Lost Cause Press offers *Anti-Slavery Propaganda* in the Oberlin College Library. In other cases, project editors develop original collections, often in consultation with recognized subject specialists. *Precurseurs Français de la Psychiatrie et de la Psychoanalyse*, prepared by Microeditions Hachette, presents 31 rare titles dealing with eighteenth and nineteenth century French psychotherapy. The same micro-publisher's *Babeuf et Babouvism* is a collection of rare books and official documents relating to early nineteenth century French socialism, selected and organized by Albert Soboul of the Sorbonne. Information Handling Services' *Historical Trials Relevant to Today's Issues* presents public records, newspapers, personal narratives, and other materials relating to the trials of Aaron Burr, Dred Scott, Charles I, and others. Bell and Howell's *The Depression Years* provides daily issues of eleven American newspapers for the period 1929-1938.

## Government Publications

Because of the difficulties inherent in their identification, acquisition, and maintenance in paper form, government publications have attracted the attention of several commercial micropublishers. Although the United States Government Printing Office is currently exploring the feasibility of simultaneously offering all or most depository publications in paper and microfiche, the Library of Congress bibliographic publications already described and the *Code of Federal Regulations* are the only items presently available in this way.[45] Readex Microprint Corporation, however, offers complete coverage of the depository and non-depository publications listed in the *Monthly Catalog*; the *U.S. Serial Set, 1817-1913,* including the *American State Papers, 1789-1838*; *Congressional*

*Hearings and Committee Prints*, 1956 to date; and the *Congressional Record*, 1957-1972. Readex offers the depository and non-depository publications as a complete collection or by individual agency. Congressional Information Service (CIS) offers two broad groups of United States government publications on microfiche: 1) Congressional working papers, including bulletins, committee prints, hearings, and reports; and 2) United States government statistical reports, regardless of creating agency.[46] Like Readex, CIS also offers the *U.S. Serial Set.* Greenwood Press, now a division of CIS, offers *U.S. Census Publications*, 1820-1967; Congressional committee prints and hearings, a number of state government publications, including documents produced by state constitutional conventions, 1776-1975; selected state labor reports to 1900; and selected state water resource reports.[47] Greenwood is also one of the few micropublishers to offer municipal documents.[48] Brookhaven Press, which intends to offer a broad range of state government publications, now has fairly full coverage for Minnesota and Wisconsin. KTO Microform has filmed a large group of pre-1930 state reports dealing with corrections, punishment, poverty, and welfare.

Coverage of international government publications is less systematic and extensive. Greenwood Press has an on-going program that will eventually make all national statistical compendia available on microfiche. Micromedia, Ltd. offers Canadian federal government publications as well as Parliamentary committee reports and minutes, statistical reports, and selected provincial and municipal publications. Readex and Pergamon both offer *Hansard's Parliamentary Debates* in Microprint and microfiche, respectively. Readex also offers the *Journal of the House of Commons*, 1547-1900, and House of Commons *Sessional Papers* from the eighteenth century. The United Nations has its own micropublishing program.[49] U.N. documents are also available from Readex Microprint Corporation.

Some commercial micropublishers offer selected publications of Third World governments. African Imprint Library Services, for example, has microfilmed government documents of the Camerouns since 1960, and selected publications of the Ivory Coast, 1957-1971. The *South African Native Affairs* collection, produced by Andronicus Publishing Company, includes reports of the South Rhodesian Chief Native Commissioner.

## Catalog Files

As with government publications, the difficulties of identifying, acquiring, maintaining, and controlling files of catalogs and related materials have led to the development of several significant commercial micropublications. For scientific and industrial libraries, the Visual Search Microfilm File (VSMF) System—mentioned in chapter two—is a collection of vendor catalogs, engineering and construction specifications, and industrial standards acquired, microfilmed, and indexed by Information Handling Services. The various subsets of the VSMF System are available on 16mm cartridges, 8mm cassettes, or NMA Type 1 Standard microfiche. Microform data files are configured in a work station with a reader and reader/printer. The VSMF System is typically cost-justified through a combination of space savings, reduced file maintenance, and faster retrieval.[50]

The same cost-justifications apply to the microform college catalog systems produced for academic libraries. The National Microfilm Library, for example, offers a complete set of general catalogs and bulletins of all institutions of higher education in the United States, plus selected catalogs of major foreign universities, on four by six inch microfiche filed inside storage panels in three-ring vinyl binders. The complete collection totals approximately 1,100 fiche, each with 495 microimages reduced 32X to 52X. The total system price is only about $400. At Western Michigan University, these microfiche catalogs replaced bulky, difficult to maintain hard copy files with resulting savings in space and clerical time.[51]

The *Micropublishers Trade List Annual*, a collection of micropublishers' catalogs on microfiche, is discussed in chapter seven.

## THE EVALUATION OF MICROPUBLICATIONS

### Technical Considerations

Since Veaner's 1968 article in *Choice* first pointed out the difficulties of examining an "invisible" product,[52] the evaluation of micropublications has been beset by controversy. The question of user acceptance of micropublications is discussed in the next chapter. The bibliographic control of microforms is the subject of chapter seven. The remaining sections of this chapter consider technical, contractual, and other considerations involved in evaluating the products of institutional and commercial micropublishers.

The technical evaluation of micropublications is concerned with the appropriateness of the microformat and reduction ratio, the relationship of the film stock to expected image stability, and the adequacy of image quality. As discussed in chapter two, the appropriateness of the microformat and reduction ratio depends on a number of factors, including the condition of the original material being filmed and the type of equipment available at the point of use. Thirty-five millimeter reel microfilm remains the dominant microform for newspapers, archives, manuscripts, rare books, and other hard-to-reproduce source documents. Most 35mm micropublications are produced at reductions in the range 9X to 17X, 14X being the most widely used. Sixteen millimeter microfilm on reels, cartridges, and cassettes is used for serial backfiles and certain original micropublications described in the preceding sections. The most popular 16mm reduction is 24X. A few commercial micropublishers offer 16mm microimages duplicated onto 35mm reel microfilm in an attempt to extend the market for their products to libraries equipped with only 35mm readers and reader/printers. Such micropublications forfeit the advantages of lower reductions typically associated with 35mm microfilm. The American Library Association has issued a statement warning libraries that this method of producing 35mm microfilm may not be adequately noted in micropublishers' advertisements. Uninformed libraries may, consequently, purchase micropublications that employ smaller image areas and higher reductions than other 35mm microforms in their collections.

As noted in chapter two, the availability of relatively inexpensive viewing equipment has attracted an increasing number of micropublishers to microfiche, even for materials that are not effectively unitized by the microfiche format. In such cases, the librarian responsible for the evaluation of the appropriateness of the fiche format must weigh any possible inconvenience necessitated by increased microform handling against the advantages of being able to provide additional readers and reader/printers for patron use. Micropublications in the fiche format are also easily duplicated for dissemination to patrons, using the equipment described in chapter three. Most micropublishers adhere to the NMA Type 1 Standard 24X fiche format. As noted in chapter two, non-standard formats—employing reductions in the range 17X to 20X—remain in use, especially by European micropublishers. Very high and ultra high reductions are employed in several large microform sets described in preceding sections of this chapter. Readex Microprint Corporation is the sole source for opaque micropublications. No institutional or commercial micropublishers offer microfilm jackets or aperture cards.

Because libraries generally expect additions to their microform holdings to last indefinitely, most micropublications produced for the library market are created on silver halide film stock. The copy sold to libraries is typically a second or third generation microform. While micropublishers are attracted by the potential economies of diazo and vesicular duplicating films, these non-archival film stocks are generally only utilized for frequently updated bibliographies and similar materials with a limited useful life. As noted in chapter three, diazo and vesicular microfilm cannot be recommended for applications requiring archival potential. In a few cases, micropublishers offer libraries a choice of diazo or vesicular microforms as a less expensive alternative to silver halide duplicates.

To assist in the evaluation of image quality, most micropublishers film one or more resolution test targets at the start of each roll or fiche. Inspection of the target and individual film frames requires the special equipment described in chapter three.

## Evaluation of Content of Microform Sets

As noted in the preceding sections, large microform sets may contain hundreds or even thousands of individual titles. The micropublication of such sets may extend over long periods of time and portions of a set may be completed and offered for sale prior to completion of the entire project. Taken together, these two factors of set size and extended period of publication make the evaluation of the actual and projected content of microform sets a difficult professional task. Data elements essential to such evaluation are specified in ANSI Z39.26-75, *American National Standard for the Advertising of Micropublications* (New York: American National Standards Institute, 1975). The librarian responsible for evaluating the content of large microform sets should consider the individual titles included in the set, especially noting titles duplicated in the library's existing holdings or available from other micropublishers at lower prices.[53] If the set is based on existing bibliographies, they should be examined. If the set is an original collection of material, the qualifications of the editor or compiler should be determined.[54] If the collection is known to be incomplete, missing titles should be noted and the likelihood of their future availability determined.

## Contractual Considerations

Because the decision to acquire library materials in microform may require the commitment of substantial financial resources for extended periods of time, careful attention should be given to the terms of the purchase agreement. The availability of discounts and time payment plans should be explored. Most micropublishers make provisions for the purchase of individual titles from large microform sets and for the return of titles duplicated in the library's holdings. Because the identification of such duplicates can itself be a formidable task, Lost Cause Press permits the return of duplicate items at any time within six months of receipt. Since few libraries will be able to inspect individual film frames immediately on receipt of a micropublication, the purchase agreement should include a provision for the replacement of defective microfilm or microfiche as discovered. The continued availability, for purchase, of individual titles damaged during use should also be determined. With the exception of edition-process microforms and micropublications produced by defunct publishers, the purchase of replacement microforms is rarely a problem. If portions of a large microform set have yet to be filmed, the library should obtain a written statement of titles to be included in subsequent filmings and delivery dates.

## REFERENCES

[1] General discussions of the field include: Allen B. Veaner, *The Evaluation of Micropublications: A Handbook for Librarians* (Chicago: Library Technology Program, American Library Association, 1971); Veaner, "Micropublication." In *Advances in Librarianship*, Melvin J. Voigt, ed., (New York: Academic Press, 1971), pp. 165-86; Veaner, "An Encyclopedia in Your Waistcoat Pocket," *Microdoc* 10 (1971): 104-106; Maynard Short, "Micropublishing of Packaged Information Systems," *Journal of Micrographics* 5 (1971): 75-80; "Twenty Questions on Micropublishing Technology: An Interview with Milton Mandel," *Journal of Micrographics* 4 (1971): 143-46; Stevens Rice, "Micropublishing," *Government Publications Review* 1 (1973): 229-30; Charles J. Koppa, "Micropublishing and the Printer," *Proceedings of the National Microfilm Association* (Silver Spring, Md.: NMA, 1972), II-109-121.

[2] Albert H. Leisinger, Jr. "Selected Aspects of Microreproduction in the United States," *Archivum* 16 (1966): 127-50.

[3] Ernst Posner, *American State Archives* (Chicago: University of Chicago Press, 1964), pp. 331-33.

[4] Brien Benson, "Hoover Institution Microfilms," *Microform Review* 3 (1974): 266-68.

[5] The problem of avoiding interesting but unmarketable materials exists for institutional micropublishers as well. See, for example, Bruce Peel, "The Microfilm Project of the Canadian Library Association," *Microform Review* 3 (1974): 106-107.

[6] David Dempsey, "The Publishing Scene," *Saturday Review* 53 (February 21, 1970): 39; Mary E. Hickey, "Inter Documentation Company: A History," *Microform Review* 3 (1974): 108-110; Ann De Villiers, "Information Handling Services: A Unique Story," *Journal of Micrographics* 10 (1976): 31-36.

[7] See Herbert S. Bailey, Jr. *The Art and Science of Book Publishing* (New York: Harper and Row, 1970), pp. 140-42.

[8] Eugene B. Power, "Microfilm as an Edition Process of Documentary Reproduction," *American Documentation* 2 (1951): 157-60; Stevens Rice, "Publishing in the Microforms," *Proceedings of the National Microfilm Association* (Annapolis, Md.: NMA, 1962), pp. 271-76; Larry Block and Richard E. Schmidt, "Demand Publishing," *Journal of Micrographics* 5 (1971): 81-82; B. J. S. Williams, "Introduction to Microforms and Microform Publishing." In *Micropublishing for Learned Societies* (Hatfield, Herts, England: National Reprographic Centre for Documentation, 1968), pp. 1-10.

[9] Eugene B. Power, "O-P Books: A Library Breakthrough," *American Documentation* 4 (1958): 273-76.

[10] John Tennant, "Readex Microprints," *Journal of Documentary Reproduction* 3 (1940): 66-70.

[11] Herbert S. Bailey, Jr., "The Limits of On-Demand Publishing," *Scholarly Publishing* 6 (1975): 291-98 concludes that on-demand publishing is clearly more cost-effective for editions of 150 copies or less.

[12] Eugene B. Power, "Microfilm and the Publication of Doctoral Dissertations," *Journal of Documentary Reproduction* 5 (1942): 37-44.

[13] Marvin E. Wilson, "Selected Research in Microfiche," *Microfiche Foundation Newsletter* No. 35 (April 1977): 12-14.

[14] Melvin J. Josephs, "Information Dissemination with Microforms," *IEEE Transactions on Professional Communication* PC-18 (1975): 164-67; H. F. Vessey, *The Use of Microfiche for Scientific and Technical Reports* (NATO, Advisory Group for Aerospace Research and Development, August, 1970).

[15] Harvey Marron, "The Educational Resources Information Center: Or How Educators Learned about Microfiche," *Journal of Micrographics* 4 (1971): 69-71.

[16] Norman Mangouni, "Micropublishing among the University Presses," *Microform Review* 3 (1974): 250-53.

[17] On the problems of university press publishing, see William B. Harvey, et al., "The Impending Crisis in University Publishing," *Scholarly Publishing* 3 (1972): 195-207; John B. Putnam, "The Scholar and the Future of Scholarly Publishing," *Scholarly Publishing* 4 (1973): 195-200.

[18] Howard M. Levin and Wendy J. Strothman, "Pictorial Microfiche and the Expansion of Scholarly Publishing: A Comprehensive Program," *Journal of Micrographics* 10 (1977): 153-58.

[19] Warren G. Bovee, "Scientific and Technical Journals on Microfiche," *IEEE Transactions on Professional Communication* PC-16 (1973): 113; Joseph H. Kuney, "Impact of Microfilms on Journal Cost," *IEEE Transactions on Professional Communication* PC-16 (1973): 80-81, 175; Frederick S. Hillier, "An Investigation of the Potential Use of Microfiche for the Publications of Two Professional Societies," *Microform Review* 4 (1975): 108-109.

[20] Constance Greaser, "Alternatives to Traditional Forms of Scientific Communication," *Scholarly Publishing* 8 (1976): 54-66, reports a warm reception for the first issues, as 46 of 50 subscribers surveyed indicated a preference for microforms over a more expensive paper journal.

[21] Horace Jacobs, "Papers and Proceedings of the Professional Meetings on Microfiche," *Microform Review* 3 (1974): 15-21; Margaret O. Sheppard, "Microfiche Preprints for Conferences," *Aslib Proceedings* 26 (1974): 435-45.

[22] Susan Martin (comp.), *Information * Politics: Proceeding of the ASIS Annual Meeting* (Washington: American Society for Information Science, 1976).

[23] The Inter Documentation Company offers the *Bibliography of Agricultural Bibliographies*, prepared by the Agricultural University of Wageninigen, the Netherlands, on source document microfiche. See *Microform Review* 5 (1976): 46-47 for a description.

[24] J. E. Linford, "Books in English," *Microform Review* 1 (1972): 207-13; also in *Canadian Library Journal* 30 (1973): 132-38.

[25] F. H. Ayres, "Books in English: A Comparative Assessment," *Journal of Librarianship* 6 (1974): 233-40.

[26] Howard Pasternack, "Microform Catalog Data Retrieval Systems," *Library Technology Reports* 12 (1976): 371-406.

[27] Nancy Hoyt Knight, "Microform Catalog Data Retrieval Systems: A Survey," *Library Technology Reports* (May 1975); D. E. Madison and J. E. Galejs, "Application of the Micrographic Catalog Retrieval System in the Iowa State University Library," *Library Resources and Technical Services* 15 (1971): 492-98.

[28] Knight, *Library Technology Reports* (May 1975); Brett Butler and John Van Pelt, "Microphotocomposition—A New Publishing Resource," *Journal of Micrographics* 6 (1972): 7-13.

[29] *Microform Review* 4 (1975): 114-15.

[30] "Microform Editions of Library of Congress Subject Heading," *Cataloging Service*, Bulletin No. 113 (Spring 1975): 7.

[31] Thomas E. Jeffrey, "The Papers of Benjamin Henry Latrobe: New Approaches to the Micropublication of Historical Records," *Microform Review* 6 (1977): 82-86, cites the production costs of producing 1,500 copies of a ten volume edited manuscript collection at $175,000 to $180,000. See also, Jeffrey, "The Papers of Benjamin Henry Latrobe: Problems and Possibilities of Editing Historical Documents on Microfiche," *Journal of Micrographics* 10 (1976): 69-75.

[32] Fred Shelley, "The Presidential Papers Program of the Library of Congress," *American Archivist* 25 (1962): 429-33; *Manuscripts on Microfilm: A Checklist of Holdings in the Manuscript Division* (Washington: Library of Congress, 1975).

[33] Robert L. Brubaker, "The Publication of Historical Sources: Recent Projects in the United States," *Library Quarterly* 37 (1967): 193-225; Waldo G. Leland, "The Prehistory and Origins of the National Historic Publications Commission," *American Archivist* 27 (1964): 187-94.

[34] L. H. Butterfield, "Vita Sine Letteris, Mors Est: The Microfilm Edition of the Adams Papers," *Library of Congress Quarterly Journal of Acquisitions* 18 (1960): 53-58.

[35] Edward Gray, "Subscriptions on Microfiche: An Irreversible Trend," *Journal of Micrographics* 8 (1975): 241-44; Gray, "Microform Concept—An Innovative Approach," *Microform Review* 1 (1972): 31-32; Gray, "Microfiche for a Simultaneous Subscription: Two Experiments," *Proceedings of the American Society for Information Science* (1975): 95-96; Ian Montagnes, "Scholarly Monographs on Microfiche: The University of Toronto Press as a Case in Point," *Microform Review* 1 (1972): 29-30.

[36] Edward Gray, "Subscriptions on Microfiche: A Progress Report," *Journal of Micrographics* 10 (1977): 169-86.

[37] Edward Gray, "Our Microform Marketing Strategy," *IEEE Transactions on Professional Communications* PC-18 (1975): 160-63, and subsequent discussion.

[38] On the relationship of micropublishing to the reprint industry, see Carol A. Nemeyer, *Scholarly Reprint Publishing in the United States* (New York: Bowker, 1972) esp. pp. 15-16.

[39] *The German Jewish Press on Microfilm* (Princeton, N.J.: Princeton Datafilm, 1974).

[40] John Y. Cole, "Foreign Official Gazette Microfilming: A Renewed Effort," *Microform Review* 4 (1975): 101-103.

[41] Leo Gruliow, "Soviet Serials on Microform," *Microform Review* 1 (1972): 203-205.

[42] *Vertical Files* (Toronto: MacLean-Hunter, 1972- ).

[43] Charles W. Evans, "High Reduction Microfiche for Libraries: An Evaluation of Collections from the National Cash Register Company and Library Resources, Inc.," *Library Resources and Technical Services* 16 (1972): 33-47; William R. Hawken, et al., "Microbook Publication—A New Approach for a New Decade," *Journal of Micrographics* 3 (1970): 188-193; Paul A. Napier, et al., "The Library Resources Inc. Library of American Civilization Demonstration at the George Washington University Library," *Microform Review* 3 (1974): 158-76; Klaus W. Otten, "Ultramicrofiche Packages for Libraries: Pros and Cons of Different Approaches," *Proceedings of the National Microfilm Association* (Silver Spring, Md.: NMA, 1971), II-110-120; Harriet K. Rebuldela, "Ultrafiche Libraries: A User Survey of the Library of American Civilization," *Microform Review* 3 (1974): 178-88.

[44] Edward A. Reno, Jr., "Some Basic Aspects of Scholarly Micropublishing," *Proceedings of the National Microfilm Association* (Silver Spring, Md.: NMA, 1973): II-282-293.

[45] James B. Adler, the Government Printing Office, and Catharine Reynolds, "Micropublishing and the Government Printing Office: Three Viewpoints," *Microform Review* 3 (1974): 80-84.

[46] *Congressional Bills on Microfiche* (Washington: Congressional Information Service, 1974); *ASI Microfiche Library* (Washington: Congressional Information Service, 1974).

[47] Beverly Railsback, "State Documents Microfilming Projects Survey," *Government Publications Review* 2 (1975): 345-50 indicates that, in 1974, only eleven states had active programs to microfilm their publications.

[48] *The Urban Documents Microfiche Collection* (Westport, Conn.: Greenwood Press, 1972- ).

[49] Allan F. Windsor, "New UN Microfiche Service Augurs Large Storage Economies," *Special Libraries* 65 (1974): 234-36.

[50] R. C. Olson, "VSMF—Billions in Low Cost Production," *Journal of Micrographics* 5 (1972): 221-27.

[51] *Microfiche College Catalog Collection* (LaJolla, California: National Microfilm Library, 1973- ). See the review by Harold E. Way in *Microform Review* 4 (1975): 294-95; also *Microform Review* 2 (1973): 126-28; 3 (1974): 126-28; 4 (1975): 135-36.

[52] Allen B. Veaner, "The Crisis in Micropublication," *Choice* 5 (1968): 444-53.

[53] To take only one example of duplication in large microfilm sets, the Readex Microprint edition of *Great Works of American Literature* includes titles also available in the Readex *Early American Imprints* and *English and American*

*Plays of the Nineteenth and Twentieth Century*; General Microfilm Company's *Victorian Fiction;* and Xerox University Microfilm's *American Fiction, 1774-1900.*

[54] For a criticism of micropublisher's selection practices, see E. M. Greider, "Ultrafiche Libraries: A Librarian's View," *Microform Review* 1 (1972): 85-100; and the rejoinder by Treadwell Ruml, "I. Ultrafiche Libraries: The Publishers Respond," *Microform Review* 1 (1972): 101-102; Charles Goldman and Harry Gunberg, "II. Ultrafiche Libraires: The Publishers Respond," *Microform Review* 1 (1972): 103-108.

# CHAPTER 6

# THE USE OF MICROFORMS

## THE TASK OF MICROFORM USE

### The Problem of User Resistance

The use of microforms created or acquired by libraries requires a reader or other display or printing device. Because microform systems are equipment-dependent, *user resistance*—the reluctance or refusal to accept microforms as an alternative to paper for information communication—is common. User resistance is related to both the manner and extent of microform use. Library microforms are used in two broad ways: for *reference* and for *study*. The reference use of microforms—typified by COM-generated holdings lists and circulation reports—involves the brief scanning of displayed microimages to retrieve small amounts of information that serve as the basis for action. The microform catalog user, for example, finds the desired entry, usually within an alphabetic arrangement on film or fiche; determines the item location from the class number or other indicator; then enters the stack area to obtain the item. Transaction time is short. Machine contact is brief. User resistance tends to be low, even among those who have had previously unfavorable experiences with microforms. A survey of microform catalog users at the Georgia Tech Library, for example, found no correlation between attitude toward microforms and frequency of use in a reference-type application.[1]

Most library-acquired micropublications, on the other hand, are intended for study—that is, the user will read or otherwise intensively examine them for their substantive content. Unlike the brief reference-type transactions described above, the use of microforms in study is a complex activity, involving prolonged machine contact. It is important to note that, even in conventional circumstances, reading—while often perceived as pleasurable—requires considerable mental and physical exertion in the form of cognition and reflection with accompanying eye movements. When the way in which such a complex activity is performed is altered or—in the case of microforms—imposed, greater neuromuscular effort is required and enjoyment is diminished.[2] The microform user must often modify long-established study habits. Posture, for example, is typically restricted. Except in research and development centers where scientists and engineers are furnished with personal readers, microform use is customarily limited to specifically designated locations within the library.

Where the user's information need is very strong, the inconveniences associated with the study use of microforms may be tolerated. In some cases, user acceptance may be facilitated by perceptions of *added value* in microforms. At MIT, for example, users recognize that the maintenance of periodicals and other library materials in microform offers the advantages of file integrity, immediate availability, and the elimination of competition for items in heavy circulation.[3] Some school children and undergraduate students appreciate the fact that use of a microform reader frees both hands for note-taking.[4] At the University of South Africa, where students enrolled in correspondence courses were provided with hard-to-obtain textbooks in convenient microfiche packages, over eighty percent of the recipients found the microform presentation acceptable.[5]

Generally, however, user resistance to study with microforms tends to be high. In 1968, when the imposition of a hardcopy charge forced the Boulder Research Laboratories library to begin ordering Defense Documentation Center reports in microfiche, a survey of scientists and engineers revealed "an over-whelming lack of enthusiasm" for conversion to microforms, with over 85 percent of the respondents opposed.[6] With few exceptions, other surveys reflect the same negative attitude.[7] At Southampton University, less than ten percent of the recipients of regular current-awareness services indicated that they frequently followed up interesting references in microform. By way of contrast, almost thirty percent of the same group frequently pursued hardcopy references in foreign languages, evidently preferring to cope with translation than with a microform in their own language.[8]

Platt undoubtedly speaks for many microform users in contending that viewing document images on a screen may be research but, for the person taught from childhood to enjoy books, it is not reading.[9] Similarly, Wooster, in an attitude survey of scientists and engineers, reported the frequent complaint that microforms lacked the "cuddly" quality of books.[10] In many cases, the user views the library's acquisition of materials in microform as a decision made solely for institutional benefit, without regard for personal inconvenience or discomfort. Some users feel that the necessity of using a microform reader is too great a price to pay for the greater availability of information. Weber reports a university library's experience with faculty members who categorically rejected research materials in microform, even when the price represented an eighty percent savings and the material was essential to departmental programs.[11] Although some of the professional decisions librarians make in the interest of greater availability of information may prove to be unpopular, user resistance cannot be dismissed lightly. Since it would obviously be irresponsible of librarians to develop extensive but unuseable microform collec-tions, the impact of microform use on work performance warrants careful examination.

## Fatigue and Microform Use

Prolonged performance of any complex task results in both objective and subjective fatigue. *Objective* fatigue manifests itself in impaired performance. There is no evidence that prolonged microform use results in a performance decrement greater than that resulting from prolonged reading of full-size documents. In a 1947 study, Charmichael and Dearborn demonstrated that subjects of good intelligence and adequate vision could maintain visual efficiency for at least six hours of continuous reading of either books or microfilm.[12] A 1969 study by Kottenstette demonstrated that undergraduate students could preserve reading rate and comprehension when using microform presentations of material ranging from descriptive to abstract.[13] A 1971 experiment by Baldwin and Bailey found no significant difference in performance when reading narrative materials in either full-size or microform.[14] Replication of the experiment by Grausneck and Kottenstette confirmed the result.[15]

These studies, taken together, indicate that library patrons can use microforms without undue objective fatigue. Ultimately, however, acceptance of microforms depends on the alleviation of *subjective* fatigue. Subjective fatigue is the *feeling* of being tired. Symptoms of subjective fatigue include headache and eyestrain. The experience and severity of subjective fatigue varies with the individual and may depend on factors, such as the need for corrective eyeglasses, that are beyond the control of microform systems designers. While subjective fatigue is the normal result of prolonged reading of full-size documents, the necessity of viewing enlarged microimages on a screen allows more scope for fatigue, causing many users to tire sooner. Furthermore, libraries acquire many micropublications to support the advanced research activities of doctoral students, faculty members, and scientists. These micropublications contain complex materials that strain the user's mind regardless of mode of presentation.[16] User resistance develops out of the resulting subjective fatigue and an awareness of *discrepancies* between microform presentations and alternative methods of acquiring needed information. The process is clearly described by Kottenstette in observations based on experiments at the Denver Research Institute:[17]

> An individual grows up using hardcopy. This form is accepted and utilized without the user having to understand what characteristics are embodied in the hardcopy that facilitates its use. Consider now what occurs when the user reads a microform presentation and the lower portion of the image is slightly out of focus. He may refocus that portion of the image many times, dismissing the problem as only "part of the system." But somewhere along the line he will begin to think: "You don't have to do this all the time with a book."

The existence of an alternative forces any process to be evaluated as a means to an end rather than in terms of end benefits alone. When the hardcopy prototype is itself inconvenient—bulky computer printouts and very large card files are obvious examples—resistance to microforms tends to be lower. Many users prefer the 16mm microfilm version of *Chemical Abstracts*, largely because the voluminous paper edition can prove unwieldy for long retrospective searches.[18] But when the hard copy alternative is familiar and attractive, as it is with most books and periodicals, microform acceptance depends on minimizing perceived discrepancies at the point where user and system meet—the reader and its surrounding environment.[19]

## EVALUATING MICROFORM READERS
### Technical Considerations

A microform *reader* is a projection device that magnifies microimages so they can be read with the unaided eye. The optical system of most microform readers is simple. A condensing lens assembly collects light and directs it through the transparent microform onto a projection lens. Depending on reader design, mirrors may be used to fold the optical path, thereby permitting more compact design. Lamps provide artificial light. As noted in chapter two, readers for Microprint and other opaque microforms use reflected, rather than transmitted light. Micrographics terminology distinguishes readers from *viewers*, which are hand-held magnifiers that operate with an ambient or battery-powered light source. Where technical manuals, charts, drawings, or maps are recorded on aperture cards, microfiche, or other unitized microforms, viewers permit convenient reference by field engineers and technical personnel in locations where the power required for other display devices is unavailable. Viewers are of questionable utility in library study-type applications.

There are several standards for microform readers.[20] These standards merely establish minimum quality expectations. Evaluation determines the suitability of a given reader for a particular application. The main technical considerations in reader evaluation involve the display method, image quality, and the film transport mechanism. Currently available microform readers employ one of two display methods.[21] *Front projection* readers, such as the Bell and Howell Micro Photo 16·35 (Fig. 6-1), display magnified microimages on an opaque surface. While a few portable front-projection readers display microimages on a table-top, the viewing surface in most models is built into the reader itself. *Rear projection* readers, like the Realist Vantage III (Fig. 6-2, p. 147), direct magnified microimages onto the back of a translucent screen which the user views from the front. Comparative performance analyses have failed to demonstrate the superiority of either display method.[22] Rear projection readers have been historically preferred in applications requiring accommodation to uncontrolled *ambient* (room) light. This is typically the case in reference-type applications—a COM-generated circulation list located at a library information desk, for example—where light levels cannot be optimized for microform display. While ambient light falling on a front projection screen may be reflected back at the user, thereby interfering with the displayed microimage, much of the ambient light falling on a rear projection screen is absorbed inside the reader itself. Several newer front projection readers, however, employ clear plastic filters to shield the screen. In both front and rear projection displays, much of the adverse effect of ambient light can be minimized with a hood.

Regardless of display method, reader image quality is evaluated in terms of resolution, contrast, and freedom from distortion. *Resolution*, applied to readers as to cameras, refers to the ability of an optical system and screen to render fine detail visible. Resolution is determined by examining an enlarged microimage of a filmed test target consisting of closely-spaced lines of decreasing size. Minimum acceptable reader resolutions vary with the material being displayed. Upper-case alphanumeric COM reports, for example, require resolution of only 2.5 lines per millimeter. The reader selected for prolonged study of microfilmed newspapers, however, must resolve more than four lines per millimeter. It should be noted that even very high resolution screens cannot enhance the quality of images degraded during microfilming or duplication.

**Figure 6-1**

**Front-Projection Microform Reader**
(Courtesy: Bell and Howell)

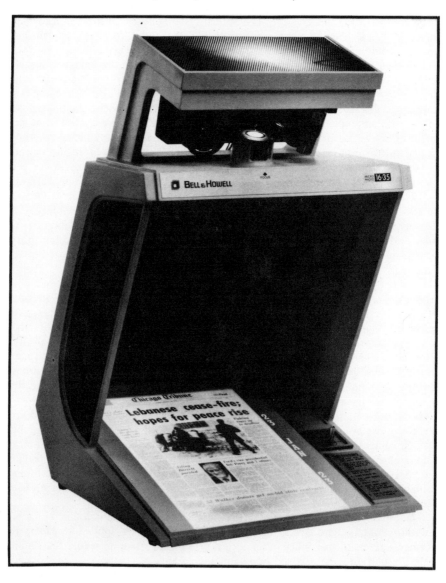

**Figure 6-2**

**Rear Projection Microform Reader**
(Courtesy: Realist, Inc.)

Screen *contrast* preserves the relationship between light and dark areas within a displayed microimage. All other reader specifications being equal, high contrast screens are preferred for viewing black-and-white microimages of textual records or line drawings. Lower screen contrast is generally preferred for viewing half-tones in black-and-white or color. Contrast is affected by screen color—the darker shades being of higher contrast. Grey is the only screen shade that adequately displays the full color spectrum.

*Distortions* are optical defects that, for example, cause straight lines at screen edges to appear curved. Slight screen distortions are inevitable and are generally significant only when maps, drawings, or other scaled originals are viewed.[23]

The *film transport* is the mechanism that moves microimages past the reader lens. In reel microfilm, cartridge, and cassette readers, the transport mechanism may be manual or motorized, the latter moving film at about ten feet per second. Motorized cartridge film transports typically provide for automatic threading onto the take-up spool as well. While motorized transports are obviously faster, manual transport systems are less vulnerable to malfunction. Whether manual or motorized, the transport mechanism should not scratch or otherwise damage the film.[24]

Microfiche readers employ a carrier-type transport mechanism that holds the fiche between two pieces of flat glass. The transport operates on a slide and must move freely in both horizontal and vertical directions. With the exception of the several automated microfiche retrieval systems described in chapter eight, fiche transports are manual in operation.

## General Engineering

The reader selected for library applications must be designed for durability and stability. The screen should be unbreakable and shatterproof. Acceptable case materials include steel, aluminum, and high-impact plastic. Portable readers must be light but well-built to withstand abuses in transport and use.

Readers intended for use in North American libraries should operate from a standard 120 volt, 60 cycle AC outlet. Alternate power supplied may be required in portable reader applications. Lamps and other replaceable parts should be easily accessible and readily obtainable. The Micro Design 4010 Microfiche Reader, for example, features an extendable modular drawer for simplified user maintenance. Several newer readers utilize ordinary automotive lamps. Others use long-life quartz-halogen bulbs that will operate for hundreds of hours before failure.

Because silver halide, vesicular, and dry silver microforms may be damaged by excessive heat, temperature at the film gate should not exceed 75°C (167°F). For user protection, metal case temperature should not exceed 50°C (142°F). Wood and plastic case temperatures should not exceed 60°C (152°F).

## Application Considerations

Factors affecting the suitability of a microform reader for a given application include microforms accepted; magnification; screen size and orientation; total reader size; and the availability of special features. In terms of microforms accepted, readers can be divided into two groups: single-purpose and multi-purpose. Single-purpose readers, as the name implies, are designed to accept one type of microform only—typically, an aperture card, an ultrafiche, or a proprietary cartridge or cassette. Most readers, while designed primarily for one microform, are multi-purpose in the sense of accepting more than one. Microfiche readers, for example, will also accept microfilm jackets and, when equipped with a tab-size carrier, aperture cards. Readers for opaque microforms will accept microfiche or microfilm jackets when an index card or other opaque barrier is placed behind them. Other popular multi-purpose reader combinations include 16mm and 35mm reels with microfiche, and 16mm reels with 16mm cartridges. The ability to accept additional microforms increases reader cost but enhances versatility which, in smaller libraries, may make the purchase of a second reader unnecessary.[25]

Although a multi-purpose reader may physically accept several different microforms, the reader magnification may not be appropriate to any or all of them. *Magnification* is a measure of the size of a given linear dimension of a displayed microimage itself. Magnification is expressed as 24X, 42X, 48X, and so on, where the displayed microimage is enlarged 24, 42, or 48 times. Alternatively, magnification—like reduction—can be expressed as a ratio—24:1, 42:1, 48:1, and so on.

Reader magnification must be appropriate to the reduction at which the microforms to be displayed were created. A document reduced 24X will be read at original size when magnified 24X. Full-size magnification is, however, rarely required. Microimages of good quality are often displayed at three-quarters of original size—a document reduced 24X is enlarged only 18X, for example. Three-quarter size readers are generally compact, requiring less desk space—an important consideration in many reference-type applications. When microimages contain small type faces or detailed graphics, higher magnifications—a 32X enlargement of a document reduced 24X, for example—may facilitate reading or close inspection of illustrations. At the Lehman College Library of the City University of New York where acquisitions librarians preferred an experimental microfiche edition of *Books in Print* to the original hard-copy version, the ability to overmagnify small type sizes was cited as an important advantage that minimized eye fatigue.[26] For library users with impaired sight, the Visualtek Microviewer (Fig. 6-3) features a specially-designed closed-circuit television camera to display microfiche images at magnifications of 200X to 650X. A split screen option allows users to simultaneously view microimages and note-taking.

Libraries with collections of microforms created at several different reductions may select a reader magnification near the middle of the reduction range. The reader recommended for use with the Microbook Library of American Civilization, for example, employs a 70X magnification to display book pages reduced 55X to 90X. This approach is effective in specially-designed systems involving microforms from a single source. But, when a library that can afford only one reader has microfiche, jackets, and aperture cards in a wide range of reductions, the fixed lens, single-magnification reader is obviously a poor choice. For such applications, the Realist Vantage microfiche reader described above features a series of interchangeable lenses, each with zoom capability over a range of magnifications from 10X to 125X. One such lens ranges from 18X to 25X and can be used to view aperture cards, NMA Type 1 Standard microfiche, and NMA Type 2 Standard microfiche. Other manufacturers offer drop-in lenses that are easily interchangeable or turret- or track-mounted, dual- or triple-magnification lenses.

*Case* size determines the amount of desk-space the reader will occupy. Reader *screen* size determines the amount of information that can be displayed at any one time. For source document microforms, typical desk-top full-size readers occupy the same area as an office typewriter and will display one letter-size page of information on a screen measuring approximately twelve (vertical) by nine (horizontal) inches. The letter-size screen is adequate for microimages of book pages or typewritten technical reports. Three-quarter size readers, as noted above,

**Figure 6-3**

**Microform Reader for Persons with Impaired Vision**
(Courtesy: Visualtek)

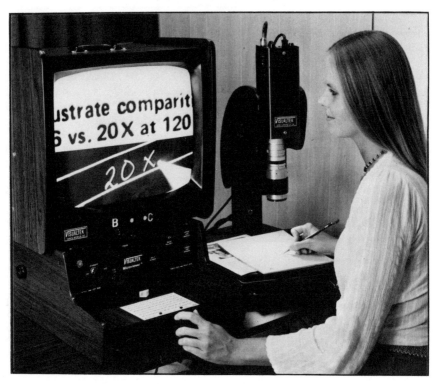

are more compact and will display the same page, at reduced size, on a smaller screen measuring perhaps nine by seven inches. Newspapers, charts, maps, and other oversize documents can be viewed in their entirety on a large-screen reader such as the Information Design Model 201 (Fig. 6-4). The large screen—in this case, measuring twenty-four by twenty-four inches—will also display two letter-size documents or book pages side by side.

Full-size COM reader screens measure approximately eleven by fourteen inches, with three-quarter size screens measuring approximately eight by eleven inches.[27] Unlike source document readers, which have vertical screen orientations, the long dimension of the COM reader screen is horizontal (Fig. 6-5, p. 152). COM readers are, consequently, slightly wider than their source document counterparts. Large-screen COM readers, while available, are seldom required. For the many COM applications, such as library catalogs and circulation lists, which are oriented toward lines rather than pages of information, the NCR model 4600-11 features a small

**Figure 6-4**
**Large-Screen Microform Reader**
(Courtesy: Information Design)

(2.6 by 12.5 inch) screen designed to display about twenty lines of data at 87 percent of original size. The reader measures 12.8 by 13.1 inches at its base and is only 11.8 inches high.

**Figure 6-5**

**COM Reader Showing Horizontal Screen**
(Courtesy: Realist, Inc.)

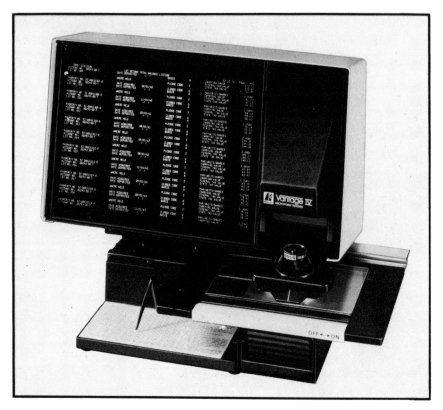

*Image rotation* is a highly desirable, and often essential, special feature that enables the user to turn displayed microimages to compensate for the varying positions of documents on film. While full 360° rotation is desirable, a minimum 90° rotation capability is required in applications utilizing both cine and comic mode roll microforms. While microfiche standards prescribe comic mode filming, technical reports often contain charts and other graphic presentations which, while filmed vertically, must be read horizontally. In the absence of image rotation, the user must turn the reader on its side—an awkward procedure that is not recommended.

*Image scanning* is a useful feature that permits the examination of the entire width of images displayed from roll microforms. Scanning allows the user to view portions of newspaper pages and other large or over-magnified documents that cannot be displayed fully within the confines of the reader screen.

To minimize microform handling and facilitate retrieval, several microfiche readers employ a double carrier that will accept two fiche or microfilm jackets simultaneously. This special feature is useful in reference-type applications where, for example, a 500-page circulation listing is reproduced on two 48X COM fiche and stored in the dual carrier, thereby eliminating the possibility that a user will have to change fiche to view a particular section of the list.

For applications requiring the display of microimages to several persons simultaneously, some microfilm readers can be converted to projectors by merely removing the screen.[28]

## Human Factors Considerations

Human factors is an interdisciplinary field that recognizes and emphasizes those elements that influence the effectiveness with which people can utilize equipment to accomplish the intended purpose of that equipment.[29] In a departure from their historic emphasis on technological innovation, micrographics equipment manufacturers and systems designers have become increasingly respectful of the significance of human factors analysis in minimizing or eliminating user resistance to microforms. While much basic work remains to be done, this section summarizes the most important human factors considerations in microform reader selection.[30]

The reader selected for library applications must minimize perceived discrepancies between microform and hard-copy presentations while reducing the amount of required accommodation to microform use. Kottenstette, following experiments in prolonged microform reading by undergraduate students, concluded that difficulties in maintaining focus and uneven screen illumination are serious reader defects which, left uncorrected, will quickly terminate microform use.[31] The microform user must be able to easily establish focus and maintain it from frame to frame. Uniform screen illumination is essential to user comfort. Even very small areas of obviously greater brightness are unacceptable. Because their light source is above the viewing surface, front projection readers typically provide fairly uniform screen illumination. Many newer rear projection readers, however, feature *high gain* screens with a powerful light source that appears much brighter at screen center. The resulting displayed images are well-suited to ambient light viewing but tend to be somewhat dark at the screen corners and may contain "hot spots," deficiencies of diffusion manifested in a halo effect. The best rear projection screens are carefully coated to diffuse light without revealing its source.[32]

The proposed revision to the *American National Standard Specification for Microfilm Readers for 16mm and 35mm Film on Reels* (New York: American National Standards Institute, 1967), submitted to members of the National Micrographics Association in draft in May 1976, recommends a minimum screen brightness of 32 foot-lamberts at the center and 10 foot-lamberts at the corners for readers to be used in ambient illumination of 50 foot-candles. Kottenstette found, however, that screen brightness preferences varied with user motivation. In studies at the Denver Research Institute, highly motivated users generally preferred higher screen illumination, while users with less pressing information needs or interests tended to prefer lower screen illumination.[33] Preferences of both groups can be satisfied by selecting a reader with variable lamp intensity. Users of positive microforms may especially prefer lower screen luminance.

The noise of the fan that dissipates reader heat can be a significant irritant in study-type applications requiring prolonged machine contact. Reader noise levels should not exceed sixty decibels above the threshold of hearing.[34] Several newer readers dissipate heat by natural convection and, having no fan, are completely silent.

Reader design must recognize the complex inter-relationship between work surface and screen display. Kottenstette found that students wearing eyeglasses or contact lenses in study-type applications could not comfortably glance from reader screen to note pad, since, in most cases, the full value of lens correction could not be obtained without tipping the head. Such students lost their place easily and could not successfully integrate the several tasks involved in study. Rear projection readers were used in the experiment.[35] Front projection readers, with their viewing surface at table-top level, preserve the customary spatial relationship between note pad and material under study, permitting both to be held in the same field of vision.

For prolonged reading, Kottenstette found that users prefer to vary their own and the reader's position. Some study-type applications may be best-served by a book-like portable reader that allows the user to assume various casual postures (Fig. 6-6). In a study of the impact of screen angle on microform reading, Lee and Buck found that, while users expressed a clear preference for tilted screens, their actual reading performance, measured in fewer eye fixations and regressions, definitely improved with a vertical screen.[36]

The need for user instruction is common to all equipment-dependent systems. In commercial applications and some special libraries, microform users constitute a closed group and can, consequently, be trained by co-workers or equipment vendors. In most public and academic libraries, however, microform readers are available to a broad user group, many of whom neither ask for, nor receive, instruction. Potential problems arising from this situation can be minimized, but not entirely eliminated, by placing step-by-step instructions, with diagrams, near the reader. Several newer readers have operating instructions permanently displayed on the reader case. Such printed instructions are most effective when accompanied by a personal demonstration that explains the reader's operating features.[37]

Operating controls should be clearly labelled and conveniently positioned near the lower front of the reader. Controls should be readily accessible by both right- and left-handed persons. Reader operation should be predictable. When the film advance knob is turned clockwise, for example, the film should move forward.

## Cost

Reader cost is more often a constraint than a selection parameter. Reader prices vary considerably and it is only possible to indicate cost ranges for various reader types. Microfiche readers are currently much less expensive than readers for roll microforms. Prices for high-quality, desk-top source document or COM fiche readers begin at slightly less than $200 and peak at around $400. The more expensive models generally feature larger screens, several lenses, and dual- or tab-size fiche carriers. The less expensive microfiche readers offer these features as extra cost options, if at all. Prices for portable microfiche readers begin at around $125.

**Figure 6-6**

**Portable Microform Reader**

(Courtesy: Library Resources, Inc.)

Prices for 16mm and 35mm reel microfilm readers begin at around $400 and peak at around $1,000. Again, higher-priced models include features such as larger screens, interchangeable magnifications, image rotation, motorized film advance, and, in some cases, an adapter for flat microforms.

Prices for self-threading cartridge and cassette readers range between $700 and $2,000. The number of available cartridge readers is, however, limited because most commercial cartridge applications require reader/printers.

## Information Sources and Selection Aids

Vendor literature is an important source of information about microform readers and related products. The *International Microfilm Source Book* (New Rochelle, N.Y.: Microfilm Publishing, Inc., 1972- ) contains an index that briefly identifies vendors, model numbers, and approximate prices for particular types of microform readers. Vendor addresses are given in a separate section. The *Source Book* is published annually.

Hubbard Ballou, ed., *Guide to Micrographic Equipment*, three volumes (Silver Spring, Md.: National Micrographics Association, 1975) is the sixth edition of a work first published in 1958. The first volume lists and describes available microform readers, giving vendor name and address, product specifications, and approximate price. Most entries include a photograph. Information is generally vendor-supplied or editorially-compiled from available product literature or other sources.

Two serial publications report the results of laboratory tests designed to evaluate the suitability of particular microform readers for library applications. *Library Technology Reports* (Chicago: American Library Association, Library Technology Program, 1965- ) has been involved in microform reader evaluation since its inception. Originally issued in loose-leaf form, LTR began publication as a paper bound bi-monthly journal in January 1976. Reader test reports are presented in selected issues. *The Sourcebook of Library Technology* is an edited cumulation, available only in microfiche, of reports issued from 1965 through 1975. While earlier reports emphasized readers for 35mm reel microfilm, much recent attention has been given to microfiche readers for source document and COM applications. Individual reports give detailed product descriptions and evaluate image quality, machine construction, and useability. Reports are currently being prepared for LTR by the R. A. Morgan Company, an optical engineering and reprographics consulting firm.

*Micrographics Equipment Review*, edited by William Saffady (Weston, Conn.: Microform Review, 1976- ) presents concise evaluations of microform readers considered to be potentially suitable for library applications. Evaluations are based on actual experience with equipment. Reports include vendor information, product specifications, and the editor's analysis, together with a photograph of the reader itself. MER is published quarterly with an annual five-part index that provides access to reports on particular readers by vendor name, model name, year of introduction, price, and function.

While *Library Technology Reports* and *Micrographics Equipment Review* emphasize reader performance in laboratory testing, *Auerbach Microform Reports* and *Input/Output Reports* (Philadelphia: Auerbach Publishers, 1972- ) analyze microform readers from the systems perspective. Reports, issued monthly in a loose-leaf format, include a product description, technical specifications, summaries of user experiences, comparison with competing products, and a price list. User experience summaries reflect a wide range of applications, including libraries. Reports on individual readers are preceded by an informative product class overview and summary specification charts that are updated periodically. Similar systems-oriented report services are offered by Datapro Research (Philadelphia, Pa.) and Alltech Publishing Company (Pennsauken, N.J.).

William R. Hawken, *Evaluating Microfiche Readers: A Handbook for Librarians* (Washington: Council on Library Resources, 1975) contains instructions and a packet of test microfiche designed to enable prospective purchasers to make an informed evaluation of reader resolution, magnification, evenness of illumination, and the appropriateness of screen size.

## READER/PRINTERS

### Purpose and Application

A reader/printer (Fig. 6-7) combines the function of a reader with the ability to make enlarged paper prints of displayed microimages. Reader/printers might be more accurately described as locator/printers since they are rarely used for prolonged reading. Several librarians report that the availability of reader/printers is essential in overcoming user resistance to microforms. This was the case, for example, at the Martland Hospital Library, where critical space problems necessitated conversion of periodical backfiles to 16mm microfilm cartridges.[38] When the Boulder Research Laboratories library first surveyed its scientific and technical personnel to determine the acceptability of DDC reports in microfiche, about half the respondents indicated acceptance, although most expressed reservations. When a second survey questionnaire, indicating that reader/printers would not be available, was distributed, respondent attitudes changed dramatically. The number of researchers considering microfiche a good medium dropped from eleven to one, while the number who considered fiche absolutely unacceptable rose from one to seven.[39]

### Printing Technology

Reader/printer evaluation and selection generally employs the criteria applicable to microform readers plus consideration of the suitability of the printing process. Special attention must be given to the quality, cost, and polarity of finished prints. There are five printing technologies in current use: dry silver, electrochemical, electrofax, xerographic, and stabilized silver.[40]

The *dry silver* process—used in the 3M 500 and 600 Series Reader/Printers— employs a specially-treated paper to expose and develop enlarged microimages using light and heat, without additional chemicals. The dry silver process is clean and convenient, requiring little operator attention. Printing speed is approximately ten seconds. Print quality is good for text and line drawings, fair for half-tones. When dry silver paper is ordered in sufficient quantities, unit costs approach five cents per

**Figure 6-7**

**Microfiche Reader/Printer** (Courtesy: Eastman Kodak Company)

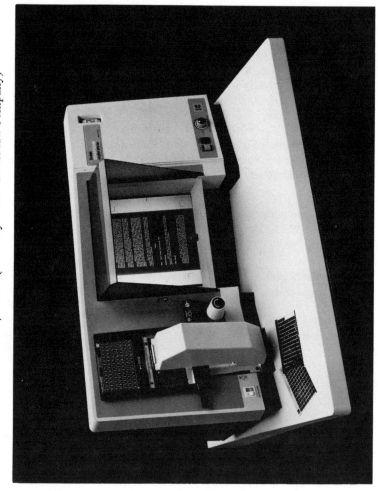

letter-size print. Equipment purchase prices begin at about $1,500 for a microfiche model, $2,000 for a reel microfilm model, and $2,500 for a cartridge model. Developed dry silver prints retain light sensitivity and are subject to fading. Print permanence, however, is rarely a user requirement. It is important to note that the dry silver process is a polarity-reversing process and will make negative prints from positive microimages. Since users prefer positive-appearing prints, the dry silver process is best-suited to negative microform collections.

The *electrochemical* process—used in the 3M 400 Series Reader/Printers—employs an electric current to create a latent image on chemically-treated paper. Development requires a liquid activator. The process is polarity-reversing. Prints are not permanent. Print speed is approximately ten seconds. Print quality is adequate for most applications. Equipment prices are generally lower than those for dry silver reader/printers, ranging from $1,000 to $2,000, depending on microforms accepted. Paper and chemicals cost about ten cents per letter-size print. Chemicals must be replenished and the machine cleaned regularly.

The *electrofax* and *xerographic* print processes are both variants of the electrostatic technology that dominates the office copier industry.[41] In the electrofax process, light transmitted through a microimage and lens forms a latent enlargement on charged photoreceptive paper coated with zinc oxide in a resin binder. The latent image is developed through the application of an oppositely-charged toner, consisting of fine carbon particles in liquid suspension. Developed prints are delivered dry and are as permanent as the paper on which they are made. Print speed is approximately ten to fifteen seconds. Print quality is good for text and line drawings, fair for half-tones. Equipment and supply costs are competitive with the dry silver process. Although the electrofax process is normally polarity-maintaining, most manufacturers modify their equipment to make positive-appearing prints from either positive or negative microimages.

In the *xerographic* process, light transmitted through a microimage and lens forms a latent enlargement on a charged photoreceptive intermediate surface such as a selenium drum. An oppositely-charged toner is applied to the drum, developing the image which is then transferred to plain paper and fused with heat. Prints are as permanent as the paper on which they are made. The Xerox Microprinter, the xerographic reader/printer most often used by libraries, is similar to the Xerox 720 copier, a first-generation plain paper copier with a print speed of twenty seconds. Xerographic print quality is good for text and line drawings, poor for half-tones. Acceptance is facilitated by the use of plain paper. Xerographic equipment is generally rented on a metered plan that charges for prints as they are made, with a minimum monthly charge for low-volume users. Paper and chemical costs are not included in meter charges, but rarely exceed two cents per letter-size print. The xerographic process is normally polarity-maintaining, although the Xerox Micro-printer will make positive-appearing prints from either positive or negative microforms.

The *stabilized silver* process is a variant of conventional silver halide photography that shortens development time by rendering undeveloped silver grains inert rather than dissolving and removing them from the print. Print speed is approximately thirty seconds. Because print quality is excellent for both line copy and half-tones, the stabilized silver process is preferred for the enlargement of maps, engineering drawings, photographs, and other documents containing fine detail. Equipment prices begin at around $5,000. Paper and chemicals for a letter-size print cost approximately 25 cents. Because undeveloped silver grains remain on the print, stabilized silver images will fade in time. The process is invariably polarity-reversing.

A few additional points for evaluation are worth noting. Reader/printers, unlike most readers, require regular inspection and preventative maintenance by the manufacturer. The price of a maintenance contract must be included in the cost of a total operating system. Service response time should also be determined. Some reader/printers allow the user to mask off areas of the displayed image prior to printing, thereby reducing print size and cost. For self-service library applications, some reader/printers can be equipped with a coin-operation attachment.

## Enlarger/Printers

Enlarger/printers are designed for automatic, high-speed single or multiple copy production of enlarged prints from microimages. Unlike reader/printers, enlarger/printers do not generally have a screen to display microimages prior to printing. The earliest enlarger/printer, the Xerox Copyflo, was designed to sequentially print enlarged images from reel microfilm onto a continuous web of plain paper which could be subsequently cut into individual pages. Although Xerox no longer manufactures the Copyflo, it remains in wide service bureau use.

The Xerox 970 is designed for the high-speed sequential enlargement of microfiche images onto letter-size plain paper. The Xerox 970 accepts 24X microfiche in the ninety-eight page NMA format. A programmable keyboard facilitates printing of selected frames. The unit, developed in prototype for report dissemination at the National Technical Information Service,[42] closely resembles the Xerox 3600 duplicator. Rated speed is 3,300 prints per hour.

Other enlarger/printers are designed for the high-speed reproduction of engineering drawings from aperture cards.[43]

## THE USE ENVIRONMENT

### The Microform Reading Room

Even when the best available microform equipment is provided, users cannot function effectively in a poorly-designed work environment. Libraries have long been notorious for relegating microforms and microform equipment to the most unattractive building areas. In a 1953 user survey, most of the 496 respondents in 76 academic libraries rated their microform facilities substandard. Not surprisingly, user attitudes toward microforms were most positive in the three libraries claiming excellent facilities.[44] Unfortunately, conditions have improved relatively little in the last quarter century. In a 1969 study sponsored by the Association for Research Libraries, interviews with eighty-nine librarians and faculty in 75 academic institutions revealed that one-half recognized their microform facilities as unacceptable. In several cases, readers were located in remote stack areas where staff assistance was unavailable to users. Where separate microform areas were established, ambient light often remained uncontrolled.[45] In a 1975 user survey at the State Library of Pennsylvania, the unattractive work environment was the most frequently-cited reason for disliking microforms. Readers there are closely confined and aligned in a single row. The microform room itself is brightly lit.[46]

In a 1976 report based on a number of site visits funded by the Council on Library Resources, Spreitzer concluded that problems of user resistance stem primarily from "a general ignorance of applied micrographics in libraries and the low position given microform users on the scale of library priorities."[47] He suggests that, rather than waiting for breakthroughs in equipment design, libraries could immediately improve their microform use environment by applying what is already known and available. The most successful library microform reading rooms, described in his report, combine a well-designed physical environment with an appropriate amount of knowledgeable professional assistance.

Integration of microform equipment cannot be achieved by merely placing a reader on a table. Careful attention to work station design is essential for comfortable prolonged study with microforms. At the Martland Hospital Library, for example, readers and reader/printers are enclosed in attractive carrel-type cubicles obtained from an open-plan office furnishings designer.[48] At the New York University Library, two-station carrels were specially designed for microform users. Each carrel is equipped with a motorized platform that permits adjustments in reader height and angle; a shelf for microform containers; a desk surface for note-taking; and a small reading lamp.[49] The LMM Superior Microfilm Reader (Fig. 6-8) is an integrated carrel-type reader/work station that projects 16mm or 35mm microimages onto a 22.25 by 24.25 inch viewing surface. A microfiche model is also available. In both cases, the projection surface is slightly tilted and can be viewed from wide angles. Both models feature an attractive walnut exterior.

Performance in difficult visual tasks, such as studying with microforms, may be favorably or adversely affected by the amount and quality of available illumination.[50] At improper levels, ambient light hinders microform use. For library microform reading rooms, Holmes recommended indirect and reflected lighting of fifteen to twenty foot-candles at the work surface.[51] Experiments by Lee and Buck, however, indicate that work performance remains insensitive to ambient light variations in the range ten to thirty foot-candles.[52] Kottenstette and Dailey reported varied user illumination preferences for prolonged study. Forty-eight percent of their subjects preferred all lights off. Forty-one percent preferred only carrel lights on. Seven percent preferred only room lights on, while four percent preferred room and carrel lights on.[53] These variations argue for work areas with locally adjustable lighting.

The relationship of lighting in a work area to illumination in its immediate and general surroundings has been the subject of several recent studies. Prolonged use of microform readers, cathode-ray-tube terminals, and other high-contrast screen displays may lead to *discomfort glare*, a form of subjective fatigue resulting from large differences in luminance between the screen and its surroundings. At a large Swedish bank, where workers using negative microforms for long periods complained of eye irritation, examination of the work area revealed luminance differences as great as 500 to 1. The recommended luminance ratio is 3 to 1 between the screen and its immediate surroundings, with an additional 3 to 1 between the immediate and general surroundings.[54] Luminance differences are easiest to control in microform reading rooms without windows. Where windows are unavoidable, users should not face them. Curtains or blinds are recommended to lower the general level of illumination and control reflection.

**Figure 6-8**

**Carrel-Type Microform Reader**

(Courtesy: Library Microfilms and Materials Company)

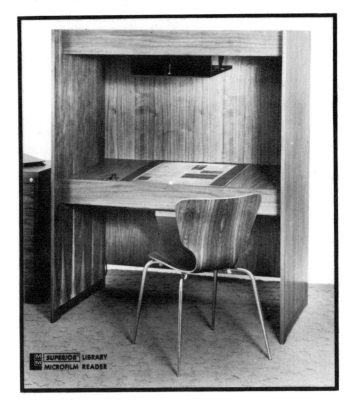

### The Librarian's Role

In addition to furnishings and lighting, consideration of the use environment extends to the level and quality of available user assistance. The librarian's own attitude toward microform use is crucial to the design of a successful work environment. Kottenstette and Dailey indicate the importance of initial impressions in prolonged microform use and stress the necessity of positive attitude-formation during the orientation period. At Hughes Aircraft Company, where a microform union catalog has served twelve technical libraries since 1963, librarians attribute good acceptance to a vigorous and positive user education program.[55] It is especially important that librarians responsible for microform collections not transmit their own negative attitudes to patrons. Library administrators must recognize the management of the microform reading room as a task requiring special professional training.[56] Librarians who understand the advantages and disadvantages of microforms will be able to deal more effectively and realistically with users.

# REFERENCES

[1] Robert J. Greene, "Microform Attitude and Frequency of Microform Use," *Journal of Micrographics* 8 (1975): 131-34.

[2] H. S. Bartley, *Fatigue, Mechanism and Management* (Springfield, Ill.: Charles C. Thomas, 1965).

[3] Susan K. Nutter, "Microforms and the User: Key Variables of User Acceptance in a Library Environment," *Drexel Library Quarterly* 11 (1975): 17-31.

[4] Catherine B. Harmon and George H. Harmon, *Microfilm in the Classroom: The Barrington School Project* (Silver Spring, Md.: National Microfilm Association, 1971); C. B. Harmon, "Microfilm in the Classroom," *Proceedings of the National Microfilm Association* (Silver Spring, Md.: NMA, 1971), II-25-27; George Harmon, "Is Microfilm Ready for Classroom Use?," *Journal of Micrographics* 5 (1972): 257-60; Robert F. Jennings and Hathia Hayes, "The Use of Microfiche Copies of Children's Trade Books in Selected Fourth Grade Classrooms," *Microform Review* 3 (1974): 189-93.

[5] John Willemse, "Microfiche as a Means of Providing Students with Literature," *Microform Review* 3 (1974): 26-29.

[6] Ralph W. Lewis, "User's Reactions to Microfiche: A Preliminary Study," *College and Research Libraries* 31 (1970): 260-68.

[7] See, for example, C. W. Christ, Jr., "Microfiche: A Study of User Attitudes and Reading Habits," *Journal of the American Society for Information Science* 23 (1972): 30-35.

[8] C. C. Parker, "The Use of External Current Awareness Services at Southampton University," *Aslib Proceedings* 25 (1973): 4-17.

[9] John Rader Platt, "Where Will the Books Go?," *Horizon* 5 (1962): 42-47.

[10] Harold Wooster, *Microfiche 1969—A User Study* (Washington: Committee on Scientific and Technical Information, 1969); Wooster, "Towards a Uniform Federal Report Numbering System and a Cuddly Microfiche Reader—Two Modest Proposals," *NMA Journal* 2 (1968): 63-67.

[11] Hans Weber, "The Librarian's View of Microforms," *IEEE Transactions on Professional Communications* PC-18 (1975): 168-73.

[12] Leonard Charmichael and Walter F. Dearborn, *Reading and Visual Fatigue* (Westport, Conn.: Greenwood Press, 1947), especially pp. 326-27.

[13] James Kottenstette, *An Investigation of the Characteristics of Ultrafiche and Its Application to Colleges and Universities* (Washington: Office of Education, Bureau of Research, August 31, 1969). See also, Kottenstette, et al., *A Guide to Instructional Uses of Microforms* (Denver: Denver Research Institute, May 1971); Robert Grausnick, Anita S. West, and James P. Kottenstette, *Microform Use in a Technical Training Environment* (Denver: Denver Research Institute, May 1971); Kottenstette, "User Behavior: Requirements," in *Microform Utilization: The Academic Library Environment* (Denver: University of Denver, 1970), pp. 158-66.

[14] T. S. Baldwin and L. J. Bailey, "Readability of Technical Training Materials Presented on Microfiche versus Offset Copy," *Journal of Applied Psychology* 55 (1971): 37-41.

[15] Robert P. Grausnick and James P. Kottenstette, *A Performance Evaluation: Microfiche vs Hardcopy* (Denver: Denver Research Institute, May 1971).

[16] G. W. W. Stevens, "Presidential Note," *Microdoc* 10 (1971): 99-101, suggests that microforms must be of especially high quality for materials in foreign languages, texts containing formulas or diagrams requiring close inspection, and other difficult materials that tax the user's faculties.

[17] Kottenstette, *An Investigation of the Characteristics of Ultrafiche . . .* , p. F-3.

[18] B. H. Weil, et al., "Esso Research Experience with Chemical Abstracts on Microfilm," *Journal of Chemical Documentation* 5 (1965): 193-200; Ann M. De Villiers and Barbara Frick Schloman, "Experiences with Scientific Journals on Microfilm in an Academic Reading Room," *Special Libraries* 64 (1973): 555-60.

[19] On the importance of the reader in user resistance to microforms, see P. R. P. Claridge, "Microfiching of Periodicals from the User's Point of View," *Aslib Proceedings* 21 (1969): 306-311. At the Warren Springs Laboratory, Herts, England, user resistance was anticipated and minimized by allowing scientists to vote on reader selection.

[20] *American National Standard Specification for Microfilm Readers for 16mm and 35mm Film on Reels* (New York: American National Standards Institute, 1967) and the proposed National Micrographics Association revision described in a subsequent section of this chapter; W. J. Barrett, "The Evaluation of Microfilm Readers," *Journal of Micrographics* 6 (1972): 51-63; G. Miles Conrad, "User Needs in a Microfacsimile Reader," *American Documentation* 2 (1951): 201-204; Gordon Wright, "Effective Reader Design," in *Microform Utilization: The Academic Library Environment*, pp. 148-57; George Tate, *Microform Readers—the Librarian's Dilemma* (Provo: Graduate Department of Library and Information Science, Brigham Young University, August 1972); Alonzo Sherman, "How to Select a Microfilm Reader or Reader-Printer," *Information and Records Management* 6 (April 1972): 62-64; David C. Weber, "Specifications for a Superior Microtext Reading Machine," *Microdoc* 5 (1966): 4-9; L. E. Walkup, et al., "The Design of Improved Microimage Readers for Promoting the Utilization of Microimages," *Proceedings of the National Microfilm Association* (Annapolis, Md.: NMA, 1962), pp. 283-310; Charles G. LaHood, Jr., "Selecting and Evaluating Microform Reading Equipment for Libraries," *Microform Review* 6 (1977): 79; Roger C. Miller, "Why Don't They Make Microform Machines for Libraries," *Microform Review* 2 (1973): 91-92; Lester O. Kruger, "Why 'They' Don't Make Microform Machines for Libraries," *South African Libraries* 43 (July 1975): 25-26.

[21] See the discussion in "Microform Readers for Libraries," *Library Technology Reports* (Nov. 1973).

[22] J. M. Judisch, "The Effect of Positive-Negative Microforms and Front-Rear Projection on Reading Speed and Comprehension," *NMA Journal* 2 (1968): 58-61.

[23] W. J. Barrett, "Microfilming Drawings and Plans," *Reprographics Quarterly* 7 (1974): 13-18.

[24] Francis Spreitzer, "Microfilm Cartridges and Cassettes," *Library Technology Reports* (May 1972) reports scratches, abrasions, and other film damage resulting from motorized cartridge transports.

[25] Harry Milligan, "Microfilm Apparatus Design Philosophy: Some Thoughts Provoked by an Exhibition," *Microdoc* 8 (1969): 11-14, suggests that European/ Japanese readers tend to be expensive, multi-purpose devices, while Anglo/ American readers tend to be modestly-priced single-function units.

[26] Harold B. Schleifer and Peggy A. Adams, "Books in Print on Microfiche: A Pilot Test," *Microform Review* 5 (1976): 10-24.

[27] Dick Enders, "COM Viewers—a Generalized Overview of Their History, Growth, and Future Direction," *Proceedings of the National Micrographics Association* (Silver Spring, Md.: NMA, 1975), pp. 165-69.

[28] On possible uses of microform readers in audiovisual presentations, see Col. Leonard S. Lee, " . . . Speak Softly But Carry a Big Fiche," *Journal of Micrographics* 7 (1974): 185-87; J. Francis Reintjes, J. O. Silvey, and S. G. Kuyamjian, "A High-Magnification, Reflective-Screen Microfiche Viewer," Ibid. 5 (1972): 117-24.

[29] For a survey of the field, see David Meister, *Human Factors: Theory and Practice* (New York: Wiley Interscience, 1971).

[30] Robert M. Landau, "Microfiche Reader Human Factors," *Journal of Micrographics* 10 (1977): 219-27.

[31] James P. Kottenstette, "Testing Student Reactions to Educational Microforms: Many Problems—A Few Answers," *Journal of Micrographics* 4 (1971): 73-78.

[32] William H. Collins, "Recent Developments in Rear Projection Screens," *Journal of Micrographics* 4 (1971): 201-207; J. T. Miller, "The Final Interface—the Readability Factor," in Don Chevert (ed.), *Micrographics Science '73: Winter Symposium* (Washington: Society of Photographic Scientists and Engineers, 1973), pp. 84-92.

[33] James P. Kottenstette and K. Anne Dailey, *An Investigation of the Environment for Educational Microform Use* (Denver: Denver Research Institute, April 1971).

[34] *Proposed Revision to American National Standard: Microfilm Readers* (Silver Spring, Md.: National Micrographics Association, May 1976).

[35] Kottenstette and Dailey, *An Investigation of the Environment . . .*

[36] David R. Lee and James R. Buck, "The Effect of Screen Angle and Luminance on Microform Reading," *Human Factors* 17 (1975): 461-69.

[37] Carl Spaulding, "Teaching the Use of Microfilm Readers," *Microform Review* 6 (1977): 80-81.

[38] Esther R. Meirboom, "Conversion of the Periodical Collection in a Teaching Hospital Library to Microfilm Format," *Bulletin of the Medical Library Association* 64 (1976): 36-40.

[39] Lewis, Ralph W. "User's Reactions to Microfiche: A Preliminary Study," *College and Research Libraries* 31 (1970): 260-68.

[40] For a description of print process technologies, see William R. Hawken, *Copying Methods Manual* (Chicago: Library Technology Program, American Library Association, 1966).

[41] William Saffady, "New Developments in Electrostatic Copiers," *American Archivist* 38 (1975): 67-75.

[42] David Farber, "Electrostatic Enlarger Aids NTIS in Dissemination of Information," *Journal of Micrographics* 7 (1973): 31-34.

[43] See, for example, Anthony Arbore, "Microfilm Speeds Print Capability," *Journal of Micrographics* 7 (1974): 155-56.

[44] W. G. Harkins, F. L. Demock, and M. E. Hanson, "Microfilm in University Libraries: A Report," *College and Research Libraries* 14 (1953): 307-316.

[45] Donald C. Holmes, *Determination of User Needs and Future Requirements for a Systems Approach to Microfilm Technology* (Washington: Office of Education, Bureau of Research, July 1969).

[46] Mary Jane Edwards, "Microforms: A View from the State Library of Pennsylvania," *Journal of Micrographics* 8 (1975): 245-50.

[47] Francis Spreitzer, "Library Microform Facilities," *Library Technology Reports* 12 (1976): 407-436.

[48] Meirboom, "Conversion of the Periodical Collection in a Teaching Hospital Library to Microfilm Format," *Bulletin of the Medical Library Association* 64 (1976): 36-40.

[49] Arthur C. Tannenbaum, "Human Engineering Factors Help Determine Microform Use in the Research Library," *Proceedings of the American Society for Information Science* (Washington: ASIS, 1975), pp. 97-98; Judy Fair, "The Microtext Reading Room: A Practical Approach," *Microform Review* 1 (1972): 199-203, 269-73; Ibid. 2 (1973): 9-13; David C. Weber, "Design for a Micro-Text Reading Room," *UNESCO Bulletin for Libraries* 20 (1966): 313-18.

[50] Terence W. Faulkner and Thomas J. Murphy, "Lighting for Difficult Visual Tasks," *Human Factors* 15 (1973): 149-62.

[51] Donald C. Holmes, *Determination of the Environmental Conditions Required in a Library for the Effective Utilization of Microforms* (Washington: Office of Education, Bureau of Research, Nov. 1970).

[52] David R. Lee and James R. Buck, "The Effect of Screen Angle and Luminance on Microform Reading," *Human Factors* 17 (1975): 461-69.

[53] James P. Kottenstette and K. Anne Dailey, *An Investigation of the Environment for Educational Microform Utilization: Phase II, "Student Use of Classroom Microform in Support of a Content Course"* (Denver: Denver Research Institute, April 1971).

[54] G. V. Hultgren and B. Knave, "Discomfort Glare and Disturbance from Light Reflections in an Office Landscape with CRT Display Terminals," *Applied Ergonomics* 5 (1974): 2-8; Hultgren, Knave, and Maud Werner, "Eye Discomfort When Reading Microfilm in Different Enlargers," *Applied Ergonomics* 5 (1974): 194-200; William B. Knowles and J. W. Wulfeck, "Visual Performance with High

Contrast Cathode-Ray-Tubes at High Levels of Ambient Illumination," *Human Factors* 14 (1972): 521-32.

[55] Clara A. Falk, B. W. Campbell, and Masse Bloomfield, "A Microfilm Catalog at Work," *Special Libraries* 67 (1976): 316-18.

[56] C. Edward Carroll, "Some Problems of Microform Utilization in Large University Collections," *Microform Review* 1 (1972): 19-24, complains that library schools have neglected micrographics education, thereby making it difficult for library administrators to find professionals capable of managing microform collections. On the status of micrographics education, see William Saffady, "Teaching Reprography," *Journal of Education for Librarianship* 15 (1975): 147-60; H. W. Axford, "Courses in Reprography Offered in Graduate Library Schools," *Library Resources and Technical Services* 17 (1973): 246-50; R. E. Stevens, "Instruction on Microform: Its Place in Library School," *Journal of Education for Librarianship* 6 (1965): 133-36; Andrew G. Torok (comp.), *Micrographics Education for Librarians* (Washington, D.C.: Library of Congress, 1977).

# CHAPTER 7

## BIBLIOGRAPHIC CONTROL OF MICROFORMS

### LEVELS OF BIBLIOGRAPHIC CONTROL

In addition to difficulties with equipment and the work environment, Kottenstette cites inadequate bibliographic control as a significant deterrent to microform acceptance and use.[1] As with conventional printed publications, an effective system of bibliographic control must indicate the availability and location of library materials in microform at three levels:

1.  *National* and *international* bibliographic controls, such as trade bibliographies and library catalogs, provide essential information about the existence of a given item in microform, whether it is in the holdings of a library or available for sale from an institutional or commercial micropublisher.

2.  *Local* bibliographic controls, such as card catalog entries and printed guides, provide potential users with information about the availability, nature, and location of microforms in a library's own holdings.

3.  *Internal* bibliographic controls, such as bibliographic targets and microfiche heading areas, are a part of the microform itself and identify it when it is removed from its storage cabinet or other container.

The bibliographic control of microforms, long a concern of librarians,[2] has been the subject of three studies funded by the Association for Research Libraries: the first by Simonton in 1962,[3] the second by Holmes in 1969,[4] and the most recent by Reichman and Tharpe in 1971.[5] These studies repeatedly found bibliographic controls for microforms inadequate at all levels. Although the bibliographic control of microforms remains far from ideal, a number of significant advances have been made since 1970, primarily at the national level. This chapter summarizes the present state of bibliographic control, emphasizing new bibliographic products and techniques.

## NATIONAL AND INTERNATIONAL CONTROLS

### Library Catalogs and Union Lists

As in the case of printed monographs and serials, the acquisition and inter-library loan of microforms are heavily dependent on the printed catalogs of national and other large research libraries.[6] In the United States, the Library of Congress assumed leadership in national bibliographic control with the publication of the first edition of *Newspapers on Microfilm* in 1948 and the establishment of a clearinghouse for reports of microfilming projects in 1949.[7] Today, four Library of Congress printed catalogs facilitate the identification and location of microforms made from various types of original materials.

The *National Register of Microform Masters*, published since 1965, is a main-entry catalog of master microforms created by both commercial and institutional micropublishers and reported on a voluntary basis.[8] The *Register* defines a master microform as one maintained *solely* for the purpose of creating duplicates. Microforms intended for use in display or retrieval equipment are specifically excluded. By listing works for which microform masters already exist, the *Register* helps to minimize needless duplication of effort and, while not intended as a for-sale listing, provides important information about the location of microform masters to prospective purchasers of duplicates. It should be noted, however, that inclusion in the *Register* does not necessarily indicate availability for sale, since reproduction may, in some cases, be prohibited by copyright law or local regulations.

Information provided for items reported in the *Register* (Fig. 7-1) includes the complete main entry, established according to Library of Congress practice; a condensed title with imprint and collation statement; the Library of Congress card number (when available); and an abbreviation indicating the location, type, and polarity of the microform master. The abbreviation *DLCm\**, for example, denotes a negative microfilm master held by the Library of Congress. A key to abbreviations appears in the front of each volume. In some cases, a series number follows the abbreviation as an aid in ordering. The *Register* reports master microforms of foreign and domestic books, pamphlets, serials, and foreign doctoral dissertations. Newspapers, technical reports, typescript translations, archives, manuscripts, American doctoral dissertations, and master's theses are excluded. Published annually, the *Register* is non-cumulative, although the 1969 edition cumulated reports of serial publications from previous issues. Libraries subscribing to the *National Union Catalog* receive the *Register* at no additional charge. It is also available as a separate purchase from the Library of Congress Card Division.

Microform masters of newspapers—specifically excluded from the *Register*— are reported in *Newspapers in Microform: United States, 1948-72* and *Newspapers in Microform: Foreign Countries, 1948-72*, both available from the LC Card Division with their respective supplements. Information in each entry includes the title, inclusive dates of publication, language, type of microform, location, and extent of holdings. As with the *Register*, reports are submitted voluntarily. It is important to note that the titles of these two publications reflect the dates when reports of available microform masters were received by the Library of Congress, not the dates of the newspaper files themselves.

## Figure 7-1

### National Register of Microform Masters

Sacro Bosco, Joannes de, fl. 1230.  Anglici uiri
clarissimi Spera mundi feliciter incipit.  [Venice,
Heilbronn, 1478]
GmC m

Sacro Bosco, Joannes de, fl. 1230.  Opus sphaeri-
cum commentis Ciechi Esculani, Francisci Capuani
et Jac. Fabri Stapulensis.  Venice, Beuilaqua,
1499.  [86] l.
MoSU m

Sacro Bosco, Joannes de, fl. 1230.  Opusculi de
Sphaera clarissimi philosophi Ioannis de Sacro
Busto.  [Viennae Pannoniae, 1518]
GmC m

Sacro Bosco, Joannes de, fl. 1230.  Sphaera
Ioannis de Sacrobosco emendata. Eliae Vineti
Santonis scholia in eandem sphaeram...  Colomiae,
Cholinum.  (1594)  [210] p.
GmC m

Sacro Bosco, Joannes de, fl. 1230.  Textus de
Sphera Johannis de Sacrobosco cum additione...
[Parisii, 1507]  63 p.
GmC m

Sacy, S.    Mémoire sur une correspondance inédite
de Temerlan avec Charles VI.  In Mémoires de
l'Académie des Inscriptions.  v.6, 1822.  pp.
470-522.
IDC mf

---

Sadler, Michael Thomas, 1780-1835.  Factory
statistics...  London, 1836.    80 p.
ResP m

Sadler, Michael Thomas, 1780-1835.  A first
letter to a reformer in reply to a pamphlet lately
published by Walter Fawkes, entitled The English-
man's manual.  London, 1817.  108 p.
ResP m

Sadler, Michael Thomas, 1780-1835.  Ireland;
its evils, and their remedies...  2d ed.  London,
Murray, 1829.  lvii, 464 p.
ResP m

Sadler, Michael Thomas, 1780-1835.  Protest
against the secret proceedings of the Factory
commission, in Leeds...  Leeds, Bingley, 1833.
16 p.
ResP m

Sadler, Michael Thomas, 1780-1835.  Reply to the
letters of John Elliot Drinkwater, esquire, and
Alfred Power, esquire, factory commissioners...
Leeds, Bingley, 1833.  23 p.
ResP m

Sadler, Michael Thomas, 1780-1835.  Speech
in the House of commons, March 16, 1832, on
moving the second reading of the Factories'
regulation bill.  3d ed.  London, Seeley, 1832.
46 p.
ResP m

---

Sämmtliche Compositionen
see Schubert, Franz Peter, 1797-1828.  Songs.
Selections.  Wolfenbüttel, Holle [185-?]

Sänger, Max.  Der Kaiserschnitt bei Uterusfi-
bromen...  Leipzig, Engelmann, 1882.
DNLM m*

Sáenz, Dalmire A    Vida sexual de Robinson
Crusoe.  [Buenos Aires, L.H. [1969]  48 p.
NN mf*    79-427440

Sáenz, José María Restrepo
see Restrepo Sáenz, José María.

Sáenz, Moisés, 1888-    Sobre el indio
ecuatoriano y su incorporación al medio nacional.
México, 1933.    vii-xvi, 195 p.    33-19444
DLC m*

Sáenz Páez, Mary Elizabeth.  La escritora
mexicana María Enriqueta.  México, 1964.
144 p.    65-42092
ICU m*

Särskilt votum
see under Sundblad, Johan, d. 1774.

Locations of microform masters and use-copies of archives and manuscripts are reported to the *National Union Catalog of Manuscript Collections* (1962- ) which, like the *Register*, accompanies subscriptions to the NUC. Locations of microform copies of monographs available for use by library patrons are reported in the NUC itself. The NUC provides the full bibliographic information for items listed in briefer form in the *National Register of Microform Masters*.

In addition to these Library of Congress printed catalogs, information about the microform holdings of American libraries can be obtained from union lists published by various cooperating institutions. *Major Microforms in the Five Associated University Libraries*, compiled and edited by Marcia Jebb (Syracuse, N.Y.: Five Associated University Libraries, 1973), is a selective union list of major series, government publications, and manuscript materials available at Cornell, Rochester, SUNY/Binghamton, SUNY/Buffalo, and Syracuse. In addition to basic bibliographic information, individual entries indicate the type of microform, series scope, location, and the availability of printed guides, internal finding aids, or reviews. For microforms made from archives or manuscripts, reference is provided to the complete entry in the *National Union Catalog of Manuscript Collections*.

*A Union List of Selected Microforms in Libraries in the New York Metropolitan Area*, edited by Morita L. Frederick (New York: Metropolitan Reference and Research Agency, 1976), contains 685 entries from the holdings of 72 libraries. The content of individual entries includes bibliographic information, and descriptive notes, together with an indication of the type of microform, location, and availability of printed guides or internal finding aids. A unique feature of this list is an index to entries by Library of Congress subject headings.

Similar lists, useful in resource sharing, include *A Union List of Microform Holdings in Ohio-Assisted Universities*, edited by Irene Schubert and Alice Weaver (Toledo: University of Toledo Libraries, 1972); *A Union List of Selected Microforms in Washington, D.C. Area Libraries* (Washington: Special Libraries Association, Washington, D.C. Chapter, 1974); *Union List of Microform Sets in O.C.U.L. Libraries*, edited by Anni Leibl and Jean S. Yolton (Toronto: Ontario Council of University Libraries, 1971); *Major Microform Holdings of ASERL Members* (New Orleans: Association of Southern Research Libraries, 1965); and *Union List of Southwestern Materials on Microfilm in New Mexico Libraries* (Albuquerque: University of New Mexico, 1957). The older *Union List of Microfilms* and its several supplements and revisions, begun in 1941 by the Philadelphia Bibliographic Center, ended with a final cumulation for the period 1949-1959 that is now primarily of historical interest,[9] as is the *Guide to Photocopied Historical Materials in the United States and Canada*, edited by Richard W. Hale, Jr. (Ithaca, N.Y.: Cornell University Press, 1961).

Librarians attempting to determine the availability and location of microforms in libraries outside of North America will experience considerable difficulty. Reichmann and Tharpe report that, as of 1971, few European, Asian, or African libraries had prepared national or regional union lists. There has been little improvement in the ensuing half-decade, even in Western European countries with advanced bibliographic controls for printed materials and well-developed microfilming facilities. Microforms, for example, are omitted from the *Bibliographie de la France* and, by definition, from the British Museum's *Catalog of Printed Books*. *South African Newspapers Available in Microform* (Pretoria: State Library, 1975), however, is a significant exception that lists the locations of master microforms made from over 150 newspapers. In addition to bibliographic information, entries include an indication of type of microform, price, and an historical description of the publication—a feature which distinguishes the South African list from the Library of Congress publication *Newspapers in Microform: Foreign Countries, 1948-72* which contains most of the same titles.

## TRADE BIBLIOGRAPHIES AND DIRECTORIES

As with printed materials, trade bibliographies are an important source of information about microforms available for sale. *The Guide to Microforms in Print* (Weston, Conn.: Microform Review, 1976- ; published by Microcard Editions, 1961-1975) is an annual cumulative alphabetical listing of books, journals, and other materials available from commercial and institutional micropublishers. Through 1976, coverage was limited to United States micropublishers. In 1977, the *Guide* incorporated *International Microforms in Print: A Guide to Microforms of Non-United States Micropublishers* (Weston, Conn.: Microform Review, 1974-1976). Entry is under author for books, title for journals, state and city for newspapers, and publishing organization for archives and manuscripts. Large microform sets consisting of titles from established bibliographies are entered under the name of the compiler of the bibliography. In addition to basic bibliographic information, such as publisher and date, entries indicate the type of microform and price. Information in the *Guide* is solicited from the micropublishers themselves.

The *Subject Guide to Microforms in Print* (Weston, Conn.: Microform Review, 1976- ), a companion volume, is an annual publication containing entries from the *Guide* arranged alphabetically under broad subject headings.

The *Microform Market Place: An International Directory of Micropublishing* (Weston, Conn.: Microform Review, 1976- ) provides, among other things, a very useful list of micropublishers, defined as any organization which markets micropublished information. This broad definition encompasses both commercial and institutional micropublishers but excludes service bureaus specializing in the micropublishing of proprietary information, such as parts catalogs, and publishers of periodicals sold in microform by other companies. Individual entries, arranged alphabetically by publisher name, indicate address, phone number, types of micropublications available, and the name and title of a responsible person within the organization. Other sections of the directory group micropublishers geographically and by broad subject specialty; report industry mergers, acquisitions, and name changes; and list reprographic centers, microform jobbers, and organizations with an interest in the educational aspects of microform use in libraries. An annotated bibliography is included.

A current and complete file of micropublishers' catalogs is an indispensible tool for librarians responsible for collection development in microform. Unfortunately, the maintenance of such a catalog file—while simplified by directories of micropublishers' addresses—remains a time-consuming task. The *Micropublisher's Trade List Annual* (Weston, Conn.: Microform Review, 1975- ) is a convenient and compact collection of annual catalogs issued by virtually all United States and foreign micropublishers. MTLA, which is published annually with six-month supplements, is available in microfiche only. Individual fiche conform to the NMA

Type 1 Standard and are stored in protective panels inside a three-ring binder. Hard-copy indexes list the fiche number for each catalog and the subject specializations of each micropublisher.

By virtue of number of entries and/or detailed descriptive content, some micropublishers' catalogs are important bibliographic tools in their own right. The *Catalog of the National Archives Microfilm Publications* (Washington: National Archives and Records Service, 1974; *Supplement*, 1976), for example, includes a roll-by-roll listing of the microfilmed papers of the Continental Congress produced by the Archives' Spindex II computer program. While the catalog now describes other microfilmed materials in briefer form, the Archives intends to extend the detailed listing in future editions. The Library of Congress, which does not publish a catalog of available microforms, advertises significant titles in detailed descriptive circulars. An index to the circulars is available from the LC Photoduplication Service. Among commercial micropublishers, Xerox University Microfilm's *Serials in Microform* is outstanding for its more than ten thousand entries with imprint dates ranging from 1669 to the present.

## Selection Aids

As noted in chapter five, the many problems inherent in the selection, evaluation, and purchase of micropublications have been described by Veaner, first in an important 1968 article in *Choice* and subsequently in a handbook entitled *The Evaluation of Micropublications* (Chicago: American Library Association, 1971). Because microforms are an essentially "invisible" product, quality-control inspection requires special equipment and expertise. Even when both are available, no librarian can examine every reel or fiche of every micropublication for missing pages, blurred images, and departures from the micropublisher's prospectus. In the case of collections containing many individual titles, micropublishers often advertise and deliver portions before the entire set is complete. In a few cases, advertised collections have failed to reach the production stage, while inferior and incomplete collections have been sold, either through carelessness or ignorance.

Prior to 1972, microform selection aids comparable to those utilized in the development of monographic or serial collections were unavailable. *Microform Review* (Weston, Conn.: Microform Review, Inc.) began publication in that year as a review journal dedicated to the evaluation of micropublications produced for the library market. Individual reviews, prepared by librarians or subject specialists, are typically divided into two parts. The substantive content of the micropublication or series is first described and analyzed in a narrative manner suited to research materials regardless of their format. The reviewer also comments on attractive or unattractive features of the microform itself, such as image quality, the suitability of the type of microform to the original material or end user, and the availability of an index or other finding aids. The second part of the review summarizes, in a standard format, characteristics of the micropublication that may or may not have been treated in the narrative section. These characteristics include the microform type; film stock, polarity, image placement, and quantity; the availability of internal and external finding aids; projected publication sequence; project editors; replacement policy; the availability of time payments, hard copy, or selected portions of larger collections; and an indication of registration with the *National Register of*

*Microform Masters.* In addition to reviews of micropublications, individual quarterly issues typically include news items and editorial comment; one or more articles on library micrographics; reviews of relevant books, technical reports, and micrographics equipment; and micropublishers' advertisements.

*Microform Review* also features highly informative bibliographic essays that analyze micropublishing activity in particular subject areas. Arne J. Arneson, "Microformats and the Music Library: A Bibliographic-Use Survey of Recent Trends," *Microform Review* 4 (1975):25-29, for example, provides an excellent overview of available research collections, noting duplication and gaps in coverage and special problems encountered by producers and purchasers of music materials in microform. Similar essays have concentrated on micropublishing in support of Soviet, African, and Asian studies.[10] Because they provide a state-of-the-art overview, these essays are particularly useful to subject bibliographers and other librarians responsible for the formulation of collection development strategies. Examples of other useful publications of this type include the *Complete Guide to Legal Materials in Microform*, edited by Henry P. Tseng (Arlington: University Publications of America, 1976); the *Guide to Russian Reprints* (New York: Pilvox Publishing Corp., 1973); and Fred Blum, "Catholica on Microforms," *Catholic Library World* 40 (1969):551-57.

## Abstracting and Indexing Services

As noted in chapter five, the bibliographic control of technical reports and other materials micropublished by ERIC and NTIS is accomplished through abstracting and indexing journals. Prior to the submission of source documents to the ERIC Document Reproduction Service (EDRS), the individual clearinghouses analyze acquired materials for subject content, assigning appropriate index terms from the *Thesaurus of ERIC Descriptors* and preparing or modifying abstracts. The results of this subject analysis are printed in *Resources in Education* (formerly *Research in Education*), a monthly index to the ERIC microform data base. Each issue of RIE is divided into two parts: document resumes and indexes. In the document resume section, entries are listed by accession number in groups corresponding to the clearinghouses which submitted them. Each entry includes a full bibliographic citation, information necessary to order the item from ERIC or other sources, a list of assigned major and minor descriptors, and an abstract. Documents unavailable from EDRS are so indicated.

The index sections provide access to document resumes and microfiche reports by assigned descriptors, author, and institution. For libraries with computer capability, RIE is available in machine-readable form on magnetic tape. Alternatively, the machine-readable RIE can be accessed, via time-sharing terminal, through Lockheed Information Systems, System Development Corporation, Bibliographic Retrieval Service, and other vendors specializing in machine-readable bibliographic data bases. Unlike the printed index, the machine-readable version provides access to minor as well as major descriptors, using a wide range of search strategies.

Similar in concept to *Resources in Education*, *Government Reports Announcements and Index* is an all-inclusive bi-weekly abstracting and indexing journal designed to support users of the NTIS data base of technical reports in microfiche. Entries are listed by accession number in the announcements section under the 22 broad subject fields endorsed by the Committee on Scientific and Technical Information in 1964. Individual entries include basic bibliographic information, such as title, personal and corporate author, date, and pagination; an order number; a list of assigned descriptors and identifiers; and an abstract. Five indexes provide access to the announcements by subject, personal author, corporate author, contract number, and accession number. Announcements of new reports in selected fields are published in *Weekly Government Abstracts*, which is currently available for 26 subjects. Abstracts are printed under as many subjects as appropriate and appear two to three weeks after receipt of the report by NTIS. The last issue of the year is a subject index.

The availability of *Government Reports Announcements and Index* simplifies much of the work associated with the maintenance of technical reports at the local level. At Calspan Corporation's technical information center, for example, *Government Announcements and Index* serves as an SDI bulletin, replacing the old accession lists prepared to announce the receipt of technical reports. As with *Resources in Education*, *Government Reports Announcements and Index* is available on magnetic tape from NTIS and can be accessed via the on-line bibliographic data base services mentioned above.

Among commercial micropublishers, Congressional Information Service (CIS) provides several excellent examples of the effectiveness of indexing and abstracting journals in the bibliographic control of large micropublished data bases.[11] The *CIS Index* provides access to congressional committee hearings, prints, reports, and other documents contained in the *CIS Microfiche Library* described in chapter five. Individual monthly issues are divided into separate abstract and index sections. Each entry in the abstract section includes full bibliographic data, the information necessary to order the item from the Government Printing Office or CIS, and a summary of the publication's scope and content. Entries for congressional hearings publications include separate bibliographic descriptions and abstracts of testimony. The abstract section is arranged by accession number. The main index is keyed to subjects and personal names. Five supplementary indexes provide access by document title, report number, document number, committee chairmen, and subcommittee chairmen. The index section cumulates quarterly. Abstract and index sections appear separately in the *CIS/Annual*, which supersedes monthly issues and includes such additional bibliographic information as LC card numbers and GPO monthly catalog numbers. The *CIS/Five Year Cumulative Index, 1970-74* is the first multi-year cumulation of index sections from the *CIS/Annual*. It is designed for use with the annual abstract volumes.

Congressional Information Service also publishes the *American Statistics Index* which provides bibliographic control of United States government statistical publications contained in the *ASI Microfiche Library*. Both the *American Statistics Index* and the *CIS/Index* can be accessed in machine-readable form through System Development Corporation's ORBIT on-line retrieval system. Orders for diazo microfiche of documents identified during an on-line search can be transmitted directly to CIS from the user's terminal.

Other examples of the use of abstracting and indexing journals in the bibliographic control of microform data bases include *Environment Abstracts*, which provides access to the full text of items in Microfiche Publications' *Envirofiche* collection, and the abstract/index section of *SAE Transactions* which references original micropublications of papers delivered at meetings of the Society of Automative Engineers.

## LOCAL BIBLIOGRAPHIC CONTROLS

### Cataloging of Microforms

While substantial recent progress has been made in national and international bibliographic control, the cataloging of microforms remains a poorly understood facet of librarianship. The 1971 survey by Reichmann and Tharpe indicated that only about sixty percent of responding research libraries describe microforms fully in catalog entries. Since the appearance of the first published treatment of the subject in 1936, library literature has emphasized the diversity of local practice and inadequacies of prevailing codes for microform cataloging. Although the development of commercial micropublishing has recently forced renewed interest, the cataloging of microforms was, for a time, almost completely neglected. In the period from 1950 to 1960, only six articles addressed the subject, three of them in foreign languages.[12] Simonton's 1961 report to the Association for Research Libraries identified the two major areas of continuing concern: 1) the physical description of microforms, and 2) depth of cataloging for large microform sets.

With respect to the physical description of retrospective micropublications and single-copy microforms made from materials previously published in printed form, the Simonton report distinguished two broad theoretical approaches. Proponents of the *edition* theory are primarily concerned with describing the work as a physical object and treat the microform as a separate edition rather than as a photographic reproduction of a previously published intellectual product.[13] Consequently, the micropublisher and date of filming accompany or replace the original publisher and publication date in the imprint statement (Fig. 7-2). The collation emphasizes the microform. Elements of the description may include the type, size, polarity, number of pieces, reduction, image placement, and location of the microform master. The collation of the original work is relegated to the notes.

Proponents of the *facsimile* theory of microform cataloging, on the other hand, are primarily concerned with the intellectual content of the work and, in description, emphasize the original publication from which the microform was made. Limited description of the microform reproduction is included in the notes (Fig. 7-3). While the *Rules for Descriptive Cataloging in the Library of Congress* (Washington: Descriptive Cataloging Division, 1949; *Supplement*, 1952) favored the edition theory for the description of retrospective micropublications, the revised chapter six of the *Anglo-American Cataloging Rules: North American Text* (Chicago: American Library Association, 1974) firmly supports the facsimile theory. Rule 156 provides that retrospective micropublications and other microform reproductions are to be described primarily in terms of the original work, insofar as the description of the original can be determined from the reproduction or other reliable source. The collation describes the original publication. The micropublication itself is described in a note following any notes pertaining to the original. The type of microform is indicated, with negative polarity specifically noted in a parenthetical expression of the form: "microfilm (Negative)." The micropublisher, place, and year are given in conventional imprint order with

Figure 7-2

**Cataloging of Micropublication According to Edition Theory**

```
Menzel, Johanna Margarete, 1930-
  German-Japanese relations during the Second
World War. Chicago [Dept. of Photoduplication,
University of Chicago Library] 1957.
  Microfilm copy (positive) of typescript.
  Collation of the original: 539 l. illus.
  Thesis-University of Chicago
  Includes bibliography.
```

Figure 7-3

**Cataloging of Micropublication According to Facsimile Theory**

```
Menzel, Johanna Margarete, 1930-
  German-Japanese relations during the
Second World War. Chicago, 1957.
  539 l. illus.
  Thesis-University of Chicago
  Includes bibliography.
  Microfilm copy (positive) of typescript
made in 1957 by Dept. of Photoduplication,
University of Chicago Library.
```

prescribed punctuation. In the case of microforms made from rare books, the specific copy of the work from which the reproduction was made is identified. The description of the microform concludes with an indication of the number of pieces (reels, cartridges, fiche, etc.) and the size. The width of microfilm is given in millimeters. Dimensions of flat microforms are given in centimeters. Thus, the standard 105 x 148mm microfiche would be described as 10.5 x 14.8 or, in round numbers 11 x 15cm. Prescribed collation punctuation is used throughout.

The distinction between the edition and facsimile theories of physical description does not apply to original micropublications as defined in chapter five. The AACR provides that such a micropublication be described "according to its own indicia of identification." The imprint thus indicates the micropublisher, place, and date (Fig. 7-4). The number of pieces and size are reported in the collation. The type of microform is given as the first note. Some original micropublishers—the State University of New York Press, for example—report their offerings to the Library of Congress for cataloging in publication.

### Figure 7-4

### Cataloging of Original Micropublication

```
Regan, Brian T      1938-

   The Gothic word / by Brian T. Regan -- 1st ed. --
Albany: State University of New York Press, 1972.
   4 sheets (364p.); 11 x 15 cm.
   Microfiche.
   Bibliography: p. 364.
```

### Alternatives to Cataloging

While the inclusion of entries for microforms in the library's public catalog provides bibliographic control in a manner familiar to both librarians and patrons, opponents of conventional descriptive cataloging for the bibliographic control of microforms question its value in terms of its expense.[14] With respect to depth of cataloging, they have been especially critical of the need for, and desirability of, separate analytic catalog entries for individual titles in large microform sets. While the inclusion of such entries in the public catalog is undoubtedly convenient for many users, the level of professional and clerical effort required to fully describe individual titles, they argue, is unjustifiably great. The number of individual titles in large microform sets, such as Xerox University Microfilm's *Early English Books* or Readex Microprint Corporation's *Early American Imprints* may well exceed the annual monographic acquisitions of some libraries. The *Early American Imprints* set contains over 42,000 titles in the first series alone.

Furthermore, because many of the titles in large microform sets are rare or esoteric, much original cataloging may be required. For example, less than fifty percent of the German books listed in *Africana Microfilms at the E. S. Bird Library, Syracuse University* (Syracuse, N.Y.: Program of East African Studies, 1974) are also listed in the NUC. Even when choice and form of entry can be established through one or more printed sources—as is the case with many of the 4,000 items in *A Bibliography of German Plays in Microcard*, edited by Norman Binger (Hamden, Conn.: Shoe String Press, 1970)—the microreproduction of the text itself must often be examined to complete the description.

Libraries acquiring large microform sets can save some professional time by purchasing catalog card sets prepared by micropublishers or other libraries. Xerox University Microfilms, for example, supports its *Early English Books* series with catalog cards prepared by the University of Michigan, while the University of British Columbia library has prepared analytic author/title entries for a number of large microform series.[15] In such cases, however, authority work remains to be done locally and the cards themselves must still be filed into the catalog. At one hundred cards per hour, inter-filing of 42,000 main entries for the *Early American Imprints* set would require three person-months of clerical effort. Depending on the hourly pay-rate, clerical support costs could approach fifteen percent of the purchase price of the microform set, which, in this case, is $10,000. Additional catalog drawers would be required, thus further increasing the initial cost of adding a large microform set to the library's holdings.

As an alternative to the expense of preparing separate entries for the public catalog, many libraries rely on printed finding aids to describe and indicate the location of individual titles in large microform sets. Critics of full analytic cataloging point out that adequate description is already available for individual titles in microform sets based on established bibliographies. Users seeking bibliographic description for the edition of *The Apology of Sir Thomas More, Knight* included in Xerox University Microfilm's *Early English Books* series, for example, need only consult the Pollard and Redgrave *Short Title Catalogue*. To locate works by Sir Thomas More in a library owning the *Early English Books* series, the user would first consult Pollard and Redgrave to determine the STC numbers for desired entries. Xerox University Microfilms provides a printed cross-index which can then be used to translate STC numbers into microfilm reel numbers within the set. Likewise, users of the Readex Microprint Corporation's *Early American Imprints* set seeking an indication of availability or bibliographic description for works by Ebenezer Parkman need only consult the alphabetic main entry listing in the *National Index of American Imprints through 1800: The Short-Title Evans*, edited by Clifford K. Shipton and James E. Mooney (Philadelphia: American Antiquarian Society, 1969).

In some cases, information in established bibliographies is supplemented by special bibliographic tools prepared by the micropublisher. These bibliographic tools generally provide additional description or improved access to individual titles within large microform sets. The individual reel guides to the *Early English Books* series, for example, provide important information about the location, paging idiosyncracies, and other characteristics of the filmed original which cannot be determined from the STC. Research Publication's *German Baroque Literature* collection is based on the holdings of the Yale University Library and contains 2,363 items filmed in the order listed in Curt von Fabur du Faur, *German Baroque Literature: A Catalogue of the Collection in the Yale University Library*, 2 vols. (New Haven, Conn.: Yale University Press, 1958; *Supplement*, 1969), which is arranged by subject. To facilitate location of individual titles, Research Publications developed its *Bibliography-Index to the Microfilm Edition of the Yale University Library Collection of German Baroque Literature* (New Haven, Conn.: Research Publications, Inc., 1971), an author-title listing which serves as both a reel guide and a supplement to von Fabur du Faur. The *Bibliography-Index* was created from photographed catalog cards prepared by the micropublisher and available as a separate purchase. Similarly, users of Research Publications' *League of Nations Documents and Serial Publications*, a microform set containing over 25,000 items filmed in official League number order within nineteen broad subjects, may be able to locate desired material by consulting Marie Carrol, *Key to League of Nations Documents Placed on Public Sale, 1920-29* (Boston: World Peace Foundation, 1930-1936) or the League's own two-volume *Catalogue of Publications* (Geneva: League of Nations, 1935). The best approach to the set, however, is through Edward A. Reno, ed., *League of Nations Documents, 1919-1946: A Descriptive Guide and Key to the Microfilm Collection* (New Haven, Conn.: Research Publications, Inc., 1973-1975), a three-volume reel-by-reel listing with full document description and abstracts.

Microform sets not based on existing bibliographies are often accompanied by specially-prepared guides that describe individual titles and provide access through author, title, and subject indexes. The printed catalog furnished with Clearwater Publishing Company's *French Theatre, 1789-1813* collection is typical. Individual entries include basic bibliographic information, a synopsis, the genre, and the date and theater of first performance. Similarly, Vincent L. Angotti, *Source Materials in the Field of Theatre* (Ann Arbor, Mich.: Xerox University Microfilms, 1967) is intended as both a researcher's guide and a cataloging aid. Individual entries provide basic bibliographic description, the Library of Congress card number, a brief content annotation, and reel location.

The printed catalogs and indexes designed to support the 19,000 ultrafiche titles in the LRI Microbook *Library of American Civilization* are perhaps the outstanding example of this alternative form of local bibliographic control.[16] The LAC features separate author, title, and subject catalogs, furnished in both book form and on fiche. The author catalog is arranged alphabetically and provides full bibliographic description and subject headings in the Library of Congress card-image format. Each entry includes the LAC number which indicates the location of the item within the microform set. The title and subject catalogs are also arranged alphabetically but provide only an abbreviated description for each entry. In addition, each separate fiche in the set is enclosed in a special envelope printed with the main entry for the work on fiche in the Library of Congress card-image format. Conventional catalog card sets are available as an extra purchase. In addition to cataloging each title, the *Library of American Civilization* includes a specially-prepared index called a *Biblioguide* which is designed to complement the subject catalog and provide more extensive access to material in the set on both broad and specific topics.

Micropublished archives and manuscript collections are typically controlled by similar book-form finding aids which provide a general description of major record series with a detailed reel inventory and indexes to subjects or correspondents. The papers of Henry A. Wallace—microfilmed separately by the Library of Congress, Roosevelt Library, and the University of Iowa—are controlled by a joint correspondents index with 125,000 entries keyed to set, reel, and frame numbers. Harvard University Press' *Province in Rebellion*, a collection of 1,140 historical documents on thirty-one microfiche, includes a contents list, an index, and an interpretive essay by L. Kinvin Wroth which discusses and references specific fiche.

The Library of Congress' Presidential Papers Microfilming Project was the first micropublishing program to employ computer-produced indexes. *The Boreal Institute Vertical Files on Northern Affairs*, produced by Micromedia Ltd., is controlled by a Keyword-In-Context (KWIC) index that references the microfiche file by date. Microfiche provided with the New York Times Information Bank are controlled by an on-line index accessed via time-sharing terminal.[17] Other microform newspaper clipping files—the *Newsbank Library*, for example—employ conventional printed indexes.

Libraries relying on alternatives to the public catalog for the bibliographic control of individual titles in large microform sets must alert patrons to the availability of printed catalogs and indexes. Some libraries place an appropriate notation on the main entry catalog card for each set, indicating the existence of more detailed finding-aids. The effectiveness of this approach is, however, yet to be demonstrated. A few libraries have prepared orientation booklets or guides to local microform holdings of which Iqbal Wagle, *A Guide to Research Collections in Microform in the University of Toronto Library* (Toronto: John P. Robarts Research Library, 1974) and Peter Olevnick, *A Guide to Selected Microform Series and Their Indexes* (Champaign-Urbana: University of Illinois, Graduate School of Library Science, Occasional Papers, May 1973) are excellent examples.[18] Subscribers to the *Library of American Civilization* receive posters and similar promotional materials designed to attract attention to the availability of the microform set and its accompanying bibliographic devices.

## Classification of Microforms

While library literature has generally emphasized the importance of full bibliographic description for microform holdings, the necessity and desirability of classification is typically questioned, since users do not generally browse in microform collections. Reichmann and Tharpe disclosed that less than thirty percent of responding libraries classify microforms, while over sixty percent filed them by some sequentially-assigned number. Those libraries which do classify microforms often employ broad, rather than close, classification, indicating the first LC letters or Dewey numbers only. The most common classification schemes combine an abbreviated class mark, an indicator of microform type, and an accession number or shelf designator.[19] Thus *QA FIC 123* would indicate the

123rd microfiche on the general subject of mathematics and computer science. A potentially significant disadvantage of non-traditional classification schemes is that microforms do not appear in the library shelflist and cannot be accessed by patrons using the shelflist as a classed catalog.

## INTERNAL BIBLIOGRAPHIC CONTROLS

Internal bibliographic controls provide identifying information within the microform itself. In the case of roll microforms, one or more identifying targets typically precede the first frame of textual material. The number and content of these targets varies with the micropublisher and the original material. *Specifications for the Microfilming of Books and Pamphlets in the Library of Congress* (Washington: Library of Congress, 1973) requires eye-legible START and END targets, together with a primary bibliographic target that identifies the author, title, place and date of publication, volume number, and class number of the original work. Secondary bibliographic targets include a printed or typed catalog card, a statement indicating the location of the original material, a credit sign identifying the micropublisher, a report of missing and mutilated pages, and a report of the volume number being filmed if more than one. Required technical targets include a National Bureau of Standards Microcopy Resolution Test Chart and an indication of reduction ratio. Missing or mutilated pages are further identified as encountered, as are changes in reduction. The best commercial micropublishers provide much the same information, sometimes employing specially-designed bibliographic targets.

As noted in chapter two, much of the essential bibliographic information on microfiche is provided in the eye-legible heading area. Typically, the heading area contains much the same information found on the title page of the hard copy original. For microfiche made from source documents, the heading area typically contains much the same information found on the title page of the hard copy original from which the microimages were made: author, title, imprint, report number, and, where applicable, a copyright statement. If the work extends over several fiche, a sequence number is generally included. The first few frames may contain a catalog card, other bibliographic targets, and a resolution test chart. Eye-legible frames may be used to demarcate and identify discrete bibliographic units within a fiche. Papers appearing in the American Chemical Society's microfiche journals, for example, are preceded by an eye-legible target indicating the first author and inclusive pagination. The same technique is used to identify individual micropublishers' catalogs in the *Micropublishers' Trade List Annual.*

# REFERENCES

[1] James P. Kottenstette, et al., *A Guide to Instructional Uses of Microform* (Denver: Denver Research Institute, 1971).

[2] H. Gordon Bechanan, "The Organization of Microforms in the Library," *Library Trends* 8 (1960): 391-406; C. Edward Carroll, "Some Problems of Microform Utilization in Large University Collections," *Microform Review* 1 (1972): 19-24; George A. Schwegmann, Jr., "The Bibliographic Control of Microforms," *Library Trends* 8 (1960): 380-90.

[3] Wesley Simonton, "The Bibliographic Control of Microforms," *Library Resources and Technical Services* 6 (1962): 29-40.

[4] Donald C. Holmes, *Determination of User Needs and Future Requirements for a Systems Approach to Microfilm Technology* (Washington: Office of Education, Bureau of Research, 1969); Holmes, "The Needs of Library Microform Users," *Proceedings of the National Microfilm Association* (Silver Spring, Md.: NMA, 1969): 256-60.

[5] Felix M. Reichmann and Josephine M. Tharpe, *Bibliographic Control of Microforms* (Westport, Conn.: Greenwood Press, 1972); Reichmann, "Bibliographic Control of Microforms," *Microform Review* 1 (1972): 279-80.

[6] For a review of available sources, see Albert Diaz, "Microreproduction Information Sources," *Library Resources and Technical Services* 11 (1967): 211-14; Diaz, "Microform Information Sources: Publications and Hardware," *Microform Review* 4 (1975): 250-61.

[7] Gloria Hsia, "Library of Congress' Contribution to the Bibliographic Control of Microforms," *Microform Review* 6 (1977): 11-14.

[8] Edmond L. Applebaum, "Implications of the National Register of Microform Masters as Part of a National Preservation Program," *Library Resources and Technical Services* 9 (1965): 489-94.

[9] Rudolf Hirsch, "Union List of Microfilms," *American Documentation* 1 (1950): 88-90.

[10] Charles R. Bryant, "Survey of Selected Current and Recent Research Materials on Southeast Asia," *Microform Review* 2 (1973): 14-22; Moore Crassey, "A Survey of Africana in Microform," *Microform Review* 3 (1974): 96-105; Leo Gruliow, "Soviet Serials on Microform," *Microform Review* 1 (1972): 9-18.

[11] James B. Adler, "Indexing as the Key to Micropublishing: The Case History of the Congressional Information Service," *Journal of Micrographics* 4 (1971): 239-45; Adler, "The Relationship between Library and Micropublisher," *Government Publications Review* 1 (1973): 226-28; John Beil, "CIS," *Illinois Libraries* 58 (1976): 194-99.

[12] Duncan Brockway, "A New Look at the Cataloging of Microfilm," *Library Resources and Technical Services* 4 (1960): 323-30. On diversities of local practice, see June Thomson, "Cataloguing of Large Works on Microform in Canadian University Libraries," *Canadian Library Journal* 26 (1969): 446-52; Suzanne Massonneau, "Cataloging Nonbook Materials: Mountain or Molehill?," *Library Resources and Technical Services* 16 (1972): 294-304; George Mitchell, "Microforms: Legerdermain

in the Library," paper delivered at the Annual Meeting of the Southwestern Library Association, Galveston, Texas, October 15, 1974 (available through EDRS as ED 105 884); Amy E. Okaro, "Bibliographic Control of Microforms in Academic Libraries in Indiana," *Focus* 28 (1973): 76-80; 1-2; H. J. Jones and J. Hagan, "Microfilm Cataloging Lacks System," *Library Journal* 72 (1947): 505-507.

[13] See, for example, Richard W. Hale, Jr., "The Cataloging of Microfilm," *American Archivist* 22 (1959): 11-13.

[14] Felix Reichmann, "Controlling the Minutiae," in Association for Research Libraries, Minutes of the 77th Meeting, January 17, 1971, Los Angeles, pp. 6-11.

[15] Margaret F. Parmalee, "Cataloging Microfilms at the University of Michigan Library," *Journal of Documentary Reproduction* 3 (1940): 121-37; J. McRee Elrod, "Author and Title Analytics for Major Microform Sets," *Microform Review* 2 (1973): 99-104.

[16] See the description in Charles Van Doren, "The Bibliographic Demands of Microbook Service," in P. S. Grove and E. G. Celement, eds., *Bibliographic Control of Non-Print Media* (Chicago: American Library Association, 1972), pp. 307-314.

[17] E. E. Duncan, "Microfiche Collections for the New York Times Information Bank," *Microform Review* 2 (1973): 269-71.

[18] See also, Suzanne Dodson, "The University of British Columbia's Guide to Large Collections in Microform: An Attempt to Minimize a Major Problem," *Microform Review* 1 (1972): 113-17.

[19] Joseph Z. Nitecki, "Simplified Classification and Cataloging of Microforms," *Library Resources and Technical Services* 13 (1969): 79-85; William L. Beck, "A Realistic Approach to Microform Management," *Microform Review* 2 (1973): 172-76; Maurice F. Tauber, "Cataloging and Classifying of Microfilm," *Journal of Documentary Reproduction* 3 (1940): 10-25.

# CHAPTER 8

## MICROFORM STORAGE AND RETRIEVAL SYSTEMS

### ROLL MICROFORMS

#### Flash Targets

The success of many microform applications depends on the ability to rapidly locate one or more specified microimages from among thousands or, in some cases, millions. This chapter describes the most widely-used manual and automated retrieval systems and techniques for both roll and flat microforms.[1]

The simplest retrieval technique for 16mm or 35mm roll microforms utilizes eye-legible flash targets with blank frames to separate groups of related microimages on film (Fig. 8-1). These flash targets function like file folder tabs or dividers,

**Figure 8-1**

**Flash Target Retrieval**

directing the user to the area in which a relevant microimage is located but not necessarily to the microimage itself.[2] In source document applications, such as a manuscript collection containing copies of outgoing correspondence or arranged alphabetically by name of recipient, flash targets consisting of one or more large characters are prepared for major alphabetic or other file divisions. Each flash target is then filmed one or more times before the group of documents to which it pertains. Groups of documents with preceding targets are separated by blank frames. To locate the microimage of a letter written to a particular person, the appropriate reel, cartridge, or cassette is first selected and mounted on a reader. The film is then advanced rapidly. The appearance of a strip of blank frames indicates that a flash target follows. Film advance is slowed or halted and the flash target consulted to determine the alphabetic grouping of the accompanying document images. If the indicated alphabetic grouping is appropriate, individual microimages are examined serially to locate the relevant document. If the indicated alphabetic grouping does not match the retrieval parameter, the film is again advanced rapidly until the next flash target is encountered and the procedure repeated.

For library catalogs, circulation reports, and other computer-output-microfilm applications, most COM recorders will generate frames containing one or more eye-legible characters. As in source document applications, these eye-legible characters typically indicate alphabetic, numeric, or other report divisions reflected in succeeding microimages. Alternatively, the COM recorder can position eye-legible characters beneath all or selected film frames. While these characters may represent large file divisions, COM software can also extract them from the data itself in order to display, for example, the inclusive catalog entries in a given frame or group of frames.

Where reports and files can be logically divided and exact frame retrieval is not required, the flash target method can be effective and economical. No special equipment is required. The retrieval procedure is straightforward. User instruction is relatively simple. Although the flash targets occupy space on the film, they do not significantly diminish microform capacity or exclude the possibility of later conversion to other retrieval systems. Many institutional and commercial micro-publications feature embedded flash targets.

### Sequential Frame Numbering

In this technique, a sequentially-assigned number appears below each document image on a 16mm or 35mm roll microform. In source document applications, the numbered frames are created by a planetary camera modified to incorporate a digital counter in the lower portion of the photographic field. The counter is automatically incremented following each exposure. Most planetary camera manufacturers offer such a sequential counter as an inexpensive option. Several rotary cameras will accept an optional accessory that imprints a sequentially-assigned number on each document prior to exposure. This numbering method takes advantage of the rotary camera's speed but, since the document is defaced in the process, it may be unacceptable for many library applications. Most COM recorders will, through software, position sequential numbers above or below each film frame. These numbers may appear in either reduced or eye-legible size.

To retrieve a particular document image, a manual or computer-stored external index must first be consulted to determine the appropriate roll and frame number. The indicated reel, cartridge, or cassette is then mounted and the film advanced until the desired frame is reached. Indexing each microimage, while time-consuming, permits exact-frame retrieval. Where retrieval requirements are less critical, only selected numbered images need be indexed. When used in this way, the sequential frame numbering method directs the user to the area in which the desired microimage is located. Document images in the area must then be examined serially.

Like the flash target method, sequential frame numbering can be effective and economical. Film preparation is uncomplicated. Many micropublications are available with numbered frames. Exact-frame retrieval is possible. Special readers are not required. The retrieval procedure is straightforward and user instruction is relatively simple. Frame numbers do not interfere with viewing, diminish microform capacity, or exclude the possibility of later conversion to other retrieval systems.

### Odometer Indexing

In odometer indexing, microimage location is a function of distance into a 16mm or 35mm roll microform. In source document applications, the film is created on any rotary or planetary camera. An index is prepared by examining processed microimages on a reader or reader/printer equipped with an odometer and associating the desired retrieval parameters with their odometer readings. As with other retrieval methods, the index may be typed on labels affixed to reel microfilm containers or cartridges (Fig. 8-2), maintained in a card file, printed, or stored in machine-readable form for computer inquiry. In COM applications, software is available to derive odometer settings prior to actual recording on film. The odometer index can then be recorded as the first microimage on the reel or cartridge to which it pertains.

**Figure 8-2**

**Odometer Retrieval**

At retrieval time, the index is consulted to determine the roll number and odometer reading corresponding to the desired subject or other search parameter. The user mounts the appropriate reel or cartridge and, watching the odometer, advances the film to the indicated reading. The user will then be at or near the desired microimage. Depending on the specificity of indexing, an additional few images may have to be examined serially.

Although its use by libraries is rarely reported, the odometer indexing retrieval method is well-suited to a wide range of 16mm and 35mm reel and cartridge applications. Index preparation is relatively simple. Specificity can be tailored to user requirements. Special cameras are not required. The method can be applied to retrospective microform collections created without odometer indexing in mind. The search procedure is straightforward and user instruction is relatively simple. Odometers are available as standard or optional equipment on the roll microform readers and reader/printers of most manufacturers.

### Code-Line Indexing

Code-line indexing—developed and marketed by Eastman Kodak under the trade name *Kodaline*—utilizes a series of short, graduated lines or bars between microimages on 16mm reel or cartridge microfilm (Fig. 8-3). The position of the lines denotes numeric information such as a sequential frame number, an account number, or a numerically-encoded subject descriptor. Line positions change with every or selected frames. Code-lines are placed on film by specially-modified rotary or planetary source document cameras. Several COM recorders will also generate 16mm microfilm with code-lines. Through software, code-line positions may be assigned sequentially or derived from the data itself. A few micropublications— *Chemical Abstracts*, for example—can be purchased with code-lines.

### Figure 8-3

### Code-Line Retrieval

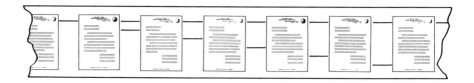

To retrieve a particular microimage, the roll number and code-line position is determined, typically by consulting a manual or computer-stored external index. When the appropriate reel or cartridge is mounted on a motorized reader and the film advanced at high speed, individual microimages are blurred and the code-lines appear continuous. A scale alongside the reader screen indicates the numeric value of each code-line position.

The code-line method is effective, although the coded film, which must be prepared by special cameras, is more expensive to create than the film used in the flash target, frame numbering, or odometer indexing methods. Code-line scales are, however, an inexpensive item available for the readers of several manufacturers. While code-lines permit fairly rapid location of desired microimages, the user orientation period may be longer than with some other methods. Consequently, code-line indexing is best-suited to the closed user groups served by scientific, technical, and other special libraries. The addition of code-lines to film does not interfere with viewing, diminish microform capacity, or—with the exception of photo-optical codes to be described in a subsequent section—preclude the use of other retrieval systems or techniques.[3] When the required cameras are available, libraries are often well-advised to prepare roll microforms with code-line indexing in anticipation of possible future use.

## Image-Count Marks

An image-count mark, often called a *blip*, is an opaque rectangular mark positioned beneath the microimage on 16mm roll microforms (Fig. 8-4). In source document applications, the recording of image-count marks requires a special rotary camera attachment. Any planetary camera can be easily modified for image count mark recording by placing a dark covering over the copyboard and positioning a small (approximately three by four inch) piece of white paper in the lower left-hand corner of the photographic field. Several planetary camera manufacturers offer a special dark copyboard for this purpose. In COM applications, a specially-prepared form slide is used to record the image count mark below each data frame. A number of micropublications can be purchased with image count marks.

**Figure 8-4**

**Image-Count Marks**

To retrieve a particular microimage, the user first consults a manual or computer stored external index to determine the appropriate roll number and frame number. The reel, cartridge, or cassette is then mounted on a special reader or reader/printer and the desired frame number entered at an operator keyboard. The film is automatically advanced while photocells and logical circuitry within the reader count the marks below each frame, stopping at the indicated microimage. The technique is thus an automated variant of sequential frame numbering. The image-count marks occupy the same position from frame to frame and have no intrinsic information content other than indicating the position a given microimage occupies from the start of the film.

Image-count marks provide an effective, reliable method for the high-speed location of exact frames. Retrieval procedures are straight-forward. User instruction is simple. Because special equipment is required for both film preparation and retrieval, image-count marking is more expensive than the methods previously described. Prices for an image-count reader with operator keyboard begin at about $5,000. Several image-count readers are available with an incrementing light-emitting-diode display rather than a keyboard. When the appropriate roll is mounted, the user, watching the display, advances the film until the desired frame number is reached. Prices for these readers begin at around $3,000. The addition of image-count marks to film does not interfere with viewing or diminish microform capacity. The presence of image-count marks does not preclude the use of code-line indexing or other retrieval methods. Where the required camera equipment is available, libraries are well advised to prepare 16mm roll microforms with image-count marks in anticipation of possible future applications.

The use of image-count marks in computer-assisted retrieval is discussed later in this chapter.

### MIRAcode

First introduced in 1964, MIRAcode (Microfilm Information Retrieval Access Code) is the trade name for a group of Eastman Kodak products that provide subject or other access to randomly recorded microimages on 16mm microfilm.[4] The name itself is derived from a photo-optical binary code which appears on film as columns of clear and opaque bits, perpendicular to the film edge and adjacent to their corresponding microimage (Fig. 8-5). Each code column uses twelve bit positions, and an optional utility bit, to represent three or four numeric digits corresponding to pre-determined subject descriptors or other retrieval parameters.[5] The present system, designated MIRAcode II, is available in two versions, Mod-12 and Mod-18, capable of encoding four or six descriptors per microimage.

**Figure 8-5**

**Photo-Optical Binary Codes (MIRAcode)**

Although retrieval parameters for purchasing records, accounts payable, and other numerically ordered files can sometimes be derived directly from the documents themselves, the design of MIRAcode applications typically begins with the establishment of a thesaurus of approved descriptors and their conversion to the numeric codes required by the system. For technical reports and other relatively common document types in well-established subject fields, existing thesauri may be adaptable to MIRAcode use. The main twelve code bits can be used to represent up to 1,000 descriptors (000 to 999). Use of the utility bit doubles the number of possible descriptors (0000 to 1999).

Once the thesaurus is established, source documents are analyzed for subject content and appropriate numeric descriptors assigned. The documents are then microfilmed using a Kodak MIRAcode II planetary camera and the numeric descriptors recorded via a key-to-film encoder. Code input via punched cards is available as an option. Certain COM recorders will also prepare film for MIRAcode retrieval, using a specially-formatted magnetic tape. In source document applications, code columns precede related microimages on film. In COM applications, the code columns follow the microimages. In either case, code columns may represent a single microimage or a group of microimages. Exposed film is processed in a conventional manner and inserted in Recordak-type 16mm cartridges.

To retrieve microimages relevant to a particular subject, the thesaurus is first consulted to determine approved descriptors and their numeric representations. A microfilm cartridge is then inserted into a MIRAcode II Retrieval Terminal and a search statement entered via the keyboard on the terminal controller (Fig. 8-6). The

**Figure 8-6**

**MIRAcode II Retrieval Terminal with Keyboard**
(Courtesy: Eastman Kodak Company)

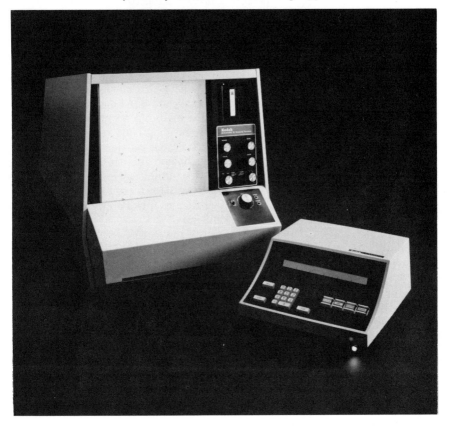

simplest searches call for an exact match of a specified numeric code and a particular code column. The MIRAcode II Retrieval Terminal advances the film at high speed, scans each code column, and stops the film to display the first microimage that satisfies the search statement. The Retrieval Terminal resembles a Recordak Microstar Reader and features a fourteen by fourteen inch rear projection screen, zoom lenses over a range of magnifications, and an optional printer. When viewing is completed, film advance is resumed until the next relevant microimage is encountered. If the ensuing search fails to disclose additional microimages meeting the search specification, the film is automatically rewound.

More complex searches, possible with the Mod-18 Controller, will match the occurrence of a specified numeric code in any code column, utilize logical OR and AND operators, and allow the operator to link two code columns to create six-digit descriptors. An interpolation option permits range searches using relational operators (greater than, less than, greater than or equal, less than or equal), a useful feature where the search statement includes a date.

MIRAcode systems offer the advantages of powerful search logic applied to randomly-filmed documents within 16mm cartridges. MIRAcode products, while marketed most heavily to commercial and criminal justice environments, have been used successfully in several important library applications. At the Detroit Free Press library, for example, MIRAcode has eliminated the problems of loss and misfiling associated with a manual clipping file while providing rapid response to received information requests.[6] Search and scan time for a single cartridge averages about 25 seconds, including film rewind. At the Medill School of Journalism of Northwestern University, a pilot MIRAcode project provided subject access to clippings from local newspapers.[7] Also at Northwestern, MIRAcode was used to control the large file of documents used in the International Comparative Political Parties Project, funded by the National Science Foundation.[8]

While the combination of microimages and code is well-suited to many applications librarians should be aware of certain constraints that must be observed in MIRAcode system design. Because the encoded descriptors accompany document images in individual cartridges, the entire index is never available for consultation at one time. To avoid the necessity of searching every cartridge in response to retrieval requests—an impossibility in large-scale applications—the source document file is typically partitioned prior to filming. At the Detroit Free Press, for example, the clipping file is divided into nineteen broad subject areas (education, politics, crime, etc.). Retrieval is consequently simplified by limiting the search to only those cartridges in appropriate areas. In this connection, it is important to note that, because code columns occupy space on film, MIRAcode applications invariably involve more cartridges than microform systems employing other retrieval techniques. MIRAcode cartridge capacity also varies inversely with the depth of indexing. Where six numeric descriptors are assigned to each microimage, for example, a cartridge of 16mm by 100 feet of microfilm typically contains less than 600 documents. Without coding, cartridge capacity exceeds 2,000 documents.

Because the file is partitioned to facilitate retrieval, newly-filmed document images must be spliced onto appropriate cartridges. The necessity of splicing—the system's most significant inconvenience—can sometimes be avoided in files partitioned by date. Any duplicate microfilms used in the system must be of silver halide stock to ensure the quality of light transmission required for accurate interpretation of code columns. The system is designed for use with negative-appearing microfilm only.

For source document applications, a MIRAcode configuration consisting of one planetary camera with key-to-film encoder and one Retrieval Terminal with Mod-18 Controller and printer costs about $40,000. Heavily-referenced files may require additional retrieval stations. Applications involving much updating or the conversion of large retrospective files may require additional cameras. Detailed systems analysis is often necessary to determine the proper balance of input versus retrieval equipment.[9]

## Oracle

Oracle is a trade name for a group of Eastman Kodak products that provide access to randomly-filmed documents using an eight-digit binary code beneath each 16mm microimage. The system which—like MIRAcode—combines encoded numeric descriptors with document images on film, consists of a special planetary camera with key-to-film unit and a retrieval station with a Recordak Starvue Reader, keyboard, and optional printer. COM film encoding is possible via the Kodak KOM-85 recorder.

Encoded 16mm film, in 215-foot lengths, is processed conventionally and loaded in a special cartridge. Because Oracle codes appear below, rather than in front of, film frames, the microimage capacity of individual cartridges remains high and the number of cartridges to be searched is correspondingly reduced. Oracle prices are approximately one-half those for comparably-configured MIRAcode systems. The search logic is, however, less powerful, although a system option permits complex search statements involving an exact match of selected code digits with interpolation of others.

## Computer-Assisted Retrieval

Several of the manual retrieval techniques described in the preceding sections require the maintenance of an index separate from the microform data base. Computer-assisted retrieval combines the space-saving and other advantages of microform storage for very large document files with the ability of computers to rapidly manipulate large amounts of index information.[10] Components in a computer-assisted microform retrieval system include a microfilm camera and reader or reader/printer; an input device for the conversion of index information to machine-readable form; a dedicated or general-purpose computer with associated disk or tape storage; and an output device—typically a line printer in batch systems, a display or printing terminal in on-line systems.

Regardless of mode of operation, a computer-produced or computer-stored index is consulted to determine the roll number and frame number of document images meeting a given search specification. A Keyword-In-Context (KWIC) index, for example, provides a simple and relatively inexpensive form of computer-assisted retrieval that is well-suited to a wide-range of library related applications.[11] For microform retrieval, a roll and frame number replaces the customary derived bibliographic code opposite the KWIC index line. The index itself can be printed directly onto roll film or microfiche via COM and updated as required. As in chapter seven, a KWIC index provides subject access to the clipping files micropublished by the Boreal Institute of Northern Affairs. Several of the original micropublications described in chapter five rely on COM-generated indexes for subject or other access to catalog card images or other bibliographic data.

In some computer-assisted retrieval systems, components are wired together in a way that permits the computer to both search the index and drive a reader or reader/printer to automatically display microimages relevant to a retrieval request. The 3M Microdisc System (Fig. 8-7) is an example of such a *computer-controlled*

**Figure 8-7**

**Microdisc Computer-Assisted Retrieval System**
(Courtesy: 3M Company)

retrieval system.[1][2] It consists of a dedicated minicomputer with disk storage, a CRT display terminal with keyboard, and a 3M 500 Page Search Reader/Printer in an integrated, desk-like configuration. Microdisc is a *turnkey* system that includes all of the application programs required for the establishment, maintenance, and search of index files as well as the system software necessary to control the various hardware components. User experience with data processing or computer programming is not required.

As with MIRAcode, the design of a subject-oriented Microdisc retrieval application begins with the establishment of a thesaurus of approved descriptors consisting of single-term keywords. Indexed source documents are then micro-filmed at random on any 16mm rotary or planetary camera capable of recording image count marks, as described in a preceding section of this chapter. COM-generated 16mm microfilm with image count marks is equally acceptable. Exposed microfilm is processed, inserted in 3M-type cartridges, and mounted on the 3M 500 Page Search Reader/Printer. An operator, seated at the CRT keyboard, places the system in *Definition Mode* and establishes a file on computer disk for the index information to be entered. Then, using both alphabetic and numeric characters, the clerk indicates the index parameters or *keynames* (subject, author, title, date, etc.) to be used and the order in which they will be entered for each item. The system is next placed in *Update Mode*, the number of the cartridge to be indexed is entered, and the reader/printer film transport advanced to display the first microimage to be indexed. Assigned descriptors or key values are then entered in the predefined keyname sequence, delimited by commas. Keynames such as author or subject may be assigned several key values. Up to 99 keynames can be used to index each item. If a keyname has no key value assigned for a given item, only the comma is entered. When the index line is completed for the first microimage, typing of a semicolon causes the system to transfer the data to the disk file and advance the film to the next frame. The process is then repeated for the remainder of the cartridge, at which time the cartridge is removed.

To retrieve microimages relevant to a particular information request, the system is placed in *Search Mode*, a search statement entered, and the index on computer disk automatically consulted for cartridge and frame numbers meeting the search criteria. The system will accept complex search statements containing logical operators, relational operators, and parenthetical expressions. As with other information retrieval programs, the system responds to each search statement with a preliminary report of the number of microimages relevant to it. The search statement can then be modified as desired. When the search statement is finalized, the operator enters a VIEW command and the system responds with instructions to mount a particular cartridge. When the cartridge is mounted, the system, using the image count marks, advances the film to display the first relevant microimage. When viewing is complete, the film is advanced to the next relevant frame. When the display of relevant frames in the mounted cartridge is complete, the film is automatically rewound and the system instructs the operator to mount the next cartridge. Alternatively, the system will display a list of all relevant cartridge and frame numbers.

The basic Microdisc system features on-line disk storage capacity for 2.5 million alphabetic or 5 million numeric characters of index information, expandable to 20 million and 40 million respectively. Because index information is stored on computer disk rather than film, it can be changed or deleted as required.

Additions to the microform data base are filmed randomly in batches, inserted in cartridges, and the index updated. Splicing is unnecessary. A single system can support up to sixteen local or remote terminals with reader/printers. An optional magnetic tape input/output unit is available to facilitate entry of index data or the periodic recording of index data on microfilm via COM.

Microdisc system prices begin at about $60,000. Similar systems are available from other manufacturers.

### Storage Containers

Whether manual or automated, most roll microform retrieval systems require the external storage of individual reels, cartridges, and cassettes when not in use. Drawer-type filing cabinets resemble office-type filing equipment and offer high storage capacities in relatively little space. A six drawer unit, measuring 36 inches wide by 30 inches high by 18 inches deep, will store up to 780 16mm reels, cartridges, or cassettes or 480 35mm reels or cartridges.

As an alternative to drawer-type files, several equipment manufacturers offer open storage racks for roll microforms. National Blank Book's Modular Storage and Retrieval System (Fig. 8-8) is configured from standard units, each with capacity

### Figure 8-8

### Modular Cartridge Storage Containers
(Courtesy: National Blank Book Company)

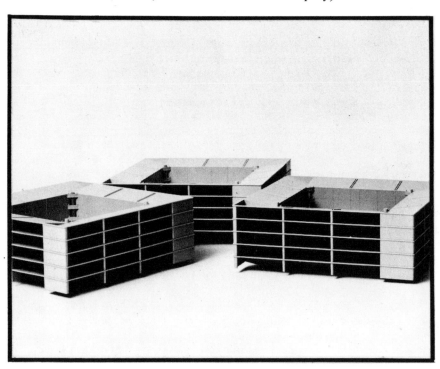

for sixty microfilm reels or cartridges. Units are expandable to a total capacity of 600 16mm microforms or 360 35mm microforms. The base incorporates a turntable and can be mounted on casters. Smaller units are well-suited to desk-top storage. Compartment-type storage eliminates the necessity of opening cabinet drawers in applications requiring the rapid retrieval of information from microfilm cartridges.

For libraries preferring to shelve roll microforms in a conventional manner, the MicroVox, developed by the Systematic Storage Company, is a binder board container measuring 9 by 9 by 4.5 inches with capacity for twelve 16mm or eight 35mm reels or cartridges. The container spine provides space for an identifying label. By using the MicroVox, librarians can physically group microform serial backfiles with recent paper issues in the same shelf location.

## FLAT MICROFORMS

### Eye-Legible Titling

The retrieval of information from microfiche and other flat microforms requires location of both the appropriate microform and the desired microimage within the microform.[13] In manual retrieval systems, location of the appropriate fiche, jacket, or aperture card is facilitated by eye-legible titling. As noted in chapter two, current standards for both source document and COM microfiche reserve the first row of frames for such titling. In source document applications, most step-and-repeat cameras will expose and position a strip of paper containing typewritten characters at the top of each fiche. For microfiche created by the strip-up method, headers are prepared separately on a typewriter or composer. These headers can be prepared in color to further highlight them. All COM recorders capable of producing microfiche will generate one or more lines of eye-legible characters in the title area. A few COM recorders will position eye-legible titling along the bottom row of frames or in either end column.

As noted in chapter seven, eye-legible titling for source document microfiche includes much of the same information found on the title page of the hardcopy original from which the microimages were made. The heading area of COM-generated microfiche catalogs, circulation lists, and similar output products typically includes the report title, date, fiche sequence number, and inclusive fiche contents in the form of a "from-to" statement of index keys extracted from the first and last data frames (Fig. 8-9). For applications with very heavy reference activity, COM fiche may provide a few additional eye-legible characters at the top of each column. Occasionally, source document microfiche feature eye-legible flash targets interspersed among conventional microimages.

Microfilm jackets, like microfiche, include a header area consisting of a matte-finished surface on which eye-legible characters can be written or typed. Because there are no standards for microfilm jackets, the amount of heading area varies considerably, from a quarter-inch to well over an inch in width. Aperture cards, of course, provide ample space for eye-legible information on both front and back.

**Figure 8-9**

**Microfiche Titling and Indexing**
(Courtesy: California Computer Products)

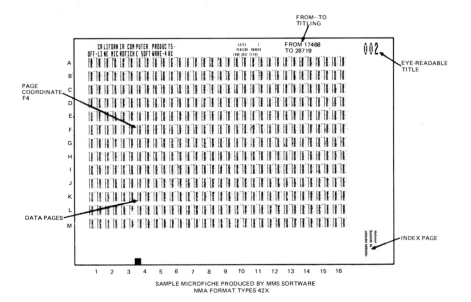

SAMPLE MICROFICHE PRODUCED BY MMS SORTWARE
NMA FORMAT TYPES 42X

As with roll microforms, manual storage and retrieval systems for flat microforms may employ drawer-type filing equipment. A typical cabinet, measuring 15 inches wide by 52 inches high by 26.5 inches deep, will hold up to 15,000 standard-size microfiche. As with paper files, groups of fiche can be separated by tabbed dividers. Smaller tray-type fiche files are available for desk-top storage. Regardless of file capacity, the user must flip through individual fiche, examining heading areas, until the desired microform is located. For very active files, panel-type storage units can eliminate much time-consuming microform handling. Panel-type files (Fig. 8-10) consist of a paper or plastic housing with pockets into which individual fiche or jackets are inserted upright, titles visible. The inclusive contents of a particular fiche are immediately apparent as are fiche sequence numbers used in refiling. Empty panel packets indicate refiling location. The panels also protect the microforms from dust and warping. The capacity of individual double-sided panels ranges from twenty to eighty fiche, depending on panel size and pocket spacing. The panels themselves can be stored in binders or mounted on desk-stands, rotary carousels, or wall racks.

**Figure 8-10**

**Panel-Type Microfiche Storage**
(Courtesy: Ring King Visibles)

## Microfiche Indexing

While eye-legible titling assists the user in identifying the appropriate microfiche, the internal microfiche index is designed to facilitate the location of the desired microimage. Information on source document microfiche and certain alphabetically or numerically sequenced COM reports can often be successfully retrieved without a specially-prepared index. Many source document microfiche prepared from technical reports and monographs include an index prepared for the original work and keyed to page numbers. Some source document applications and many COM reports, however, require a special index to associate data with its location in a particular microfiche frame, typically expressed as an alphanumeric row and column address. In source document applications, the microfiche index is prepared manually and filmed with the documents. In COM applications, software is utilized to extract user-specified index keys from each data frame and list them in the index with their associated microfiche grid coordinates. A grid on the microfiche reader facilitates the display of particular microimages.

The most prevalent source document and COM formats provide for an index as the last frame on a fiche, positioned in the lower right-hand corner. Placement of the index in this position is essential in applications anticipating the use of the automated microfiche retrieval and display equipment discussed later in this chapter. If more than one index frame is required, they customarily occupy the last few corner frames. In COM applications, there is an increasing trend toward the placement of index frames at the top of each fiche column. These column indexes may be identical with, or more detailed versions of, the corner index. The column index technique sacrifices a few data frames to facilitate retrieval by keeping the user in close proximity to an index.

Another increasingly popular technique provides for a randomly-recorded microfiche or microfilm data base—of catalog entries, for example—controlled by a master index on one or more separate fiche. Each index entry delivers a fiche number and grid coordinates or a roll number and frame number. The index is re-issued periodically to reflect changes or additions to the data base. This master microfiche index technique is used with MARCFICHE and other bibliographic micropublications described in chapter five. If both the data base and index are on fiche, a dual-carrier reader can be used to facilitate rapid referral from one microform to the other. For data bases on 16mm microfilm with a microfiche index, the COR 701 reader will accept a 16mm cartridge and a fiche simultaneously. A version of the COR 701 is available for film containing image count marks.

## Automated Retrieval and Display Systems

Automated microfiche retrieval and display systems are designed to minimize or eliminate user involvement in the location of a specified microfiche and frame.[14] The CARD (Compact Automated Retrieval and Display) reader (Fig. 8-11), for example, stores up to 750 microfiche in an interior carousel. Each microfiche bears a numerically-coded notched metal clip, supplied by the manufacturer, Image Systems Incorporated. The reader itself has two keyboards. To retrieve a particular microfiche and frame, the user enters the fiche number at the left-hand keyboard and the frame coordinates at the right-hand keyboard. The carousel is then searched, the desired fiche located by its clip notches, and the requested frame displayed. Retrieval time averages less than five seconds. Failure to enter frame coordinates at the right-hand keyboard causes the system to display the last frame on the specified fiche—the last frame being customarily reserved for an index.

The system's total microimage capacity varies with the internal format of the fiche utilized. With 98-page, NMA Type 1 Standard source document fiche, for example, a fully-loaded carousel would contain 73,500 microimages. With 208-page, 42X COM fiche, total system capacity increases to 156,000 microimages. Other acceptable fiche formats include 60-page, 18X COSATI; 80-page, 27X COM; and 100-page, 30X Decimal. Because of the requirement for precise microimage registration, a given CARD reader will accurately display one pre-selected microfiche format only. Fiche of varying formats and reductions cannot be mixed within the carousel.

**Figure 8-11**

**Automated Microfiche Display Device**
(Courtesy: Image Systems, Inc.)

As with other retrieval systems, the appropriate fiche and frame number must first be determined by consulting a manual or automated external index. For applications utilizing a machine-readable index maintained on a disk file associated with a large-scale or minicomputer, an optional feature allows the CARD reader to interface with any ASCII or EBCDIC terminal. The terminal is used to query the disk file index which, in turn, delivers the appropriate fiche and frame number directly to the CARD reader, thereby eliminating the necessity of additional key-entry. CARD is also available in several turnkey configurations utilizing a minicomputer and retrieval software for different types of applications. One such system, called ANCIRS (Automated News Clipping Indexing Retrieval System) is designed expressly for subject-oriented retrieval in newspaper libraries.[15]

Since its introduction in 1968, CARD has been a successful component in several library-based retrieval systems. At the Space Photography Laboratory of the California Institute of Technology, for example, a CARD reader interfaced to a minicomputer is used to access a file of lunar and planetary photographs on microfiche.[16] At MIT, modified CARD units were used for full-text storage in Project Intrex, described in chapter one.

### Random Access Files

As noted in chapter two, the flat microforms are vulnerable to loss through misfiling. The GAF 4000 (Fig. 8-12) is an example of a system that offers misfile protection by accessing a file of aperture cards at random. Cards to be entered in

**Figure 8-12**

**Random Access Aperture Card File**
(Courtesy: GAF Corporation)

the system are first notched along their bottom edge, using a special device that encodes a patent number, drawing number, or other numeric retrieval parameter up to eight digits in length. Encoded cards are then inserted in the file in any order. The basic system's capacity is 4,000 cards, expandable to 40,000 in increments of 4,000. To retrieve a given card, the identifying number or other retrieval parameter is key-entered at the system controller. The file is then automatically searched, the coded notches interpreted, and those cards meeting the search parameter ejected from the file. Ejected cards can then be duplicated, viewed, or used in a reader/printer or enlarger/printer. Following use, the cards are re-inserted anywhere in the file. Because the entire file is searched in parallel, retrieval time is a constant six seconds regardless of card location. Because the internal system code is Binary-Coded-Decimal (BCD), the GAF 4000 can interface with a computer. The basic system for 4,000 cards costs approximately $12,000. Equipment for each additional 4,000 cards costs approximately $9,000. Other manufacturers offer similar systems for microfiche or microfilm jackets.[17]

## REFERENCES

[1] The literature on microform retrieval system theory and practice is not extensive. For general information, see Clyde H. Aaron, "Retrieval Techniques—Flexibility for the Analyst," *Proceedings of the National Microfilm Association* (Silver Spring, Md.: NMA, 1974), II-24; G. S. Baker, "Information Access Methods for Microfilm Systems," *Microdoc* 13 (1974): 100-112; B. J. S. Williams, *Miniaturised Communications* (London: Library Association, 1970): 115-33; Bruce Bartos, *Microform-Based Information Storage and Retrieval Systems* (Los Alamitos, Calif.: Southwest Regional Laboratory for Educational Research and Development, April 1971); Vannevar Bush, "As We May Think," *Atlantic Monthly* 176 (July 1945): 101-108, is the classic statement on the automated microform retrieval system. See also, Ralph R. Shaw, "The Rapid Selector," *Journal of Documentation* 5 (1949): 164-71; James L. Pike and Thomas C. Bagg, "The Rapid Selector and Other NBS Document Retrieval Studies," *Proceedings of the National Microfilm Association* (Annapolis, Md.: NMA, 1962): 213-27; A. W. Tyler, W. L. Meyers, and J. W. Kuipers, "The Application of the Kodak Minicard System to Problems of Documentation," *American Documentation* 6 (1955): 18-30; David R. Wolf, "Automated Microimage Files and Other Advanced Techniques," *Proceedings of the National Microfilm Association* (Silver Spring, Md.: NMA, 1967): 87-89; Carl E. Nelson, "Micrographics—State of the Art," *Proceedings of the National Microfilm Association* (Silver Spring, Md.: NMA, 1969): 353-63; Alfred S. Tauber, "A Review of Microphotographic Techniques and Graphic Storage and Retrieval Systems," *Drexel Library Quarterly* 5 (1969): 234-40; Rodd S. Exelbert and Mitchell Badler, "Automatic Information Retrieval: A Report on the State of the Art," *Information and Records Management* 8 (1974): 23-29, 33-34.

[2] L. A. Smitzer, "The Art of Roll Film Look-Up," *Proceedings of the National Microfilm Association* (Silver Spring, Md.: NMA, 1968): 57-61.

[3] R. W. Johnson, et al., *Multi-Coded Microfilm Feasibility Study* (Dover, N.J.: Picatinny Arsenal, August 1975).

[4] The best system description is Stephen H. Wilcox, "Kodak MIRAcode II Products: Concepts and Applications," in Don Chenevert, ed., *Micrographics Science, 1973: Winter Symposium* (Washington: Society of Photographic Scientists and Engineers, 1973): 13-28. For application descriptions, see Leo G. Volkheimer, "Application of an Automated Microfilm System to Nuclear Weapons Operation," *Proceedings of the National Microfilm Association* (Annapolis, Md.: NMA, 1966): 63-74; Gerald C. Benedict and Thomas Buckley, "Random Access Retrieval with Microfilm," *Proceedings of the National Microfilm Association* (Silver Spring, Md.: NMA, 1971): II-39-43; James R. Miller, "A Brief Description of a Sophisticated University Alumni Marketing Information System," *Journal of Micrographics* 7 (1974): 223-29.

[5] Descriptors are represented on film in the Excess-3 code, a variant of binary-coded decimal (BCD) in which all numbers are three more than their natural BCD representation. Once understood, the code is not difficult to interpret.

[6] Jacques Fournier and Alison Schoenfeld, "The Development of an Electronic Film Retrieval System for a Newspaper Library," in *Proceedings of the American Society for Information Science* 10 (1973): 67-69.

[7] Kenneth Janda and David Gordon, "A Microfilm Information Retrieval System for Newspaper Libraries," *Special Libraries* 61 (1970): 33-41.

[8] Kenneth Janda, "Political Research with Miracode: A 16mm Microfilm Information Retrieval System," *NMA Journal* 1 (1968): 41-47.

[9] L. H. Foster, "Effective Systems Design and Analysis for Large-Scale Source Document Miracode Applications," *Journal of Micrographics* 7 (1974): 223-29.

[10] The advantages of segregating index information and document images have long been recognized. See, for example, Mortimer Taube, "Trends in Microfilm Applications Today and Tomorrow," *Proceedings of the National Microfilm Association* (Annapolis, Md.: NMA, 1965): 37-43; J. L. Simonds, "Information Technology for Network Operations," *Proceedings of the National Microfilm Association* (Silver Spring, Md.: NMA, 1969): 51-58; R. I. Tomlin and R. G. Brunner, "A Total Information Concept: Rapid Retrieval of Microfilmed Documents Using an Optical Coincidence System," *NMA Journal* 2 (1968): 102-104; Donald D. Jenkins, "Magnetic Indexing, Microfilm Storage, and Information Retrieval," *Proceedings of the National Microfilm Association* (Annapolis, Md.: NMA, 1962): 205-212; Paul W. Larson, "CRIS: Command Retrieval Information System," *Proceedings of the National Microfilm Association* (Annapolis, Md.: NMA, 1962): 41-49; Norman A. Vogel, "Walnut Document Storage and Retrieval System," *Proceedings of the National Microfilm Association* (Annapolis, Md.: NMA, 1962): 27-29; Donald R. Knudson and Richard S. Marcus, "The Design of a Microimage Storage and Transmission Capability Into an Integrated Transfer System," *Journal of Micrographics* 6 (1972): 15-20; R. J. D. Johnson, "An Experimental On-Line Retrieval System Using Ultrafiche," *Program* 9 (1975): 56-63.

[11] Alonzo Sherman, "Keyword Indexing for Microfilm," *NMA Journal* 2 (1968): 89-91.

[12] Arthur A. Teplitz, "Computer-Controlled Retrieval: A Primer," *Journal of Micrographics* 5 (1971): 35-40; Robert M. Landau, "New Economic Factors in the System Integration of Computer Terminal On-Line Retrieval Systems and Large Microform Data Banks," *Journal of Micrographics* 5 (1972): 125-30; Joseph W. Shepard, "Retrieval Systems Considerations," *Journal of Micrographics* 8 (1975): 285-89; L. P. Rinehart, "Retrieval: A New Dimension for Management," *Proceedings of the National Microfilm Association* (Silver Spring, Md.: NMA, 1971): III-7-12; R. W. Burnham, "Interfacing Microfilm and the Computer in a Technical Information System," *Proceedings of the National Microfilm Association* (Silver Spring, Md.: NMA, 1967): 131-43; Roy L. Merwin, "Benefits of Multi-Terminal Fast Automatic Random Access to Integrated Computer and Microfilm Information," *Proceedings of the American Society for Information Science* 10 (1973): 149-50; Merwin, "One Manufacturer's Approach to Automated Information Storage and Retrieval," *Journal of Micrographics* 6 (1973): 159-66.

[13] The best survey is Robert Judd Smith, "Microfiche Indexing Systems," *Proceedings of the National Micrographics Association* (Silver Spring, Md.: NMA, 1975): 244-53.

[14] George W. Tressel, Patricia L. Brown, and Richard E. Krohn, "Automated Retrieval and Remote Viewing of COSATI Microfiche—Problems and Prospects," *Proceedings of the American Society for Information Science* 7 (1970): 123-28; A. S. Tauber, "The Dynamic Use of Microfiche," *Proceedings of the National Microfilm Association* (Annapolis, Md.: NMA, 1966): 41-51; Tauber, "Document Retrieval Facts of Life," *Proceedings of the National Microfilm Association* (Annapolis, Md.: NMA, 1965): 216-22.

[15] Leon Bloom, "Information Retrieval Using Micrographics," *Journal of Micrographics* 8 (1974): 55-62.

[16] R. G. J. Zimmerman, "A Computer-Accessed Microfiche Library," *Journal of Library Automation* 7 (1974): 290-306.

[17] See Robert J. Kalthoff, "Automated Document Storage and Retrieval: A Perspective," *Journal of Micrographics* 9 (1975): 61-72; Henry D. Patterson, "Automation of Engineering Documentation Files," *Proceedings of the National Microfilm Association* (Annapolis, Md.: NMA, 1965): 129-35.

# CHAPTER 9

## MICROGRAPHICS AND LIBRARIES: The Future

### NEW TECHNOLOGIES

#### Computer-Input-Microfilm

Two types of innovative micrographic technologies are of significance to libraries: 1) those that employ radically different recording methodologies; and 2) those that link mocrographics to other technologies, especially data processing and data communications technologies. Computer-Input-Microfilm (CIM), a variant of optical character recognition technology, belongs to the second type. A CIM device scans, interprets, and translates human-readable information on microfilm into machine-readable digital data on magnetic tape or other media. Thus, CIM is conceptually the opposite of COM. The advantages of CIM are obvious. Tape, disk, and drum storage are expensive, bulky, and vulnerable to deterioration over time. Microfilm is economical, compact, and, when properly processed, archivally stable. Widespread availability of CIM technology would permit the maintenance of library catalogs and other data bases in microform while allowing rapid computer re-entry for additional data manipulation. The compactness of microforms would also permit significant economies in the mailing or other interchange of potentially machine-readable bibliographic information.

Although CIM technology is still developing, the advantages of microfilm over paper in optical character recognition systems have been recognized for many years. Compact microfilm is easier to handle than bulky paper. Input documents need not be of uniform size or thickness—an important consideration in many library applications. The elimination of paper jamming permits higher document transport speeds. In addition, microfilm character recognition is accomplished by transmitted rather than the more powerful reflected light required in OCR systems reading opaque paper documents. FOSDIC, one of the earliest CIM devices, has been used, in several improved versions, since 1953 at the United States Census Bureau.[1] For the broad range of CIM applications, however, Grafix I, a complex and powerful device developed by Information International Incorporated, represents the state-of-the-art today.[2]

Using a unique combination of hardware and software, Grafix I will read microfilmed source documents or COM microimages in a variety of fonts and formats, including hand printing. Character recognition is accomplished through a masking technique enhanced by a probability algorithm. Broken type faces and hand printing are recognized by feature extraction. Rejected characters are displayed, with context, at an operator terminal for key-entered correction. Although any microfilm input can be accepted, the system performs most reliably with high-quality COM microimages generated by graphics-type recorders.

The first Grafix I was built for the United States Navy. The system has since been used in several library-related applications. For the DATUM Information Retrieval System, an automated legal data base developed at the University of Montreal, a Grafix I device converted 16,000 bi-lingual pages of printed Exchecquer Court Proceedings to machine-readable form. At the University of California at Irvine, Grafix I has been used to encode Greek text for computer processing. The Hydrologic Data Laboratory at the Agricultural Research Service in Beltsville, Maryland, uses Grafix I for computer re-entry of data previously recorded via COM. A data-entry error rate of less than one percent is reported.[3]

## Microfacsimile Transmission

*Facsimile*, or *Fax*, is a technology that permits the transmission of document images to remote locations via telephone wires or other appropriate data communication facilities.[4] A typical facsimile equipment configuration consists of a transmitter capable of analyzing and translating a given document or document image into a pattern of digital or analog signals suitable for transmission and a receiver equipped with logical circuitry capable of decoding the signal and driving a recording device to construct an image of the original document. Facsimile equipment for the transmission of paper documents has been commercially available since the mid-1960s and has gained increasing acceptance since 1975. In libraries, facsimile equipment has been used for the transmission of inter-library loan materials and other time-sensitive documents.[5]

*Microfacsimile*, as the name implies, is a technology that permits the transmission of microimages to remote locations. Microfacsimile devices accept microimages as input and reconstruct the transmitted signals as either microimages or, more commonly, full-size documents. There are several potential library applications for microfacsimile. Several librarians have suggested the formation of multi-library consortia to acquire large research collections to be stored on film or fiche in centralized repositories. Microfacsimile would appear to be of considerable potential value in transmitting requested microimages from the central collection to participating libraries.

In contrast to the rapidly developing market for facsimile equipment capable of transmitting images of full-size paper documents, microfacsimile equipment is commercially available from only one source—the Alden Electronic and Impulse Recording Equipment Company of Westboro, Massachusetts.[6] Customized micro-facsimile devices have been developed for special applications, primarily in the military. To ensure preservation of legibility in transmitted microimages and enlarged prints, microforms intended for use in microfacsimile systems must be of very high quality, low in density and high in contrast. The microfacsimile transmitter must be able to scan very small points on film and translate recorded information into a signal suitable for reconstruction by the receiver. Technical considerations, however, have proven less of an impediment to the development of microfacsimile systems than the failure of a clear market for microfacsimile products to present itself. The potential microfacsimile market has, in fact, been narrowed by the minimal space requirements and ease of duplication that are characteristic of microform storage and retrieval systems. As an alternative to maintaining a centralized collection of microimages to be transmitted to remote users on demand, microfilm and microfiche collections can be inexpensively duplicated for decentralized storage at multiple locations. While copyright restrictions make this approach impractical in the potential library application described above, no such restrictions limit the duplication and decentralization of proprietary data in the more lucrative commercial sector for which microfacsimile systems would be initially developed. In such applications, however, microfacsimile would remain a viable system for the transmission of centralized files updated very frequently. Frequent updating would render wholesale file duplication impractical in many applications. The recent development of updateable microfiche systems, described in chapters two and three, may make such applications increasingly common.

### New Recording Methods

While the updateable microfiche systems already described employ unconventional micro-recording media, their approach to the positioning of microimages on fiche has largely conformed to prevailing standards and practices. The IZON 200 Reader System represents a new approach to microrecording that is of considerable interest and potential significance to libraries.[7] The IZON 200 Reader System will display microimages recorded by a proprietary process on an eight by ten inch sheet of IZON Film.™ Unlike conventional single-lens microfilm cameras, the recording device used to expose IZON film contains 504 molded plastic micro-lenses. These 504 lenses, arranged in rows and columns on a lens sheet, operate together to record an entire source document or existing microimages. The first lens, in the upper left corner, views only the first 504th part of the original material. Each subsequent lens exposes only that portion of the material directly before it. Recorded images, reduced 25X, are deposited in designated areas called *domains* on IZON film. The film is divided into 504 domains, one for each lens, and each domain contains 195 bins. The capacity of one sheet of IZON film is, thus, 195 pages. To the unaided eye, the 504 segmented sub-images appear as black dots on film. A half-inch area along the right hand film margin is reserved for eye-legible information.

The IZON 200 Reader System contains a corresponding system of 504 lenses designed to re-assemble the source document image and display it on a seven by nine inch screen. Individual lenses display 1/504th portion of the image. The images themselves overlap slightly, eliminating segmentation lines. The design implications of this display method are of particular significance to libraries. While conventional microform readers require a twelve to seventeen inch projection distance between lens and screen, the distributed optics of the IZON 200 Reader System permit compact design. The reader itself weighs only six pounds and measures just 10 inches wide by 13.5 inches high by 2.5 inches deep. It is suitable for lap use and can be handled like a book. The screen itself can be turned for proper orientation of microimages filmed in either the cine or comic mode. As noted in chapter six, book-like qualities are an important factor in overcoming user-resistance to microform readers intended for study-type applications.

# NEW UNDERSTANDING

## Micrographics Education

Chapter six also emphasized the importance of educating librarians for the design and management of microform applications. Librarians can obtain micrographics education in several ways. Among professional organizations, the National Micrographics Association accomplishes its educational objectives through a program of meetings, seminars, and publications.[8] While the NMA serves the broad micrographics user community, sessions at the annual meeting are typically devoted to library applications. The *Journal of Micrographics*, the NMA's primary publication, often contains articles of direct or tangential interest to librarians. The NMA also publishes a series of inexpensive, illustrated booklets on such basic subjects as selecting display equipment, computer-output-microfilm, and microform retrieval systems. The NMA publication list also includes two micrographics textbooks.

The American Library Association, the Special Libraries Association, the American 'Society for Information Science, and the Association of Records Managers and Administrators are among the other professional organizations including sessions on micrographics as a regular feature of their annual and other meeting programs. Micrographics courses are an increasingly common component in the offerings of organizations specializing in continuing education. The Continuing Engineering Education Division of the George Washington University, for example, offers courses in Microfilm Information Systems and Automated Document Storage and Retrieval Systems, both of which emphasize the design of micrographic systems. Similar courses are offered by the American Management Association and the Institute for Graphic Communication.

The Columbia University School of Library Service first offered a course in micrographics in 1939.[9] Despite this early beginning, library schools have generally neglected micrographics in the design of curricula for the education of future professionals. A 1972 survey indicated that only 7 of 44 accredited library schools offered special courses related to micrographics. A 1975 examination of the catalogs of 65 accredited library schools indicated that only 12 offered courses specifically incorporating micrographics-related terminology in their titles. An additional nine incorporated such terminology in one or more of their course descriptions.

## The Need for Research

While opportunities for micrographics education have increased significantly in recent years, there is little widespread understanding of the relationship of micrographics to other information management technologies, especially computers. The development of COM and automated microform retrieval systems has highlighted the need for systems analysts trained in both micrographics and computer technologies. Acceptance and use of micrographics has been deterred, however, by data processing personnel's unfamiliarity with the advantages of microforms or even the most rudimentary principles of micrographics systems design. Many data processing specialists are openly contemptuous of micrographics as a solution to complex information management problems. Their attitude is shared by some librarians who view microforms as a second-rate interim technology that will eventually be displaced by increasingly less-expensive direct access computer storage.[10] These attitudes will only be overcome through research that analyzes the cost/performance advantages of microforms in particular kinds of applications. As an example of this much-needed research, Levine analyzed the information-seeking behavior of persons using a microfiche data base consisting of 6,000 pages pertaining to foreign naval activities. Full-text storage on fiche was supported with both an on-line index, permitting complex logical searches, and a printed KWOC index. Fiche themselves were stored in desk-top automatic retrieval units designed to eliminate manual handling. As users became more familiar with fiche retrieval, expensive on-line searches gradually gave way to browsing of fiche. Users often found that they could view fiche faster than their on-line terminals could print the accession numbers of fiche meeting the stated search criteria. Levine concluded that users having access to entire documents in rapidly retrievable microfiche form could tolerate lower relevance in indexing, with resulting savings in indexing costs. Further, the availability of full text on fiche may eliminate the need for abstracts entirely.[11] Such studies, indicating areas of cost displacements and savings in micrographics systems, are unfortunately few in number. Ultimately, however, the continued viability of micrographics systems as an information management alternative may depend on the understanding that only such research can provide.

# REFERENCES

[1] Masey Volk, "Automated Input for the 1970 Census," *Journal of Micrographics* 3 (1969): 57-62; James L. McPherson and Masey Volk, "FOSDIC Microfilm Problems and Their Solutions," *Proceedings of the National Microfilm Association* 11 (1962): 193-203.

[2] Alfred L. Fenaughty, "Demand Printing: A Revolution in Publishing," *Journal of Micrographics* 8 (1975): 201-206; Arnold K. Griffith, "From Gutenberg to Grafix I—New Directions in OCR," *Journal of Micrographics* 9 (1975): 81-89; Roger Holland, "CIM—the Present and the Future," *Microdoc* 15 (1976): 52-55.

[3] J. B. Burford and J. M. Clark, "Hydrologic Data—Computer-Microfilm Storage and Retrieval," *Journal of Micrographics* 8 (1975): 147-51.

[4] The only survey, now somewhat dated, is Daniel M. Costigan, *Fax: Principles and Practice of Facsimile Communication* (Philadelphia: Chilton Book Co., 1971).

[5] For an excellent review of library fax experiments, see Sharon Schatz, *Facsimile Transmission in Libraries—a State of the Art Survey* (Washington: Library of Congress Information Systems Office, 1967), reprinted in *Library Resources and Technical Services* 12 (1968): 5-15; also D. W. Heron, "Telefacsimile in Libraries: Progress and Prospects," *UNESCO Bulletin for Libraries* 23 (1969): 8-13; "Facsimile Transmission," *Advanced Technology/Libraries* 1 (March 1972): 1-7.

[6] Daniel M. Costigan, "Microfacsimile: A Status Report," *Journal of Micrographics* 4 (1971): 189-99.

[7] William L. Wallace, "Developing a Book-Size Reader System," *Journal of Micrographics* 10 (1977): 161-68.

[8] Don M. Avedon, "Micrographics Education for Librarians," in Andrew G. Torok, ed., *Micrographics Education for Librarians*, RLMS Microfile Series, Vol. 3 (Washington: Library of Congress, 1977).

[9] R. E. Stevens, "Instruction on Microform: Its Place in Library School," *Journal of Education for Librarianship* 6 (1965): 133-36; Hubbard W. Ballou, "Micrographics Education at Columbia," in Torok, ed., *Micrographics Education for Librarians.*

[10] See, for example, J. E. Crow, "Microforms and Technical Information," *Journal of Chemical Documentation* 8 (1968): 204-207.

[11] Emil H. Levine, "Effect of Instantaneous Retrieval on Indexing Criteria," *Journal of the American Society for Information Science* 25 (1974): 199-200; Levine, "Potential Savings in Indexing Costs through the Use of High-Speed Random Access Microfiche," in Frances Spigai, ed., *Information Roundup: Proceedings of the Fourth ASIS Mid-Year Conference* (Washington: American Society for Information Science, 1975): 105-107.

# GLOSSARY

This glossary defines essential terms used throughout the book. Definitions are necessarily abbreviated. The numbers in parenthesis indicate chapter locations where fuller discussions of listed terms can be found. The glossary is intended primarily for readers who encounter unfamiliar terms in early chapters which are not fully defined or discussed until subsequent chapters. Readers seeking a more extensive listing of micrographics terminology should consult *The Glossary of Micrographics* (Silver Spring, Md.: National Micrographics Association, 1973).

**Aperture card** (2). A tabulating-size card with a chip of 35mm microfilm mounted in a rectangular aperture. In an eighty column card, the standard aperture spans columns 53 through 77 and measures 1.304 by 1.908 inches.

**Archival quality** (3). Refers to the ability of an entire processed microform to retain its original characteristics and resist deterioration over time.

**Camera, planetary** (3). A microfilming device in which source documents are exposed while positioned on a flat copyboard or glass platen; also called a flat-bed camera.

**Camera, rotary** (3). A microfilming device in which source documents are exposed as they rotate past a narrow slit aperture; also called a flow-type camera.

**Camera, step-and-repeat** (3). A microfilming device capable of creating microfiche by sequentially exposing source documents in a predetermined format of rows and columns on 105mm microfilm.

**Camera-original microform** (3). The microform that comes out of the camera, as opposed to microforms created by duplication.

**Camera/processor** (3). Integrated units designed to expose and develop microimages as one continuous operation without external processing.

**Card jacket** (2). A four by six inch card with polyester sleeves for the insertion of 16mm or 35mm microfilm strips.

**Cartridge** (2). A plastic single-core container for 16mm or 35mm microfilm. When mounted on an appropriate reader, microfilm from the cartridge is automatically threaded onto a take-up spool built into the reader.

**Cassette** (2). A plastic double-core container for 16mm microfilm which encloses both a supply and take-up spool in a single housing.

**Cine mode** (2). Method of image placement in which the text of the document is perpendicular to the edges of the film.

**Comic mode** (2). Method of image placement in which the text of the document is parallel to the edges of the film.

**Computer-assisted retrieval** (8). A retrieval technique in which a computer-stored index is searched to determine the location of specific images within a microform data base.

**Computer-output-microfilm** (4). The end product of a process that converts machine-readable, computer-processable digital data to human-readable textual or graphic information on microfilm or microfiche without first creating paper documents.

**Contrast** (3, 6). An expression of the relationship between high and low density areas of a photographic image or screen display.

**COSATI** (2). Acronym for the Committee on Scientific and Technical Information, used to denote a microfiche format consisting of 60 images reduced 18X and arranged in 5 rows and 12 columns; now the NMA Type 2 Standard for microfiche of documents.

**CRT photography** (4). Method of generating computer-output-microfilm by photographing data pages displayed on a cathode-ray-tube screen inside a COM recorder.

**Diazo process** (3). Method of microform duplication in which film employing an emulsion of diazonium salts is exposed to ultraviolet light transmitted through a master microform. Salts are dispersed in areas of the microfilm corresponding to light areas of the original microimage, while dark areas remain unaffected, forming a latent image that is developed with ammonia fumes.

**Dry silver process** (3, 4, 6). Process by which full-size or micro-images are recorded by exposure to light and development by heat alone without wet chemicals. Dry silver microfilms are available for both source document and computer-output microfilming. Dry silver print papers are used in certain reader/printers.

**Duo** (3). A rotary camera microfilming technique in which one half of the width of a roll of 16mm microfilm is masked and the remainder exposed. When the full length of the film has passed through the camera, it is removed and reloaded. The previously exposed portion is masked and the previously masked portion exposed. The duo microfilming technique is used to increase the microimage capacity of a single reel by recording documents at high reductions.

**Duplex** (3). A rotary camera microfilming technique in which mirrors are used to simultaneously record the front and back of source documents, each occupying one-half the width of 16mm film.

**Duplicate microform** (3). A microform created by duplicating an existing microform.

**Duplicating microfilms** (3). Microfilms designed for the creation of duplicate microforms rather than for use in cameras.

**Electrochemical process** (6). A method of microimage enlargement which employs an electric current to create a latent image on chemically-treated paper. Development is accomplished via a liquid activator. The process is employed in reader/printers.

**Electrofax process** (6). A method of microimage enlargement which employs electrostatic charges to create a latent image on charged photoreceptive paper coated with zinc oxide. The image is developed by applying an oppositely-charged toner, consisting of fine carbon particles in liquid suspension. The process is employed in reader/printers.

**Electron beam recording** (4). Method of generating computer-output-microfilm in which a deflected electron beam strokes individual characters on dry silver microfilm.

**Enlarger/printer** (6). A device designed for the automatic, high-speed, single- or multiple-copy production of enlarged prints from microimages.

**Eye-legible images** (2, 4, 7, 8). Images on microfilm that are large enough to be read by the unaided eye. Eye-legible images are generally employed in the first few target frames on microfilm or in the title row on microfiche and serve to identify the microform and indicate its content.

**Flat microforms** (2). A grouping of microforms by physical shape. The flat microforms include microfiche, microfilm jackets, aperture cards, ultrafiche, and micro-opaques.

**Generation** (3). A measure of the remoteness of a particular microform from the original source document or computer-output. The camera-original microform is a first-generation microform, a duplicate microform made from it is a second-generation microform, and so on.

**Image rotation** (6). A reader feature that enables the microform user to turn displayed microimages to compensate for the varying positions of documents on film.

**Jacket card** (2). A tabulating-size card with polyester sleeves for the insertion of 16mm or 35mm microfilm strips.

**Laser-beam recording** (4). Method of generating computer-output-microfilm in which a deflected laser beam shapes individual characters by illuminating selected points on special silver halide or dry silver microfilm.

**Latent image** (3). An image that requires development to become visible.

**Light-emitting-diode recording** (4). Method of generating computer-output-microfilm in which light-emitting-diodes are used to create a line of up to 132 characters which is subsequently exposed to microfilm.

**Magnification** (6). A measure of the size of a given linear dimension of a displayed microimage compared to the size of the corresponding linear dimension of the microimage itself. Magnification is expressed as 24X, 42X, 48X, and so on, where the displayed microimage is enlarged 24, 42, or 48 times.

**Magnification ratio** (6). Magnification expressed as a ratio—1:24, 1:42, 1:48, and so on.

**Microcard** (1). An opaque microform, three by five inches in size, on which microimages are affixed in rows and columns. The reverse side of the card may contain additional microimages or eye-legible bibliographic data.

**Microfiche** (2). A sheet of microfilm containing multiple microimages in a two dimensional grid pattern of rows and columns. The term is both singular and plural.

**Microfilm** (1, 2, 3, 4). Used as a noun to denote fine-grain, high resolution film containing, or capable of containing, images greatly reduced in size. Used as a verb to denote the recording of microimages on film.

**Microfilm jacket** (2). A transparent acetate or polyester carrier with one or more sleeves designed to hold 16mm or 35mm microfilm in flat strips.

**Microform** (2). A generic term for any information communication or storage medium containing images too small to be read without magnification.

**Micrographics** (1). A general term used to denote all activities relating to the creation or use of microforms.

**Microimage** (2). Image too small to be read without magnification.

**Micro-opaque** (2). A microform distinguished by a paper rather than a film image support.

**Microprint** (2). Trade-name for opaque microform created by the Readex Microprint Corporation. Unlike other microforms, Microprint is created by printing reduced document images on rag content card stock.

**Micropublishing** (1, 5). The production of information in multiple-copy microform for sale or distribution to the public.

**Micropublishing, original** (5). The publication of information in microform in place of, or prior to, its publication in paper form.

**Micropublishing, retrospective** (5). The re-publication in multiple-copy microform of material previously published in paper form.

**Micropublishing, simultaneous** (5). Micropublications issued at the same time as paper form publication of the same material.

**Photochromic microimagery** (2). Trade-name used by NCR to denote the technology used to create ultrafiche.

**Polarity** (3). Term used to denote the change or retention of the dark-to-light relationship of corresponding areas of a microimage and the original source document or COM-generated display from which the microimage was made.

**Processing** (3). The series of mechanical and chemical operations required to make latent microimages visible.

**Reader** (6). A projection device that magnifies microimages so they can be read with the unaided eye.

**Reader/printer** (6). A projection device that both magnifies microimages for screen display and prints paper enlargements of displayed images on user demand.

**Reduction** (2). A measure of the number of times a given linear dimension of a document is reduced through microfilming. Reduction is expressed as 14X, 24X, 42X, and so on, where the reduced linear dimension is 1/14, 1/24, or 1/42 the length of its full-size counterpart.

**Reduction ratio** (2). The expression of reduction as a ratio—14:1, 24:1, 42:1, and so on.

**Reel** (2). A plastic or metal flanged holder for wound microfilm in 16mm and 35mm widths.

**Resolution** (3, 6). As applied to microfilms and display devices, a measure of the ability of optical systems and photographic materials to render fine detail visible. Resolution is typically expressed as the number of lines per millimeter discernable in a microimage and is determined by examining a microfilmed test target consisting of closely spaced lines of progressively decreasing size.

**Roll microform** (2). A generic term which encompasses microfilm on reels, in cartridges, and in cassettes.

**Silver halide process** (3). The dominant microfilming technology in which film coated with a light-sensitive emulsion of silver halide crystals suspended in gelatin is exposed to light reflected from a source document or generated by COM recorders. When exposed to light, silver halide crystals are converted to silver nuclei in areas of the film corresponding to light areas of the original. These altered crystals are converted to black silver grains during development.

**Small office microfilm** (1). Name given to microfilm products intended for use in relatively low volume installations.

**Simplex** (3). Microfilming method in which a single document image appears in each film frame.

**Transparent electrophotography** (2). The process used to create updateable microfiche by the A. B. Dick/Scott System 200 Record Processor. Transparent Electrophotographic (TEP) film has the capacity to withstand exposure but retain sensitivity.

**Turnkey** (8). A computer-based system in which the customer purchases all hardware and software as a single functioning unit and need only turn on the key to put the system into operation.

**Ultrafiche** (2). Microfiche created at reductions in excess of 90X. In library applications, the term is often loosely used to denote fiche created at reductions in excess of 55X.

**Vesicular process** (3). Method of microform duplication in which film employing a light sensitive emulsion suspended in a thermoplastic resin is exposed to ultraviolet light which creates pressure pockets that deform the emulsion, creating a latent image that is developed through heat.

**Viewer** (6). A hand-held magnifier which operates with an ambient or battery-powered light source.

**Viewer/inserter** (3). A device used to strip up roll microfilm for conversion to microfilm jackets.

**Xerographic process** (6). A method of microimage enlargement which employs electrostatic charges to create a latent image on a charged intermediate surface and subsequently transfer the image to an oppositely-charged sheet of ordinary paper. The process is employed in reader/printers and enlarger/printers.

# SELECTED BIBLIOGRAPHY ON
# LIBRARY APPLICATIONS OF MICROGRAPHICS

Adler, James A. "Indexing as the Key to Micropublishing: The Case History of the Congressional Information Service," *Journal of Micrographics* 4 (1971):239-45.

Adler, James A. "The Relationship between Library and Micropublisher," *Government Publications Review* 1 (1973):226-28.

Applebaum, Edmond L. "Implications of the National Register of Microform Masters as Part of a National Preservation Program," *Library Resources and Technical Services* 9 (1965):489-94.

Aschenborn, H. J. "UNICAT—the South African Joint Catalogue of Monographs on Microfiche," *Microdoc* 11 (1972):76-78.

Aschenborn, H. J. "The Use of Microfilm in South African Libraries," *Journal of Micrographics* 6 (1972):33-37.

Ayres, F. H. "Books in English: A Comparative Assessment," *Journal of Librarianship* 6 (1974):233-40.

Boni, Albert. "Readex Microprint—How It Began," *Microdoc* 11 (1972):5-10.

Butterfield, Lyman H. "Vita Sine Literis, Mors Est: The Microfilm Edition of the Adams Papers," *Library of Congress Quarterly Journal of Acquisitions* 18 (1960):53-58.

Bailey, Herbert S., Jr. "The Limits of On-Demand Publishing," *Scholarly Publishing* 6 (1975):291-98.

Basile, Victor A., and Reginald W. Smith. "Evolving the Ninety Percent Pharmaceutical Library," *Special Libraries* 61 (1970):81-86.

Beck, William L. "A Realistic Approach to Microform Management," *Microform Review* 2 (1973):172-76.

Beil, John. "CIS," *Illinois Libraries* 58 (1976):194-99.

Buckle, David. "The Cost of a COM Catalogue System at Birmingham University Library," *Microdoc* 13 (1974):15-18.

Buckle, David, and Thomas French. "The Application of Microform to Manual and Machine-Readable Catalogues," *Program* 5 (1971):41-66.

Bush, Vannevar. "As We May Think," *Atlantic Monthly* 176 (July 1945):101-108.

Carroll, C. Edward. "Microfilmed Catalogs: A More Efficient Way to Share Library Resources," *Microform Review* 1 (1972):274-78.

Carroll, C. Edward. "Some Problems of Microform Utilization in Large University Collections," *Microform Review* 1 (1972):19-24.

Chillag, J. P. "Problems with Reports, Particularly Microfiche Reports," *ASLIB Proceedings* 22 (1970):201-216.

Chinn, Marion. "A Microfiche System for Legal Material at the Consumer's Association Library," *Microdoc* 14 (1975):109-111.

Christ, C. W., Jr. "Microfiche: A Study of User Attitudes and Reading Habits," *Journal of the American Society of Information Science* 23 (1972):30-35.

Clapp, Verner W., and Robert T. Jordan. "Re-Evaluation of Microfilm as a Method of Book Storage," *College and Research Libraries* 24 (1963):5-15.

Claridge, P. R. P. "Microfiching of Periodicals from the User's Point of View," *ASLIB Proceedings* 21 (1969):306-311.

Corya, William L. "The Integration of Formats to Provide Catalog Access Services." In Frances Spigai, ed., *Information Roundup* (Washington: American Society for Information Science, 1975): 96-104.

Daghita, Joan M. "A Core Collection of Journals on Microfilm in a Community Teaching Hospital Library," *Bulletin of the Medical Library Association* 64 (1976):240-41.

Doebler, Paul. "Libraries on Microfiche: LRI's Experience in the Field," *Publishers Weekly* 202 (Dec. 18, 1972):27-30.

De Villiers, Ann M., and Barbara F. Schloman. "Experiences with Scientific Journals on Microfilm in an Academic Reading Room," *Special Libraries* 64 (1973):555-60.

Duncan, Virginia L., and Frances E. Parsons. "Use of Microfilm in an Industrial Research Library," *Special Libraries* 61 (1970):288-90.

Dugger, Gordon L., Ruth F. Bryans, and William T. Morris, Jr. "AIAA Experiments and Results on SDD, Synoptics, Miniprints, and Related Topics," *IEEE Transactions on Professional Communications* PC-16 (1973):100-104, 178.

Darling, Pamela. "Developing a Preservation Microfilming Program," *Library Journal* 99 (1974):2803-2809.

Darling, Pamela. "Microforms in Libraries: Preservation and Storage," *Microform Review* 5 (1976):93-100.

Edwards, Mary Jane. "Microforms: A View from the State Library of Pennsylvania," *Journal of Micrographics* 8 (1975):245-50.

Elrod, J. McRee. "Author and Title Analytics for Major Microform Sets," *Microform Review* 2 (1973):99-104.

Elrod, J. McRee. "Is the Card Catalogue's Unquestioned Sway in North America Ending?," *Journal of Academic Librarianship* 2 (1976):4-8.

Evans, Charles W. "High Reduction Microfiche for Libraries: An Evaluation of Collections from the National Cash Register Co. and Library Resources, Inc.," *Library Resources and Technical Services* 16 (1972):33-47.

Fair, Judy. "The Microtext Reading Room: A Practical Approach," *Microform Review* 1 (1972):199-203, 269-73; 2 (1973):9-13.

Falk, Clara A., Bell W. Campbell, and Masse Bloomfield. "A Microfilm Card Catalog at Work," *Special Libraries* 67 (1976):316-18.

Forbes, Edward J., and Thomas C. Bagg. *Report of a Study of Requirements and Specifications for Serial and Monograph Microrecording for the National Library of Medicine* (Washington: National Bureau of Standards, 1966).

Fournier, Jacques, and Alison Schoenfeld. "The Development of an Electronic Film Retrieval System for a Newspaper Library," *Proceedings of the American Society for Information Science* 10 (1973):67-69.

Gaines, Katherine. "Undertaking a Subject Catalog in Microfiche," *Library Resources and Technical Services* 15 (1971):297-308.

Goldman, Charles C., and Harry Grinberg. "II. Ultrafiche Libraries: The Publishers Respond," *Microform Review* 1 (1972):103-108.

Gray, Edward. "Our Microform Marketing Strategy," *IEEE Transactions on Professional Communications* PC-18 (1975):160-63.

Greene, Robert J. "Microform Attitude and Frequency of Microform Use," *Journal of Micrographics* 8 (1975):131-34.

Greene, Robert J. "Microform Library Catalogs and the LENDS Microfiche Catalog," *Microform Review* 4 (1975):30-34.

Gregory, Roma S. "Acquisition of Microforms," *Library Trends* 18 (1970):373-84.

Grieder, E. M. "Ultrafiche Libraries: A Librarian's View," *Microform Review* 1 (1972):85-100.

Harvey, William B., et al. "The Impending Crisis in University Publishing," *Scholarly Publishing* 3 (1972):195-207.

Hawken, William R., et al. "Microbook Publication—A New Approach for a New Decade," *Journal of Micrographics* 3 (1970):188-93.

Hawken, William R. "Microform Standardization: The Problem of Research Materials and a Proposed Solution," *NMA Journal* 2 (1968):14-27.

Hawken, William R. "Systems Instead of Standards," *Library Journal* 98 (Sept. 15, 1973):2515-25.

Hawken, William R. "Technical Reports on Microfiche—What Price Unitization," *National Micro-News* no. 69 (April 1964):195-207.

Heilprin, Laurence B. "The Economics of On-Demand Library Copying," *Proceedings of the National Microfilm Association* (Annapolis, Md.: National Microfilm Association, 1962): 311-39.

Heim, Kathleen M. "The Role of Microforms in the Small College Library," *Microform Review* 3 (1974):254-59.

Holmes, Donald C. *Determination of User Needs and Future Requirements for a Systems Approach to Microfilm Technology* (Washington: Office of Education, Bureau of Research, 1969).

Holmes, Donald C. *Determination of the Environmental Conditions Required in a Library for the Effective Utilization of Microforms* (Washington: Office of Education, Bureau of Research, 1970).

Jacobs, Horace. "Papers and Proceedings of Professional Meetings on Microfiche," *Microform Review* 3 (1974):15-21.

Janda, Kenneth, and David Gordon. "A Microfilm Information Retrieval System for Newspaper Libraries," *Special Libraries* 61 (1970):33-47.

Josephs, Melvin J. "Information Dissemination with Microforms," *IEEE Transactions on Professional Communications* PC-18 (1975):164-67.

Knight, Nancy H. "Microform Catalog Data Retrieval Systems: A Survey," *LTR* (May 1975).

Kozumplik, W. A., and R. T. Lange. "Computer-Produced Microfilm Library Catalog," *American Documentation* 18 (1967):67-80.

Kristy, Norton F. "System Design for Microbook Publishing," *Proceedings of the American Society for Information Science* 7 (1970):221-23.

Kuney, Joseph H. "Impact of Microfilms on Journal Costs," *IEEE Transactions on Professional Communications* PC-16 (1973):80-81, 175.

Kunkel, Barbara, et al. "The Impact of Modern Technology on a Technical Library," *Proceedings of the American Society for Information Science* 12 (1975):121-22.

Leisinger, Albert H., Jr. "Selected Aspects of Microreproduction in the United States," *Archivum* 16 (1966):127-50.

Lewis, Ralph W. "User's Reaction to Microfiche: A Preliminary Study," *College and Research Libraries* 31 (1970):260-68.

Logie, Audrey. "Access to Readex Microprint U.S. Government Depository Collection," *Government Publications Review* 2 (1975):103-110.

Lynden, Frederick C. "Replacement of Hard Copy by Microforms," *Microform Review* 4 (1975):9-14.

Madison, D. E., and J. E. Galejs. "Application of the Micrographic Catalog Retrieval System in the Iowa State University Library," *Library Resources and Technical Services* 15 (1971):492-98.

Martin, Susan K. "Mixed Media for a Serial System: Hardcopy, Microform, and CRT's." In Frances Spigai, ed. *Information Roundup* (Washington: American Society for Information Science, 1975): 111-17.

Massey, Don W. "The Management and Reorganization of the Photographic Services at Alderman Library, University of Virginia," *Journal of Micrographics* 4 (1970):35-39.

Maxin, Jacqueline A. "The Open Shelving of Journals on Microfilm," *Special Libraries* 66 (1975):592-94.

McGrath, William E., and Donald Simon. "Regional Numerical Union Catalog on Computer Output Microfiche," *Journal of Library Automation* 5 (1972):217-29.

Meirboom, Esther R. "Conversion of the Periodical Collection in a Teaching Hospital Library to Microfilm Format," *Bulletin of the Medical Library Association* 64 (1976):36-40.

Meyer, Richard W., and John F. Knapp. "COM Catalog Based on OCLC Records," *Journal of Library Automation* 8 (1975):312-21.

Miele, Anthony W. "The Illinois State Library Microfilm Automated Catalog (IMAC)," *Microform Review* 2 (1973):27-31.

Mislovitz, Maryann J. "Control and Dissemination of Drug-Related Literature," *Proceedings of the American Society for Information Science* 10 (1973):157-58.

Montagnes, Ian. "Scholarly Monographs on Microfiche: The University of Toronto Press as a Case in Point," *Microform Review* 1 (1972):29-30.

Napier, Paul A., et al. "The Library Resources, Inc., Library of American Civilization Demonstration at the George Washington University Library," *Microform Review* 3 (1974):158-76.

Nutter, Susan K. "Microforms and the User: Key Variables of User Acceptance in a Library Environment," *Drexel Library Quarterly* 11 (1975):17-31.

Oliva, John J. "Microfilm Cartridge System at Prince George's Community College," *Journal of Micrographics* 6 (1972):89-92.

Otten, Klaus. "A Hypothesis: Microform Will Become the Major Medium for 'New Information' in Reference Libraries," *Journal of Micrographics* 4 (1971):265-74.

Otten, Klaus. "Microform in the Research Library of the Future," *Journal of Micrographics* 6 (1973):121-27.

Otten, Klaus. "Ultramicrofiche Packages for Libraries: Pros and Cons of Different Approaches," *Proceedings of the National Microfilm Association* (Silver Spring, Md.: National Microfilm Association, 1971): II-110-20.

Overhage, Carl F. J., and J. F. Reintjes. "Project Intrex: A General Review," *Information Storage and Retrieval* 10 (1974):157-88.

Peele, David. "Bind or Film: Factors in the Decision," *Library Resources and Technical Services* 8 (1964):168-71.

Pickford, A. G. A. "FAIR (Fast Access Information Retrieval) Project: Aims and Methods," *ASLIB Proceedings* 19 (1967):79-95.

Power, Eugene B. "O-P Books: A Library Breakthrough," *American Documentation* 4 (1958):273-76.

Pritsker, Alan B., and J. William Sadler. "An Evaluation of Microfilm as a Method of Book Storage," *College and Research Libraries* 18 (1957):290-96.

Raffel, Jeffrey A., and Robert Shishko. *Systematic Analysis of University Libraries: An Application of Cost-Benefit Analysis to the MIT Libraries* (Cambridge: MIT Press, 1969).

Rebuldela, Harriet K. "Ultrafiche Libraries: A User Survey of the Library of American Civilization," *Microform Review* 3 (1974):178-88.

Reichmann, Felix. "Bibliographic Control of Microforms," *Microform Review* 1 (1972):279-80.

Reichmann, Felix, and Josephine Tharpe. *Bibliographic Control of Microforms* (Westport, Conn.: Greenwood Press, 1972).

Reid, Jutta R. "Cost Comparison of Periodicals in Hard Copy and on Microform," *Microform Review* 5 (1976):185-92.

Reno, Edward A., Jr. "Some Basic Aspects of Scholarly Micropublishing," *Proceedings of the National Microfilm Association* (Silver Spring, Md.: National Microfilm Association, 1973): II-202-93.

Roberts, E. G., and J. P. Kennedy. "The Georgia Tech Library's Microfiche Catalog," *Journal of Micrographics* 6 (1973):245-51.

Rochlin, Philip. "Micro Media in the Library: A Once Over Lightly," *Journal of Micrographics* 6 (1973):99-104.

Rogers, Kenneth A., and Earl C. Vogt. "Cost Benefits of Computer Output Microfilm Library Catalogs," *Proceedings of the American Society for Information Science* 10 (1973):199-200.

Ruml, Treadwell. "I. Ultrafiche Libraries: The Publishers Respond," *Microform Review* 1 (1972):101-102.

Saffady, William. "A Computer Output Microfilm List of Serials for Patron Use," *Journal of Library Automation* 7 (1974):263-66.

Saffady, William. *Computer Output Microfilm Hardware and Software: The State of the Art* (Washington: Library of Congress, 1977).

Saffady, William. "Microfilm Cameras: A Survey of Features and Functions," *Special Libraries* 68 (1977):1-6.

Saffady, William. "Microfilm Equipment and Retrieval Systems for Library Picture Collections," *Special Libraries* 65 (1974):440-44.

Saffady, William. "Small Office Microfilm (SOM) Products: A Survey," *Microform Review* 5 (1976):266-71.

Saffady, William. "Teaching Reprography," *Journal of Education for Librarianship* 15 (1975):147-59.

Salmon, Stephen R. "User Resistance to Microforms in the Research Library," *Microform Review* 3 (1974):194-99.

Schleifer, Harold B., and Peggy A. Adams. "Books in Print on Microfiche: A Pilot Test," *Microform Review* 5 (1976):10-24.

Scott, Peter. "Project Intrex and Microphotography." In *Intrex: Report of a Planning Conference on Information Transfer Experiments* (Cambridge: MIT, 1965): 203-215.

Scott, Peter. "Scholars and Researchers and Their Use of Microforms," *NMA Journal* 2 (1969):121-26.

Simmons, Peter. "Library Automation at the University of British Columbia: A Ten-Year Progress Report." In Frances Spigai, ed. *Information Roundup* (Washington: American Society for Information Science, 1975): 87-95.

Simonton, Wesley. "The Bibliographic Control of Microforms," *Library Resources and Technical Services* 6 (1962):29-40.

Spaulding, Carl. "Teaching the Use of Microfilm Readers," *Microform Review* 6 (1977):80-81.

Spencer, John R. *An Appraisal of Computer Output Microfilm for Library Catalogues* (Hatfield, Herts, Eng., National Reprographic Centre for Documentation, 1973).

Spreitzer, Francis. "Library Microform Facilities," *Library Technology Reports* 12 (1976):407-436.

Starker, Lee N. "User Experiences with Primary Journals on 16mm Microfilm," *Journal of Chemical Documentation* 10 (1970):5-6.

Stecker, Elizabeth. "RMIT COM Catalogue Study Results," *Australian Library Journal* 24 (1975):9-10.

Stevens, Rolland E. "The Microform Revolution," *Library Trends* 19 (1971):379-95.

Tannebaum, Arthur C. "Human Engineering Factors Help Determine Microform Use in the Research Library," *Proceedings of the American Society for Information Science* 12 (1975):97-98.

Teague, J. "Microform: A Developing Medium," *New Library World* 76 (1975):119-22.

Tebbel, John. "Libraries in Miniature: A New Era Begins," *Saturday Review* 54 (Jan. 9, 1971):41-42.

Teplitz, Arthur. "Library Fiche: An Introduction and Explanation," *Proceedings of the National Microfilm Association* (Silver Spring, Md.: National Microfilm Association, 1968): 125-32.

Teplitz, Arthur. "Microfilm Libraries—Service Levels and Impact of Copyright on These Levels," *Journal of Micrographics* 6 (1972):67-70.

Thomas, Peter A. "Microfiche in a Special Library," *New Library World* 76 (1975):43-44.

Thompson, Lawrence A. "Microforms as Library Resources," *Library Trends* 8 (1960):359-71.

Thomson, June. "Cataloguing of Large Works on Microform in Canadian University Libraries," *Canadian Library Journal* 26 (1969):446-52.

Torok, Stephen. "Microform Utilization in Europe—a Librarian's Observations," *Journal of Micrographics* 8 (1975):215-22.

Tylicki, E. "Preparation of a Microfilm File of Company Technical Reports," *Journal of Chemical Documentation* 10 (1970):20-22.

Ungerleider, S. Lester. "A Study of COM Usability in the Technical Processing Area of the Yale University Library," *Journal of Micrographics* 7 (1973):81-89.

Van Doren, Charles. "The Bibliographic Demands of Microbook Service." In P. S. Grove and E. G. Clement, eds. *Bibliographic Control of Nonprint Media* (Chicago: American Library Association, 1972), 307-314.

Veaner, A. B. "The Crisis in Micropublication," *Choice* 5 (1968):448-53.

Veaner, A. B. "Microfilm and the Library: A Retrospective," *Drexel Library Quarterly* 11 (1975):3-16.

Veaner, A. B. *The Evaluation of Micropublications: A Handbook for Librarians* (Chicago: American Library Association, 1971).

Veaner, A. B. "Microreproduction and Micropublication Standards: What They Mean to You, the User," *Microform Review* 3 (1974):80-84.

Veit, Fritz. "Microforms, Microform Equipment and Microform Use in the Educational Environment," *Library Trends* 19 (1971):444-46.

Vessey, H. F. *The Use of Microfiche for Scientific and Technical Reports.* (NATO: Advisory Group for Aerospace Research and Development, 1970).

Weber, David C. "Specifications for a Superior Microtext Reading Machine," *Microdoc* 5 (1966):6-9.

Weber, Hans H. "The Librarian's View of Microforms," *IEEE Transactions on Professional Communications* PC-18 (1975):168-73.

Weil, Ben H., and Lee N. Starker. "Introduction to the Microfilm Forum: Experiences, Problems, and Plans of Microform Users," *Journal of Chemical Documentation* 10 (1970):3-4.

Weil, Ben H., et al. "Esso Research Experiences with Chemical Abstracts on Microfilm," *Journal of Chemical Documentation* 5 (1965):193-200.

Wicker, Roger, Ray Neperud, and Arthur Teplitz. *Microfiche Storage and Retrieval Study* (Falls Church, Va.: System Development Corporation, 1970).

Wilber, Alan. "Microfiche Systems for the Small User," *Journal of Micrographics* 5 (1972):131-36.

Williams, B. J. S. "Introduction to Microforms and Microform Publishing." In *Micropublishing for Learned Societies* (Hatfield, Eng., National Reprographic Centre for documentation, 1968): 1-10.

Williams, B. J. S. "Microforms in Information Retrieval and Communication Systems," *ASLIB Proceedings* 19 (1967):223-31.

Williams, B. J. S. *Miniaturized Communications* (London: Library Association, 1973).

Williams, B. J. S. "NRCd—a British Contribution to International Micrographics," *Microform Review* 5 (1976):34-39.

Williams, B. J. S. "Progress in Documentation: Micrographics," *Journal of Documentation* 27 (1971):295-304.

Williams, B. J. S., and G. H. Wright. "Microforms—an Active Tool for Library Systems," *Microdoc* 6 (1967):3-14.

Windsor, Allan F. "New UN Microfiche Service Augurs Large Storage Economies," *Special Libraries* 65 (1974):5-6.

Wooster, Harold. *Microfiche 1969—a User Study* (Washington: Committee on Scientific and Technical Information, 1969).

Wooster, Harold. "Towards a Uniform Federal Report Numbering System and a Cuddly Microfiche Reader—Two Modest Proposals," *NMA Journal* 2 (1968):63-67.

Yerkes, Charles P. "Micropublishing: An Overview," *Journal of Micrographics* 5 (1971):59-61.

# INDEX